THE CAMBRIDGE ANCIENT HISTORY

PLATES TO VOLUME VII PART 1

THE CAMBRIDGE ANCIENT HISTORY

PLATES TO VOLUME VII PART 1

The Hellenistic World to the Coming of the Romans

NEW EDITION

Edited by
ROGER LING

*Reader in the History of Art,
University of Manchester*

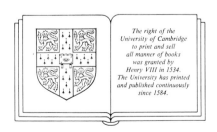

CAMBRIDGE UNIVERSITY PRESS
CAMBRIDGE
LONDON NEW YORK NEW ROCHELLE
MELBOURNE SYDNEY

Published by the Press Syndicate of the University of Cambridge
The Pitt Building, Trumpington Street, Cambridge CB2 1RP
32 East 57th Street, New York NY 10022, USA
296 Beaconsfield Parade, Middle Park, Melbourne 3206, Australia

First published 1984

Printed in Great Britain by the University Press, Cambridge

Library of Congress catalogue card number: 83-5186

British Library Cataloguing in Publication Data
The Cambridge ancient history.—New ed.
Vol. 7, pt. 1
Plates
1. History, Ancient
I. Ling, Roger
930 D57

ISBN 0 521 24354 8

CONTENTS

MAPS

PREFACE

This collection of plates is intended, like the plates volumes of the first edition of the *Cambridge Ancient History*, and that which appeared with volumes I and II of the new edition, to be a companion to the text-volume which covers the relevant period. In contrast with its predecessors, however, it is also intended to be able to stand alone. It thus adopts a new format in which the illustrations are accompanied by fuller and more analytical captions (rather like those in Rostovtzeff's *Social and Economic History of the Hellenistic World*) and are arranged in sections with brief introductory comments. In this way it is hoped to provide a reasonably coherent picture of the Hellenistic period which will be of some interest to archaeologists, to art-historians, or simply to the average reader who, for one reason or another, wants a survey of the material remains rather than a more strictly historical approach.

Inevitably this means that the stress may be laid in different areas from that of the text-volume. Some aspects of the discussion in the latter cannot be readily illustrated because of the thinness of the archaeological evidence; others cannot be fully illustrated for fear of upsetting the balance of the visual documentation. For example, to do complete justice to the Egyptian papyri would result in a very uneven coverage. Similarly with art and architecture. A conscious decision has been taken not to illustrate works of art and buildings, as in the first edition, for their own sakes, but rather to use them as historical and sociological documents. This is not to decry their intrinsic value or artistic importance. The study of art and architecture from more purely aesthetic and stylistic standpoints is a worthy exercise, but it is not primarily the stuff of which history is made: much more important is the information which art can give us about the interaction of Greeks and natives, about patronage and propaganda, about the beliefs and interests of householders, and generally about the quality of life. Something of the way in which this information can be extracted will emerge in the course of this volume.

In compiling this book the editor is conscious of his debt to innumerable friends and colleagues – notably, of course, to the other contributors, but also to the editors of *CAH* and to those authors of chapters in *CAH* VII.1 who have given assistance. Others who must be singled out for thanks are M. Andronikos, P. Bernard, Nancy Bookidis, L. Casson, H. W. Catling, H. Döhl, M. N. Filgis, P. M. Fraser, M. L. Katzev, Glenys Lloyd-Morgan, A. Mallwitz, H. Meyer, Stella G. Miller, Stephen G. Miller, V. Nutton, K. S. Painter, Ph. M. Petsas, A. J. N. W. Prag, D. J. de Solla Price, S. Price, A. J. Spawforth, Veronica Tatton-Brown, Helen Townsend, A. D. Trendall, Fanie-Marie Tsigakou,

T. R. Volk and D. Williams. In addition to these, I must thank generally all those representatives of museums, institutions and archaeological services who have helped in obtaining photographs or providing information, and apologize that there is not space to name them all. Final thanks are due to the staff of the Cambridge University Press, to Jane Wilkinson for her excellent and percipient typing, to Lesley Ling for her usual patience and unfailing helpfulness, and to Dr E. B. French and the staff of the Museum of Classical Archaeology in Cambridge for their hospitality, without which the project could not have been completed.

Manchester 1982 R. J. L.

ACKNOWLEDGEMENTS

Acknowledgement is due to the following for their permission to reproduce the illustrations indicated.

French Archaeological Delegation in Afghanistan: 6, 17, 26, 27, 30, 31, 258; Alexandria, Graeco-Roman Museum: 254b; Alinari-Anderson: 8, 188; R. E. Allen: 43, 57; M. Andronikos: 101; Athens, American School of Classical Studies, Agora Excavations: 120, 121a, b, 122a, b, 127a–c, 128b, c, 161, 167, 170, 174, 175, 205, 224; Athens, American School of Classical Studies, Corinth Excavations: 214, 225, 235; Athens, Benaki Museum: 155, 156; Athens, Epigraphical Museum: 192; Athens, French School of Archaeology: 79 (drawing F. Courby), 129, 130, 135, 137b (drawing Y. Fomine), 138, 141, 142, 177, 178, 184, 200, 209, 215, 222, 223, 226; Athens, German Archaeological Institute: 42, 72, 85, 182a, b, 187, 194, 195a, 203a–f, 232, 233, 234, 248; Athens, National Museum: 163, 189, 261a, 266; Baghdad, Directorate General of Antiquities: 21; Barcelona, Archaeological Museum (photo S. Ripoll López): 111a; Basel, Antikenmuseum (photo Claire Niggli): 191; Berlin, State Museums (Pergamon Museum): 63, 99, 145, 265; A. D. H. Bivar: 35; Boston, Museum of Fine Arts: 199; Brussels, Musées Royaux d'Art et d'Histoire (© A.C.L. Bruxelles): 83; Cairo, Egyptian Museum: 10; Cairo, French Institute of Oriental Archaeology: 179; Cairo, German Archaeological Institute: 5, 9, 251; Cambridge, Fitzwilliam Museum (courtesy of the Syndics): 4a–d, 11, 14, 22a, b, 28, 36, 45a, b, 56a, 65a, b, d, 70a–f, 78a–g, 211a, b; Cambridge, Museum of Classical Archaeology: 60, 213; Christie, Manson and Woods: 95; P. Clayton: 15; P. Connolly: 104, 106, 107, 108, 111b, c, 112, 113; Copenhagen, National Museum: 164; Copenhagen, Ny Carlsberg Glyptotek: 77; Dublin, Trinity College Library: 257; Egypt Exploration Society: 2; N. Filgis: 46, 176a–c, 198, 243a; Florence, Biblioteca Laurenziana (photos G. B. Pineider): 267; P. M. Fraser: 41; Freiburg im Breisgau, Universitätsbibliothek: 180; V. R. Grace: 128a (courtesy of the Graeco-Roman Museum, Alexandria), 128d, e (courtesy of the National Museum, Athens); Government of India, Archaeological Survey of India: 37; Government of India, Survey of India: 33; Istanbul, German Archaeological Institute (photo W. Schiele): 38; K. Jeppesen: 18; M. Katzev: 132a (photo J. Veltri), 132b, c (photo Susan Katzev); A. Koudoura and Chr. Lephakis (courtesy Ph. Petsas): 67; Leiden, Rijksmuseum van Oudheden: 239; L. A. Ling: 75, 252; R. J. Ling: 231, 262a; London, British Library: 1; London, British Museum (courtesy of the Trustees) (Coins Department): 56b, 65c, 94a–f, 109; (Egyptian Antiquities): 3, 13, 260; (Greek and Roman Antiquities): 40, 55, 123, 126, 134, 146, 150, 151, 152, 153, 154, 157, 158, 159, 160, 162a–d, 168, 169, 171, 172, 207, 221, 264; (Prehistoric and Romano-British Antiquities): 102; Manchester, History of Art Department Collection, University: 256; Manchester, John Rylands Library: 263; Manchester Museum: 165, 204b; Bildarchiv Foto Marburg: 47, 59, 61; M. Mellink: 12; Stella G. Miller: 100; Stephen G. Miller: 71; Munich, Antikensammlungen: 237 (photo C. H. Krüger-Moessner); Munich, University Institute of Classical Archaeology: 62, 246; Naples, Archaeological Superintendency: 201, 202, 208; New York, Metropolitan Museum of Art: 185; Oxford, Ashmolean Museum: 230, 240; A. Pandermalis: 69; Paris, Louvre Museum: 24 (photo Chuzeville), 105, 110, 117, 204a (photo London Institute of Classical Studies Webster Archive); Paris, University of Paris-Sorbonne Institute of Papyrology: 119; A. Perissinotto: 249; Ph. Petsas: 66; Potenza, Archaeological Superintendency of Basilicata: 89 (photo A. La Capra), 93, 96b–d; A. J. N. W. Prag: 181, 219; Princeton University: 16, 97; Princeton University Art Museum: 206; Reggio Calabria, Archaeological Superintendency of Calabria: 91; Rome, German Archaeological Institute: 29, 125, 144, 149, 187; Rome, Istituto Centrale del Restauro: 96a; Salerno, Archaeological Superintendency: 92; S. Sherwin-White: 39, 44, 49, 54; H. Schleif: 183; D. De Solla Price: 261b (drawing B. Pope), 262b; S. T. D. Spittle: 217; Wim Swaan: 7, 23, 48, 50, 51, 52, 53, 58, 64, 86, 87, 88, 103, 118, 124, 131, 133, 137a, 139, 140, 143, 147, 148, 173, 186, 193a, 196, 197, 212, 220, 227, 228, 229, 242, 244, 247, 255, 268; Syracuse, Archaeological Superintendency: 98, 190; Taranto, Archaeological Superintendency: 90; Tehran, Iran-e Bastan Museum (courtesy of Ministry of Culture and Arts): 19, 20; R. A. Tomlinson: 73, 74, 76, 80, 81, 82, 84, 210; Venice, Archaeological Superintendency: 216; M. Vickers: 68; Vienna, Austrian Archaeological Institute: 243b (drawing E. Fossel), 245; Vienna, Kunsthistorisches Museum: 238, 241; Vienna, Nationalbibliothek: 259; A. J. B. Wace (courtesy of Mrs Wace): 136; Anna Wachsmann (courtesy of Mrs Lehmann): 218; D. White (courtesy of Libyan Department of Antiquities): 253; F. E. Winter: 114, 115, 116; Yale University Art Gallery: 25; N. Yalouris: 166, 236

The following illustrations are reproduced from the works listed: 32: K. V. Trever, *Pamiatniki Greko-Baktriiskogo Isskustva* (1940) pl. 1; 34: H. P. Francfort, *Mém. Dél. Arch. Française en Afghanistan* 23 (1979) pl. XIV.27; 193b: A. v. Gerkan, *Das Theater von Priene* (1921) pl. 35; 195b: E. Fiechter, *Das Theater in Oropos* (1930) pl. 8; 250: E. H. Minns, *Scythians and Greeks* (1913) fig. 235; 254a: A. Adriani, *Repertorio d'arte dell' Egitto greco-romano* C 1–2 (1966) fig. 181

ABBREVIATIONS

AAA	*Athens Annals of Archaeology*
AJA	*American Journal of Archaeology*
Akurgal	E. Akurgal, *Ancient Civilizations and Ruins of Turkey*, 4th ed. (1978)
Ant. Denk.	*Antike Denkmäler*
Ant. K.	*Antike Kunst*
APB	Excavations of the Athenian Agora Picture Book
Arch. Anz.	*Archäologischer Anzeiger*
Arch. Eph.	*Ephemeris Archaiologiki*
Arch. J.	*Archaeological Journal*
ASAtene	*Annuario della Scuola Archeologica di Atene*
Ath. Mitt.	*Mitteilungen des Deutschen Archäologischen Instituts. Athenische Abteilung*
AZ	*Archäologische Zeitung*
BABesch.	*Bulletin van de Vereeniging tot Bevordering der Kennis van de Antike Beschaving*
BCH	*Bulletin de correspondance hellénique*
BdA	*Bollettino d'arte*
Bean, *AT*	G. E. Bean, *Aegean Turkey*, 2nd ed. (1979)
Berve and Gruben	H. Berve and G. Gruben, *Greek Temples, Theatres and Shrines* (1963)
BICS	University of London, Institute of Classical Studies, *Bulletin*
Bieber, *Denkmäler*	M. Bieber, *Die Denkmäler zum Theaterwesen im Altertum* (1920)
Bieber, *History*	M. Bieber, *The History of the Greek and Roman Theater*, 2nd ed. (1961)
Bieber, *Sculpture*	M. Bieber, *The Sculpture of the Hellenistic Age*, revised ed. (1961)
BIFAO	*Bulletin de l'Institut Français d'Archéologie Orientale*
BM Coins	*A Catalogue of the Greek Coins in the British Museum*
Bruneau and Ducat	P. Bruneau and J. Ducat, *Guide de Délos* (1965)
Bruneau, *Recherches*	P. Bruneau, *Recherches sur les cultes de Délos à l'époque hellénistique et à l'époque impériale* (1970)
Brunn-Bruckmann	*Brunn-Bruckmann's Denkmäler griechischer und römischer Sculptur* (1902–47)
Bulle, *Untersuchungen*	H. Bulle, *Untersuchungen an griechischen Theatern* (1928)
CAH	*Cambridge Ancient History*
CRAI	*Comptes rendus de l'Académie des Inscriptions et Belles Lettres*
CVA	*Corpus Vasorum Antiquorum*
Davis and Kraay	N. Davis and C. M. Kraay, *The Hellenistic Kingdoms. Portrait Coins and History* (1973)
Deltion	*Archaiologikon Deltion*

Dinsmoor	W. B. Dinsmoor, *The Architecture of Ancient Greece* (1950)
Dörpfeld and Reisch	W. Dörpfeld and E. Reisch, *Das griechische Theater* (1896)
EAD	*Exploration archéologique de Délos*
Fiechter, *Entwicklung*	E. R. Fiechter, *Die baugeschichtliche Entwicklung des antiken Theaters* (1914)
Fraser	P. M. Fraser, *Rhodian Funerary Monuments* (1977)
GIBM	*The Collection of Ancient Greek Inscriptions in the British Museum* (1874–1916)
ID	*Inscriptions de Délos*
IG	*Inscriptiones Graecae*
IGD	A. D. Trendall and T. B. L. Webster, *Illustrations of Greek Drama* (1971)
ILN	*Illustrated London News*
JdI	*Jahrbuch des Deutschen Archäologischen Instituts*
JGS	*Journal of Glass Studies*
JHS	*Journal of Hellenic Studies*
JNES	*Journal of Near Eastern Studies*
JOAI	*Jahreshefte des Österreichischen Archäologischen Instituts*
JRS	*Journal of Roman Studies*
Karouzou	S. Karouzou, *National Archaeological Museum, Collection of Sculpture: a Catalogue* (1968)
Kurtz and Boardman	D. C. Kurtz and J. Boardman, *Greek Burial Customs* (1971)
Lullies	R. Lullies, *Griechische Plastik* (1979)
Marcadé	J. Marcadé, *Au Musée de Délos. Étude sur la sculpture hellénistique en ronde bosse découverte dans l'île* (1969)
McClean	S. W. Grose, *Fitzwilliam Museum. Catalogue of the McClean Collection of Greek Coins* (1923–9)
Mon. Piot	Fondation Eugène Piot, *Monuments et mémoires publiés par l'Académie des Inscriptions et Belles Lettres*
NC	*Numismatic Chronicle*
OGIS	W. Dittenberger, *Orientis Graeci Inscriptiones Selectae* (1903–5)
Ol. Bericht	*Bericht über die Ausgrabungen in Olympia*
Opus. Arch.	*Opuscula archaeologica*
PECS	*Princeton Encyclopedia of Classical Sites* (1976)
PCG	*A Guide to the Principal Coins of the Greeks* (British Museum, 1932)
Pickard-Cambridge, *Theatre*	A. W. Pickard-Cambridge, *The Theatre of Dionysus in Athens* (1946)
Pickard-Cambridge, *Festivals*	A. W. Pickard-Cambridge, *The Dramatic Festivals of Athens*, 2nd ed. (1968)
Praktika	*Praktika tis en Athinais Archaiologikis Hetairias*
REG	*Revue des études grecques*
Rend. Pont. Acc.	*Atti della Pontificia Accademia Romana di Archeologia, rendiconti*
Rev. Arch.	*Revue archéologique*
Richter, *Portraits*	G. M. A. Richter, *The Portraits of the Greeks* (1965)
RN	*Revue numismatique*
Robert, *Masken*	C. Robert, *Die Masken der neueren attischen Komödie* (Hallisches Winckelmannsprogram xxv) (1911)
Robertson	C. M. Robertson, *A History of Greek Art* (1975)
Röm. Mitt.	*Mitteilungen des Deutschen Archäologischen Instituts. Römische Abteilung*

Rostovtzeff	M. I. Rostovtzeff, *Social and Economic History of the Hellenistic World* (1941)
SIG	W. Dittenberger, *Sylloge Inscriptionum Graecarum*, 3rd ed. (1915–24)
SNG	*Sylloge Nummorum Graecorum*
SNG IV	*Sylloge Nummorum Graecorum* IV. *Fitzwilliam Museum. Leake and General Collections*
Svoronos, *Ath. Mus.*	J. N. Svoronos, *Das Athener Nationalmuseum* (1908–13)
Svoronos, *Nom. Ptol.*	J. N. Svoronos, *Ta nomismata tou kratous ton Ptolemaion* (1974)
Webster, *MNC*	T. B. L. Webster, *Monuments Illustrating New Comedy* (*BICS* suppl. XI) (1961)

Abbreviations for classical authors and their works follow the conventions in *Oxford Classical Dictionary*, 2nd ed. (1970).

INTRODUCTION

The conquests of Alexander irrevocably changed the pattern of Greek history. On a superficial level, of course, the major change was the greatly enlarged area of the Greek world, in which the centre of gravity shifted from European Greece to centres further east – to the coastal cities of Asia Minor, Rhodes, Antioch on the Orontes, Seleucia on the Tigris, and Alexandria, all of which benefited from the new resources and trade-routes opened to the Greeks. Along with this went the inevitable political and sociological changes. On the political stage kings and kingdoms became a fundamental feature of the Greek world, and a leitmotiv of the new age is the relationship between kings and the old cities and sanctuaries – a relationship expressed on the one hand by the efforts of those cities to win the favour and patronage of the kings, and on the other hand by the concern of the kings to advertise their munificence and to gain the support of the cities (or to 'sugar the pill' of their lost liberty) by bestowing buildings and other favours upon them. At the same time the rivalries between the kings produced wars which were conducted, thanks to the use of mercenary armies and developments in siegecraft and weaponry, on a bigger and more professional scale than before. But the establishment of stable governments and a broad balance of power in the eastern Mediterranean meant that, on the whole, the Greek world enjoyed a greater degree of security and freedom from disruption than had ever been possible in the days of the city-states.

The sociological changes are more complex and difficult to evaluate. The relationship between the Greeks and Macedonians on the one hand and the native peoples of the newly conquered territories on the other is a particularly interesting theme. It seems that, whatever the intentions of Alexander himself, there was never any real partnership in government: the ruling classes continued to be drawn largely from people of Greek or Macedonian stock. Nonetheless a degree of cultural cross-fertilization was inevitable. The current of Hellenization was the stronger influence: thus the term 'Hellenistic' used to describe the age. By means of the newly founded cities, especially in the east, all of which were characterized by Greek-style constitutions and institutions, the kings set up enclaves from which Greek culture radiated to surrounding areas. The Greek language became the lingua franca of the whole world from southern Italy to Afghanistan; a money economy was carried to areas where it had never previously existed; and Greek art and artefacts spread to wholly new regions, where their influence was long to outlive the Greek political presence (for example in the Buddhist Gandhâra civilization of north-west India). Conversely the Greeks could not help but be tainted by the culture of the civilizations which they had supplanted. This is revealed by architectural and artistic borrowings in the eastern kingdoms and in particular by the influence of oriental and Egyptian religions upon Greek circles, whether this took the form of a fusion between the Greek and native gods or simply of a more or less direct adoption of a native deity (as happened with Isis).

The interplay of Greek and native is an aspect of Hellenistic civilization which has helped to dictate the structure of the present volume. While the world of Alexander's successors is united, in many respects, by a universal 'Hellenistic' culture, it is also affected by strong regional peculiarities; the situation is very different, for instance, in European Greece, where the city-state tradition remained alive and the kings of Macedonia had to tread warily in their dealings with the old cities and more especially with the new federal leagues, and in Egypt, where the Ptolemies inherited a long-established monarchical civilization with a highly individual social and economic system. The first part of the book (chapters 1 to 6) therefore reviews the main regions of the

Hellenistic world in turn, picking out the political and social features which characterize each of them, in so far as they can be illustrated from the material record. First comes Ptolemaic Egypt, the first of the kingdoms to become firmly established in the turmoil following Alexander's death. The Seleucid kingdom, which was confirmed by the battle of Corupedium in 281 B.C. and was focused on Syria and Mesopotamia, comes next, while a third chapter deals with the kingdoms in Bactria and India which split off from the Seleucid empire in the mid-third century. Chapter 4 covers Asia Minor, where Seleucid influence was confined mainly to the third century and to the southern half of the peninsula while independent kingdoms established themselves in Cappadocia, Pontus, Bithynia, and, expanding to take over much of Asia Minor during the second century, in Pergamum. Chapter 5 deals with Macedonia, Greece and the Cyclades, and chapter 6 with Italy and Sicily, where a period of prosperity under the hegemony of Tarentum and Syracuse soon gave way to the relentless advance of the Romans.

In the second part of the volume the Hellenistic world is taken as a whole and universal aspects are examined: warfare in chapter 7, and various facets of civilization in chapter 8. Even here, as will be seen, the picture is never uniform: to take an example, forms of burial and grave-monuments are very different in Macedonia, Athens, Asia Minor and Alexandria. But overriding the regional variations is a general community of culture. Institutions such as the Greek language, the gymnasium and its sports, the theatre, and the Greek styles of columnar architecture travelled wherever the colonists did, turning up in such remote sites as Kandahar and Aï Khanum in Afghanistan. It is these, even more than the physical control of rulers of Greek or Macedonian stock, that enable us to define the Hellenistic world and to treat it as a single cultural phenomenon.

1. THE PTOLEMAIC KINGDOM

DOROTHY J. THOMPSON

Egypt, conquered by Alexander the Great in 332 B.C., on his death in 323 B.C. fell to the control of Ptolemy son of Lagus. The family of this Macedonian general (**4**, **11–14**) ruled the country for almost three centuries until in 30 B.C. Octavian took Egypt for Rome and Cleopatra VII, the last of the Ptolemies, met her self-inflicted death at the bite of a royal asp. At first Ptolemy I kept his capital in the historic centre of Memphis (**2–3**) but in 313 B.C. he moved it to Alexandria, Alexander's Greek foundation on the coast (**5–6**). Alexandria became the centre of the highly developed, bureaucratic administration through which the Greeks controlled the country. Further, endowed with Museum and Library (cf. **257**), it was the flourishing centre of Greek cultural activity, of literature, the arts (**5**; cf. **7**, **12**, **123**, **151–3**) and of science. Greek was adopted as the language of government and in its upper ranks the administration was staffed by immigrants from all parts of the Greek-speaking world.

The traditional wealth of Egypt depended on agriculture. At the village level Egyptians were employed for dealings with the peasants, for the control of the annual Nile flood and for the cultivation of the Nile valley, where for the most part village life went on unchanged (**8**). In the third century B.C. large areas of land, especially in the Fayûm Basin, were reclaimed for cultivation and new settlements were established (**1**). Soldiers were given land-grants, individuals benefited from gift-estates. From all over the Greek-speaking world immigrants flocked to Egypt and the interaction of these with the native population is of central historical interest (**9–10**; cf. **251**).

In Pharaonic Egypt the strength of the temples had provided an important counterweight to royal power; the Ptolemies faced the same problem complicated by cultural differences. The temples were complex institutions providing large-scale employment; cultic activity, offerings and religious processions (**8**) were a regular part of life in the Egyptian countryside. Alexander was accepted into the temples as an Egyptian Pharaoh and the Ptolemies took on the traditional role as protectors of the Egyptian gods and as temple-builders (**15**). A series of decrees (**3**) regulates the changing relations of the Ptolemies and the Egyptian priesthood. From the reign of Ptolemy II Philadelphus a new ruler cult was instituted with a Greek priesthood based in Alexandria (**14**). Ptolemy II's second wife, Arsinoe Philadelphus (**1**, **11**, **14**), was the first Ptolemy to be introduced into the Egyptian temples as a temple-sharing goddess.

The written evidence for Ptolemaic Egypt is exceptionally rich since the dry climate has preserved a large number of papyri and ostraca, the everyday writing material for both Greeks and Egyptians (**1–2**; cf. **27**, **119**, **179–80**, **257**, **259**, **263**). These are supplemented by official decrees on both papyrus and stone (**3**) which illuminate the interaction of peoples and culture in this country.

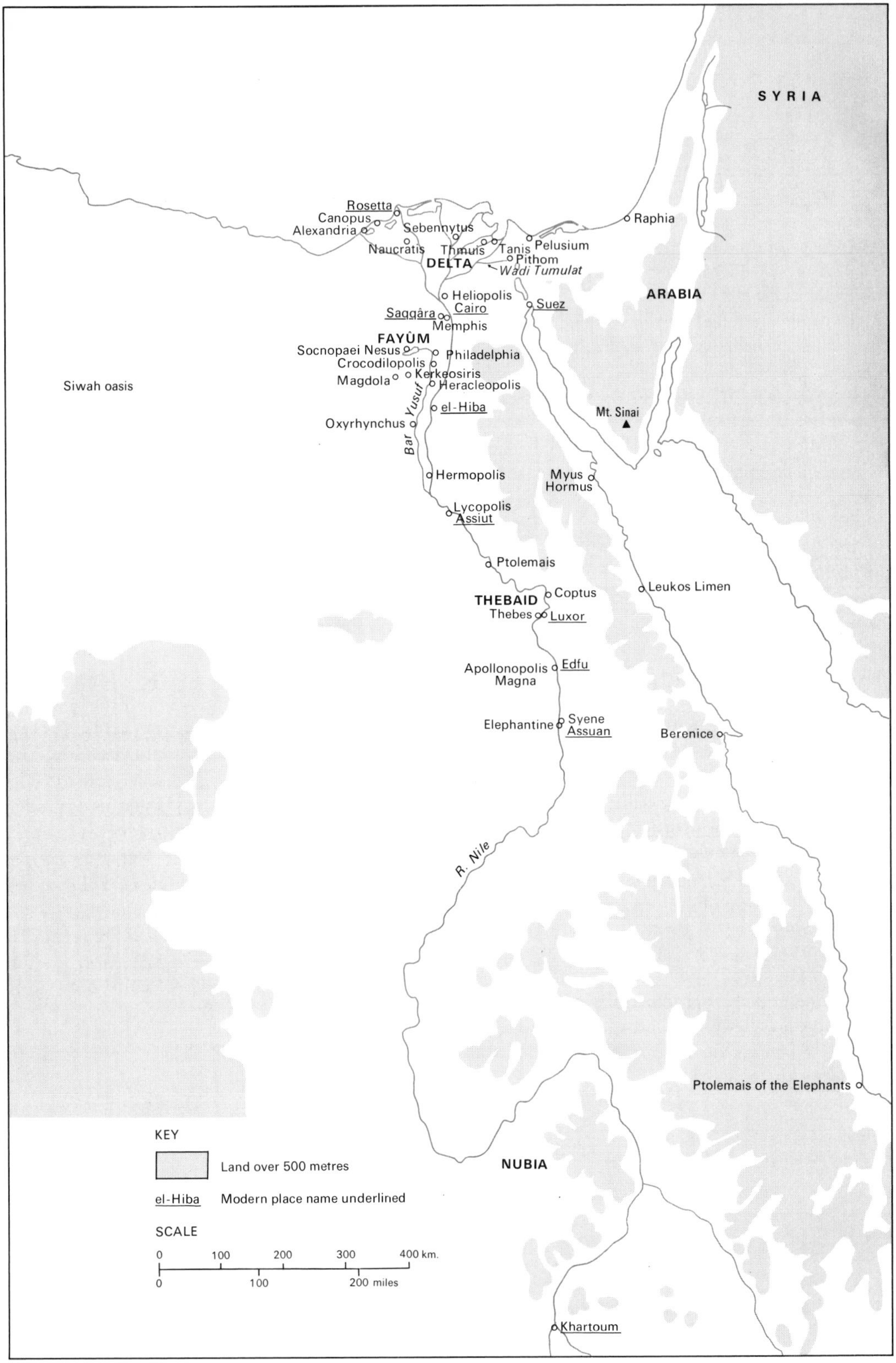
SYRIA
Rosetta
Canopus
Alexandria
Sebennytus
Naucratis
Thmuis
Tanis
Pelusium
Raphia
Pithom
DELTA
Wadi Tumulat
Heliopolis
Cairo
Suez
ARABIA
Saqqâra
Memphis
FAYÛM
Socnopaei Nesus
Philadelphia
Crocodilopolis
Kerkeosiris
Magdola
Heracleopolis
Siwah oasis
el-Hiba
Bar Yusuf
Oxyrhynchus
Mt. Sinai
Hermopolis
Myus Hormus
Lycopolis
Assiut
Ptolemais
THEBAID
Coptus
Leukos Limen
Thebes
Luxor
Apollonopolis Magna
Edfu
Elephantine
Syene
Assuan
Berenice
R. Nile
Ptolemais of the Elephants
KEY
Land over 500 metres
el-Hiba
Modern place name underlined
SCALE
0 100 200 300 400 km.
0 100 200 miles
NUBIA
Khartoum

1. Egypt

1

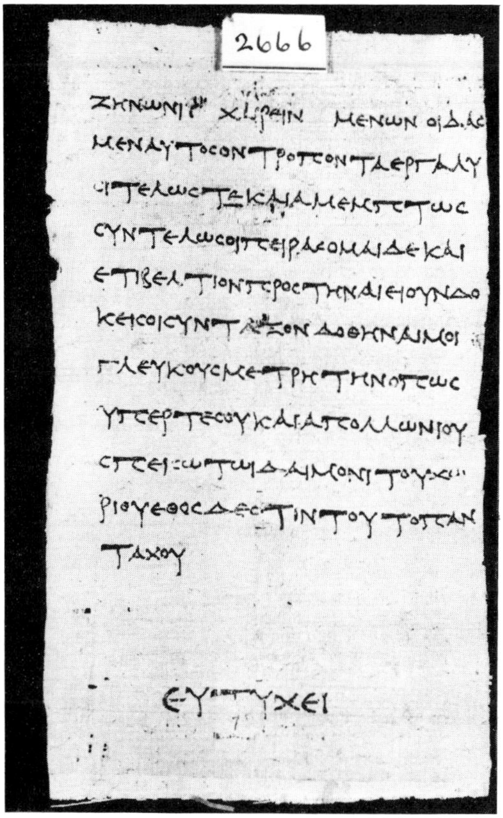

2

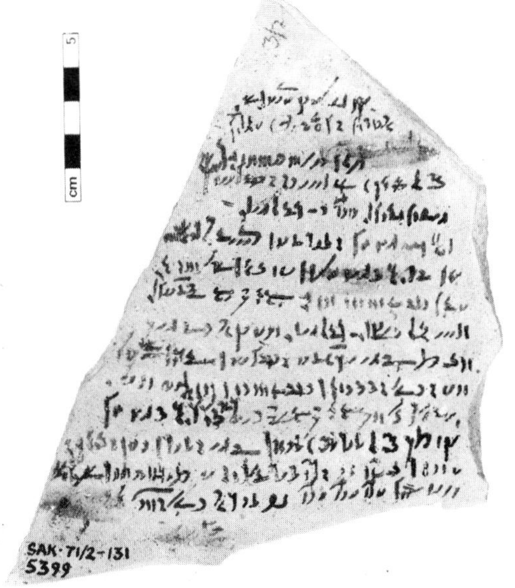

1. A Greek papyrus from the papers of Zenon, estate-manager of Apollonius, *dioiketes* of Ptolemy II Philadelphus (cf. **9**). Menon writes to Zenon with a request for a measure of sweet wine with which he may pour a libation to the *daimon* of Philadelphia, probably the goddess Arsinoe after whom the town was named, on behalf of Zenon and Apollonius. Philadelphia in the Fayûm was one of many Ptolemaic foundations and Arsinoe Philadelphus (the brother-loving) the object of particular veneration (cf. **11**, **13–14**).

(London, British Library 2666. 15.6 cm × 9.5 cm.)

C. Préaux, *Les grecs en Égypte d'après les archives de Zénon* (1947) 72; T. C. Skeat, *Greek Papyri in the British Museum* VII (1974) no. 2041.

2. A demotic ostracon. On the back of a broken pot Ḥor, who came from the Delta to serve in the Ibis sanctuary in the Memphis necropolis, wrote a draft account of his personal involvement in the Sixth Syrian War. He had a dream foretelling the departure of Antiochus IV (*ʾtyks*) from Egypt by the last day of Pauni in Year 2, 30 July 168 B.C. On 11 July, at a date when Antiochus' representative Cleon (*Gry(n)ʾ*) was still in Memphis, Ḥor reported his dream prophesying the salvation of Alexandria to Eirenaios (*Hrynys*), the *strategos*. The recto of this ostracon further records an audience on 29 August 168 in the Great Serapeum at Alexandria with 'the Pharaohs', the brothers Ptolemy VI Philometor and Ptolemy VIII Euergetes.

The recent discovery of Ḥor's private ostraca from the sacred animal necropolis at Saqqâra has added important details to the historical accounts of this war. Antiochus' governor at Memphis and the date of his departure from Egypt (required by Rome) were not previously known.

(Saqqâra, in store. Height 17.8 cm; width 14.9 cm; thickness 1.0 cm.)

J. D. Ray, *The Archive of Ḥor* (1976) 14–20 Text 2 verso, pl. III; D. J. Crawford, *Studia Hellenistica* 24 (1980) 36–7.

3. The Rosetta stone. This black basalt inscription, found by the Napoleonic expedition of A.D. 1799, in A.D. 1824 formed the key for Champollion's decipherment of hieroglyphic. Written in hieroglyphic, demotic and Greek, the

3

decree was published in March 196 B.C. by the priests who had met in Memphis for the coronation of Ptolemy V Epiphanes in November 197 B.C. Nominally celebrating the recent defeat of rebels the decree records significant concessions made by Epiphanes to the temples and marks a development in relations between king and priests. Epiphanes was the first recorded Ptolemy to receive an Egyptian coronation at Memphis and this synodal decree was probably first drafted in Egyptian.

(London, British Museum EA 24, from Rosetta. Height 1.14 m; width 72.5 cm; thickness 28 cm.)

OGIS no. 90; K. Sethe, *Hieroglyphische Urkunden* II (1904) 183 no. 36; W. Spiegelberg, *Der demotische Text der Priesterdekreten von Kanopus und Memphis* (1922); F. Daumas, *Les moyens d'expression du grec et de l'égyptien* (1952); C. Andrews, *The Rosetta Stone* (1981); for a translation see E. R. Bevan, *A History of Egypt under the Ptolemaic Dynasty* (1927) 263–8.

4

a

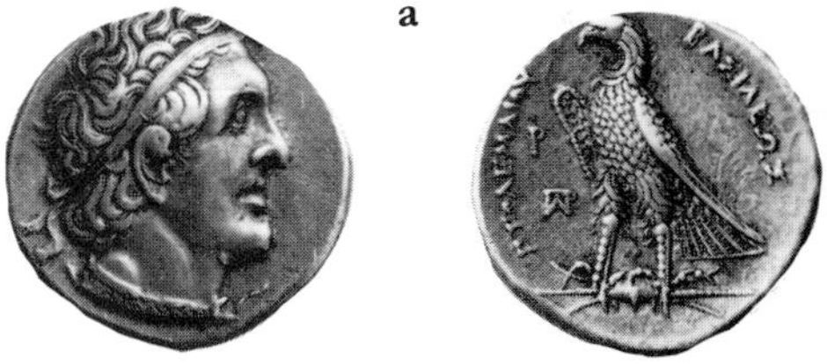

4. Ptolemaic coins.

(**a**) Silver tetradrachm of Ptolemy I Soter (*c.* 304–283 B.C.). *Obv.* Diademed head of Ptolemy I facing right, with aegis. *Rev.* Eagle facing left on thunderbolt; in front P and monogram; around ΠΤΟΛΕΜΑΙΟΥ ΒΑΣΙΛΕΩΣ.

Unpublished (Hart collection). For the type see Svoronos, *Nom. Ptol.* 43 no. 255, pl. IX.11; *SNG Copenhagen* XL (1977) nos. 72–5 (var.)

b

(**b**) Gold octadrachm of Ptolemy IV Philopator (221–205 B.C.) portraying Ptolemy III Euergetes (246–221 B.C.). *Obv.* Bust of Ptolemy III facing right, wearing radiate crown and aegis; behind his shoulder a trident sceptre; border of dots. *Rev.* Radiate cornucopia bound with fillet; border of dots; around ΠΤΟΛΕΜΑΙΟΥ ΒΑΣΙΛΕΩΣ.

McClean III, 423 no. 9783, pl. 364.8; cf. Svoronos, *Nom. Ptol.* 178 no. 1117, pl. XXXVI.6; *SNG Copenhagen* XL, no. 196.

c

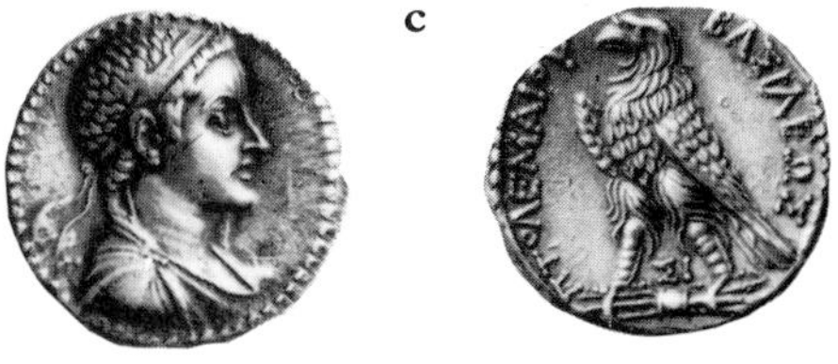

(**c**) Silver tetradrachm of Phoenicia for Ptolemy V Epiphanes. *Obv.* Diademed head of king facing right, with *chlamys*, border of dots. *Rev.* Eagle facing left on thunderbolt with ΣΙ (Sidon) between legs; around ΠΤΟΛΕΜΑΙΟΥ ΒΑΣΙΛΕΩΣ.

McClean III, 426 no. 9802, pl. 366.8; cf. Svoronos, *Nom. Ptol.* 215 no. 1294, pl. XLIII.8; *SNG Copenhagen* XL, no. 466.

(**d**) Base silver tetradrachm of Phoenicia for Cleopatra VII, *c.* 34 B.C. *Obv.* Bust of Cleopatra facing right, wearing diadem, pearl necklace, dress embroidered with pearls; border of dots; around ΒΑϹΙΛΙϹϹΑ ΚΛΕΟΠΑΤΡΑ ΘΕΑ ΝΕΩΤΕΡΑ. *Rev.* Bust of Antony facing right; border of dots; around ΑΝΤΩΝΙΟϹ ΑΥΤΟΚΡΑΤΩΡ ΤΡΙΤΟΝ ΤΡΙΩΝ ΑΝΔΡΩΝ.

d

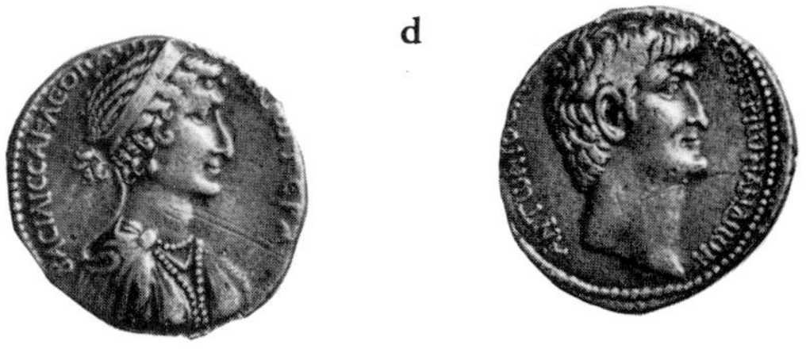

T. V. Buttrey, *American Numismatic Society Museum Notes* 6 (1954) 95–109, pl. XV.1–2; cf. Svoronos, *Nom. Ptol.* 316 no. 1897, pl. LXIII.22.

(Cambridge, Fitzwilliam Museum. Actual size.)

5

5. Alexandria as mistress of the seas. On this panel from a mosaic pavement signed by Sophilus, a female bust probably represents the naval power of Alexandria. She wears a headdress in the form of a ship's prow and a military cloak, and carries a mast and yard. The mosaic, possibly a copy of a painting, stands in an elaborate border with a double maeander pattern (not shown here) and is of a wide range of delicate colours in tiny *tesserae* (cf. **140**, **201**). It has been variously dated but probably belongs to the second century B.C.

(Alexandria, Graeco-Roman Museum 21739, from Thmuis (Delta). Height 2.80 m; width 2.61 m.)

Rostovtzeff 254, pl. XXXV with earlier bibliography; B. R. Brown, *Ptolemaic Paintings and Mosaics* (1957) 67–8, pls. XXXVIII and XL; K. Parlasca, in *La Mosaïque gréco-romaine* II (1975) 364.

6. The Pharos of Alexandria. On this Hellenistic beaker of colourless glass found in Afghanistan, the lighthouse of Alexandria, one of the seven wonders of the world, is depicted on one face with three ships on the other. The embossed glass ornaments were attached under heat and the beaker seems to be a souvenir from the city, a centre of glass-making. The lighthouse building, simplified in form with small windows, is attached to a fortification wall. Above the crenellations of the tower stands a colossal male nude statue, with an oar or rudder signifying maritime power in the crook of his left arm.

6

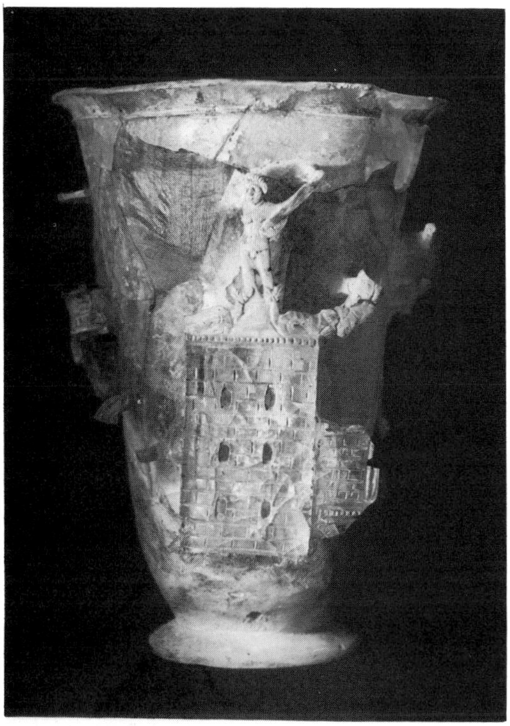

Although beardless, the figure is identified as Zeus Soter by an early-third-century B.C. epigram of Posidippus which also records the dedication of the lighthouse by the Ptolemaic courtier, Sostratus son of Dexiphanes of Cnidus. The statue is flanked by tritons of which only the tails survive. The statuary is later portrayed on Alexandrian coins of Domitian which, as do other representations, show a more elaborate, three-tiered structure for the lighthouse.

(Kabul Museum, from Begram. Height 17.25 cm; width, at rim 11.8 cm, at base 6.4 cm.)

H. Thiersch, *Pharos* (1909); J. Hackin, *Recherches archéologiques à Begram* (1939) 42–4 no. 203, figs. 37–40; H. Seyrig, *Syria* 22 (1941) 262 n. 2; Ch. Picard, *BCH* 76 (1952) 61–95; O. Kurz in J. Hackin, *Nouvelles recherches archéologiques à Begram* (1954) 101–2, 107–9, figs. 359–63; M. J. Price and B. L. Trell, *Coins and their Cities* (1977) 180–2, 238.

7. Interior of the so-called Tazza Farnese, a dish, probably of the first century B.C., carved from sardonyx in the cameo technique. This technique is new to Hellenistic times and the banded agates (onyx or sardonyx) from Arabia and India were particularly well suited to producing striking colour-effects. Here the tones range from white through cream to red and dark brown. The subject seems to be the fertility of the Nile, the personification of which is shown seated against a tree at the left, holding a cornucopia, while a figure of Abundance (or Isis) reclines with one elbow on the head of a sphinx beneath. The dish was certainly made in Alexandria. Attempts to identify a deeper symbolism, involving members of the ruling family, have not produced very convincing results.

(Naples, National Museum 27611, formerly Farnese collection. Diam. 20 cm.)

A. Furtwängler, *Die antike Gemmen* (1900) 253–6, pls. LIV, LV; J. Charbonneaux, *Mon. Piot* 50 (1958) 85–103; F. L. Bastet, *BABesch.* 37 (1962) 1–24; G. M. A. Richter, *Engraved Gems of the Greeks and the Etruscans* (1968) 151 no. 596 (with further bibliography); D. B. Thompson, in H. Maehler and V. M. Strocka, eds., *Das ptolemäische Ägypten* (1978) 113–22, figs. 97–109.

8. A Nile landscape from the Palestrina mosaic. The section illustrated is from what is now the bottom right-hand corner of the mosaic and shows a religious procession, a regular feature of Egyptian life, passing through a small shrine with ornamental roof and sun disk and uraei above the pediment. A sacred bier is followed by standard-bearers and a group of worshippers with garlanded hair and musical instruments. A small pedestal with Anubis stands nearby and in front, at the left, a standard-bearer is seated close to an opening in the wall. In the surrounding water are boats, a pleasure boat with cabin and sails of the type used on the Nile, two light fishing canoes (the left one of bound reeds), and a warship full of armed men. Below, on an island in a rural landscape, a peasant wearing a peaked cap and rustic tunic stands at a gateway, with a protective tower to the right. His wife works in the garden close to the large dovecote (pigeons being an important source of both food and manure). A palm and water-plants identify the Egyptian landscape, possibly in flood time. The mosaic is originally from a hall below the sanctuary of Fortuna at Praeneste in Italy. In its entirety it presents a landscape with animals, figures and buildings stretching from Ethiopia to the Delta. It probably dates from the first century B.C. but parts of the mosaic were reworked in the seventeenth century. Here the strange emblem on the bier, originally carried by four priests, is a later addition.

7

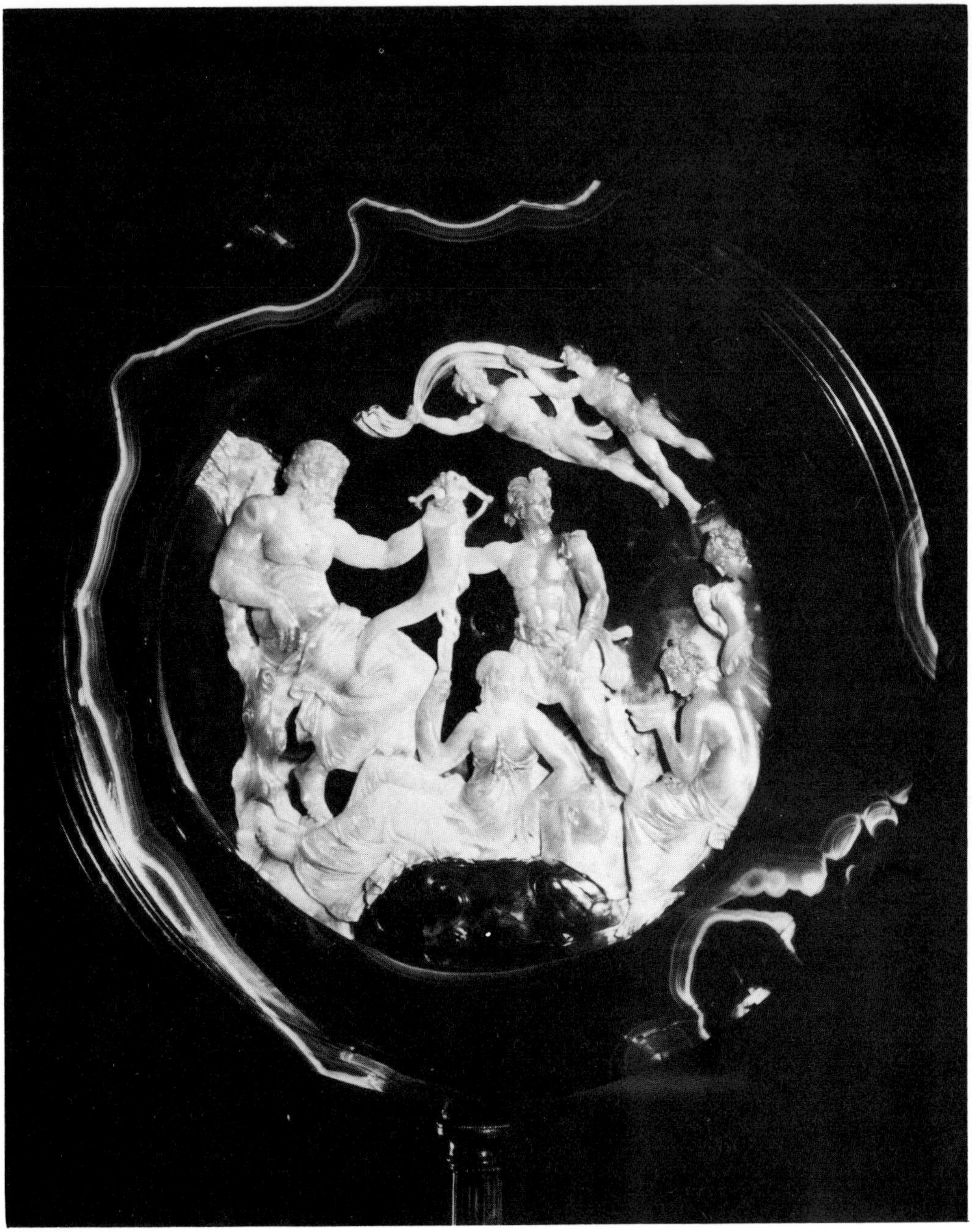

(Palestrina, National Museum (Palazzo Barberini).)

Rostovtzeff, pl. XXXVIII; id. *The Social and Economic History of the Roman Empire*, 2nd ed. (1957) pl. LI; G. Gullini, *I mosaici di Palestrina* (1956) 42, pl. XIX; S. Aurigemma, *Rend. Pont. Acc.* 3. 30–1 (1957–9) 72–4; H. Whitehouse, *The Dal Pozzo Copies of the Palestrina Mosaic* (1976) 5, 21–2, 82, pls. 16–17.

9. Dedication to Anubis. The stele (*c.* 250 B.C.) portrays Anubis to whom it is dedicated, carrying a *wꜣs*-sceptre in his left hand and sign of life (*ankh*) in his right, in front of an altar. He wears a typical Egyptian kilt and has the jackal's tail; his hieroglyph is above. The inscription below, in a semi-cursive hand, reads:

ὑπὲρ Ἀπολλωνίου

8

καὶ Ζήνωνος
Πασῶς κυνοβοσκὸς
Ἀνούβι εὐχήν.

(On behalf of Apollonius and Zenon, Pasos, feeder of the sacred jackals, (makes this) dedication to Anoubis.) Apollonius, the *dioiketes* of Ptolemy II Philadelphus, was the recipient of a 10,000 *aroura* gift-estate at Philadelphia (from where this stele comes), Zenon was manager of the estate, and both were Carians by origin. It is interesting to find an Egyptian, Pasos, employed in the native Anubis cult making such a dedication in Greek upon a stele of Greek form. Anubis was god of the embalmers, and jackals might be the recipients of cult, both alive and themselves mummified.

(Cairo, Egyptian Museum J.E. 44048. Height 47 cm; width 18 cm.)

G. Grimm, *Kunst der Ptolemäer- und Römerzeit im Ägyptische Museum Kairo* (1975) 18 no. 11, pl. 12;

9

Papyrologica Lugduno-Batava xx: P. W. Pestman, ed., *Greek and Demotic Texts from the Zenon Archive* (1980) 274–5.

10. Advertisement for a Cretan dream-interpreter from Saqqâra. This unusual painted limestone stele from the Serapeum area advertises a Cretan dream-interpreter of *c.* 2000 B.C. A Greek

10

pediment is supported by two Egyptian pilasters with caryatids facing front, and on the painted surface an Apis bull faces a stepped, horned altar of Hellenistic type. The inscription above reads:

ἐνύπνια κρίνω
τοῦ θεοῦ πρόσταγ-
μα ἔχων. τύχ' ἀγα-
θᾶι. Κρής ἐστιν ὁ
κρίνων τάδε.

(I interpret dreams having orders from the god. Good fortune. A Cretan is the interpreter.) The cult of the bull Osiris–Apis was the central cult of the sacred animal necropolis of Memphis but many other shrines and temples shared the site, with its busy community of priests, embalmers, temple employees and pilgrims. Incubation, dream-oracles and the description of dreams (in both Greek and demotic) are recorded in the Ptolemaic papyri and ostraca from the area (see **2**). The record of a Cretan settled here illustrates the international repute of Memphis and its necropolis.

(Cairo, Egyptian Museum 27567. Height 35 cm; width 25 cm.)

Rostovtzeff 900, pl. CI, 1; J. Quaegebeur, *BIFAO* 69 (1971) 195–7; Grimm, *op. cit.*, 18 no. 12, pl. 13 with bibliography.

I

12

11. Silver decadrachm of Ptolemy II or III for Arsinoe II continuing the earlier type of Arsinoe I. *Obv.* Head of Arsinoe II facing right, wearing diadem, *stephane* and veil; behind ΜΜ; border of dots. *Rev.* Double cornucopia bound with fillet; border of dots; around ΑΡΣΙΝΟΗΣ ΦΙΛΑΔΕΛΦΟΥ.

(Cambridge, Fitzwilliam Museum. Actual size.)

SNG III, no. 3415; cf. Svoronos, *Nom. Ptol.* 143 no. 947, pl. XXVIII.12; *SNG Copenhagen* XL (1977) no. 136.

12. A faience queen vase of Berenice II. The queen figure is dressed in a Greek *chiton* and *himation*; in her left arm she carries a cornucopia with fruit and two spikes and with her right hand she pours a libation from a decorated *phiale*. The inscription above reads:

Βερενίκης βασιλίσσης
ἀγαθῆς τύχης

and to the left, not visible, on a large altar a further inscription θεῶν εὐεργετῶν dates the vase after 243 B.C. when Ptolemy III Euergetes and his wife, Berenice II, first entered the dynastic cult as the Theoi Euergetai. The vase is of light blue faience, an Egyptian material, with dark blue on the queen's hair (bound by a light fillet), green lettering, and gilding on the base, the *phiale* and the rim of the horn. Such figured *oinochoai* were probably used in the Greek ruler cult introduced when Ptolemy II Philadelphus and Arsinoe II were deified as the Theoi Adelphoi.

(Antalya Museum 571, from Xanthos, Lycia. Height 24 cm; diameter 18.8 cm.)

P. M. Fraser, *Ptolemaic Alexandria* (1972) 140, 240–3; D. B. Thompson, *Ptolemaic Oinochoai and Portraits in Faience* (1973) 149f. no. 75, pls. B, XXV–XXVII, with earlier bibliography and discussion.

13. Arsinoe II as an Egyptian goddess. On this block from Tanis Ptolemy II Philadelphus faces his queen and sister Arsinoe II. Arsinoe, on the left, wears a long, clinging robe, the vulture headdress and her typical, composite crown (with the red crown of Lower Egypt surmounted by the high plumes of Isis, the lyriform cow's

13

horns of Hathor embracing the solar disk and the ram's horns of Amon with the uraeus). In her left hand she carries a papyriform sceptre and in her right the sign of life (*ankh*). Ptolemy II, crowned with the double red and white (*pschent*) crown of Lower and Upper Egypt with the uraeus in front, wears a short kilt and collar. In his left hand he holds up a ritual object and in his right carries a *wꜣs*-sceptre. Hieroglyphs identify Ptolemy as a traditional king of Egypt and Arsinoe as queen and daughter of Amon, god of Thebes. Arsinoe was introduced to the Egyptian temples after her death by the Mendes stele of 270 B.C. and regularly shared worship with the chief god of an area. Here she is shown as a goddess in her own right and the representation belongs to the period 270–246 B.C., during her brother's lifetime.

(London, British Museum EA 1056, from Tanis (Sân el-Ḥagar). Height 43 cm; width 35 cm; thickness 5 cm.)

J. Quaegebeur, *BIFAO* 69 (1971) 191–217, esp. 213 no. 25, pl. XXVIII; *JNES* 30 (1971) 239–70; id. in H. Maehler and V. M. Strocka, eds., *Das ptolemäische Ägypten* (1978) 245–62; D. J. Crawford, *Studia Hellenistica* 24 (1980) 23–7; K. Sethe, *Hieroglyphische Urkunden* (1904) 41 no. 13 for Mendes decree.

14

14. Gold octadrachm of Ptolemy Philadelphus (285–246 B.C.) showing Ptolemy and Arsinoe as the Theoi Adelphoi. *Obv.* Jugate busts facing right of Ptolemy II, diademed and wearing *chlamys*, and Arsinoe II, diademed and veiled; behind monogram; border of dots. *Rev.* Jugate busts facing right of Ptolemy I, wearing diadem and aegis (?), and Berenice I, diademed and veiled; behind, spearhead; border of dots.

(Cambridge, Fitzwilliam Museum, Young gift. Actual size.)

For the type see Svoronos, *Nom. Ptol.* 29 no. 169, pl. VI.8; *SNG Copenhagen* XL (1977) no. 132.

15. The temple of Horus at Edfu (Apollonopolis Magna). The building of the great south-facing pylon of the Edfu temple, together with the enclosure wall, commenced in 116 B.C.; the hanging of the wooden gates in 57 B.C. concluded a temple-building programme which had lasted 180 years. The temple, started in 237

15

B.C., is the most complete of the surviving Ptolemaic temples and under the last Egyptian pharaoh (Nectanebo II) owned 13,209 *arourai* (3,402 ha) in Upper Egypt. On the top two registers of the 33.50 m-high pylon Ptolemy XII Neos Dionysos (Auletes) is shown making offerings to various gods and in the main scene adopts the traditional pose of pharaoh smiting his enemies in the presence of Horus and Hathor. The perpendicular recesses were for flagstaffs and the pediment of the pylon door is decorated with a sun disk with uraei. Colossal statues of hawks (the bird of Horus) flank the entrance.

B. Porter and R. L. B. Moss, *Topographical Bibliography of Ancient Egyptian Hieroglyphic Texts, Reliefs and Paintings* VI (1939) 121–2; H. W. Fairman, *BIFAO* 43 (1945) 93; D. Meeks, *Le grand texte des donations au temple d'Edfou* (1972).

2. THE SELEUCID KINGDOM

M. A. R. COLLEDGE

The area of western Asia appropriated by the Seleucids was one in which a variety of previous cultures, Semitic based on Syria and Mesopotamia, and Iranian based on Iran, had each left a powerful living legacy. The conquering Greeks under Alexander, Seleucus and the Seleucid rulers introduced their own material culture, adding one more to the many pre-existing. Of prime importance to the newcomers were urban settlements. Seleucus I founded two new capitals: Seleucia on the Tigris in Babylonia, and Antioch on the Orontes in western Syria (**16**); Hellenistic levels have been excavated on each site, particularly Seleucia, illustrating street and building forms. Greek settlements were scattered across the realm for military and commercial purposes, as new colonies, refoundations or additions to existing townships; such sites as Syrian Dura-Europus, Iranian Susa and most notably north Afghan Aï Khanum on the Oxus (**17**), as well as others, have yielded important Seleucid remains, comprising defensive walling, an acropolis, streets usually laid out on a 'Hippodamian' grid plan, agoras, palaces, temples, *heroa*, houses, theatres, baths, a fountain and tombs. Executed normally in local materials these structures often echoed those of the Greek homeland, but sometimes, as for instance with the religious *asylon* (?) of *c.* 250–240 B.C. on the Persian Gulf island of Icarus (Faïlaka, **18**), Greek and oriental traditions were blended, and elsewhere, particularly as regards religious buildings, whether in Syria, in Babylonia, at Persepolis or at Aï Khanum, Asiatic traditions predominated. Other Greek cultural imports included inscriptions, sarcophagi, metalwork, jewellery and pottery of normal Hellenistic types, and a unique sundial at Aï Khanum for calculating both time and equinoxes (**258**). Sculptors long maintained Hellenic traditions, using local materials (especially clay and limestone) or occasionally imported marble to produce statuary (often acrolithic or acrometallic) and reliefs in stone or bronze (**19**, **20**), or figurines (**21**), mostly in terracotta but sometimes in bronze or various stones. Mints were established by Alexander and the Seleucids across the region for the production of Attic-standard coinage of Greek type (**22**). Many Greek themes (especially divinities) entered the iconographic repertoire. Seleucid rulers also commissioned buildings (**87**) and apparently portraits (**23–4**) of normal Hellenistic kinds in Mediterranean Greek areas, for propaganda purposes. Meanwhile Asiatic workshops continued to produce traditional eastern figurines, rock reliefs (in west Iran), cuneiform tablets (in Mesopotamia), jewellery, textiles and pottery mainly for Asiatics. Here, too, blending occurred, as in pottery, an Iranian rock relief of Heracles (**25**), or figurines at Seleucia. As Seleucid political control loosened, so its cultural thrust diminished, with complex cultural results.

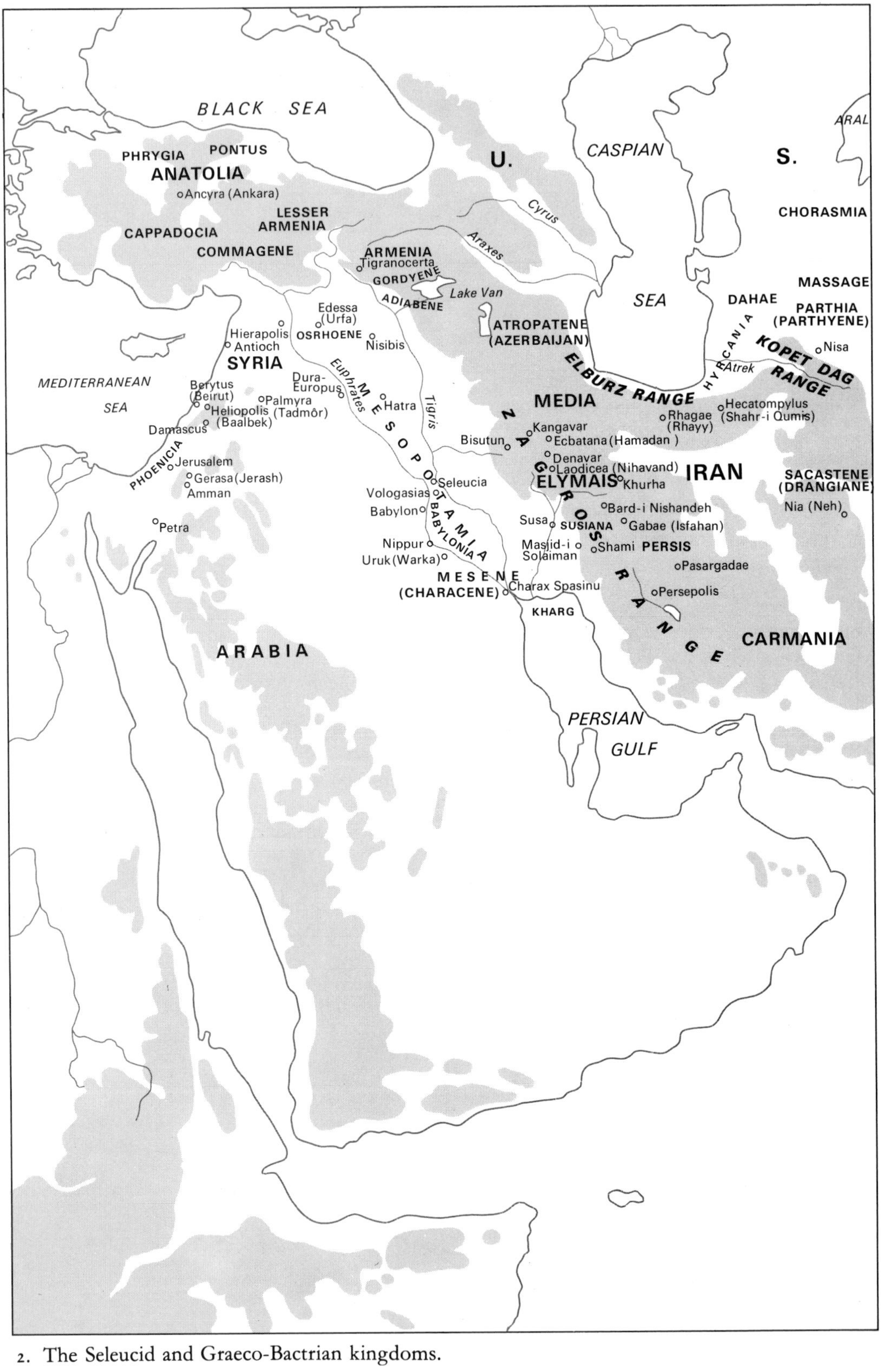

2. The Seleucid and Graeco-Bactrian kingdoms.

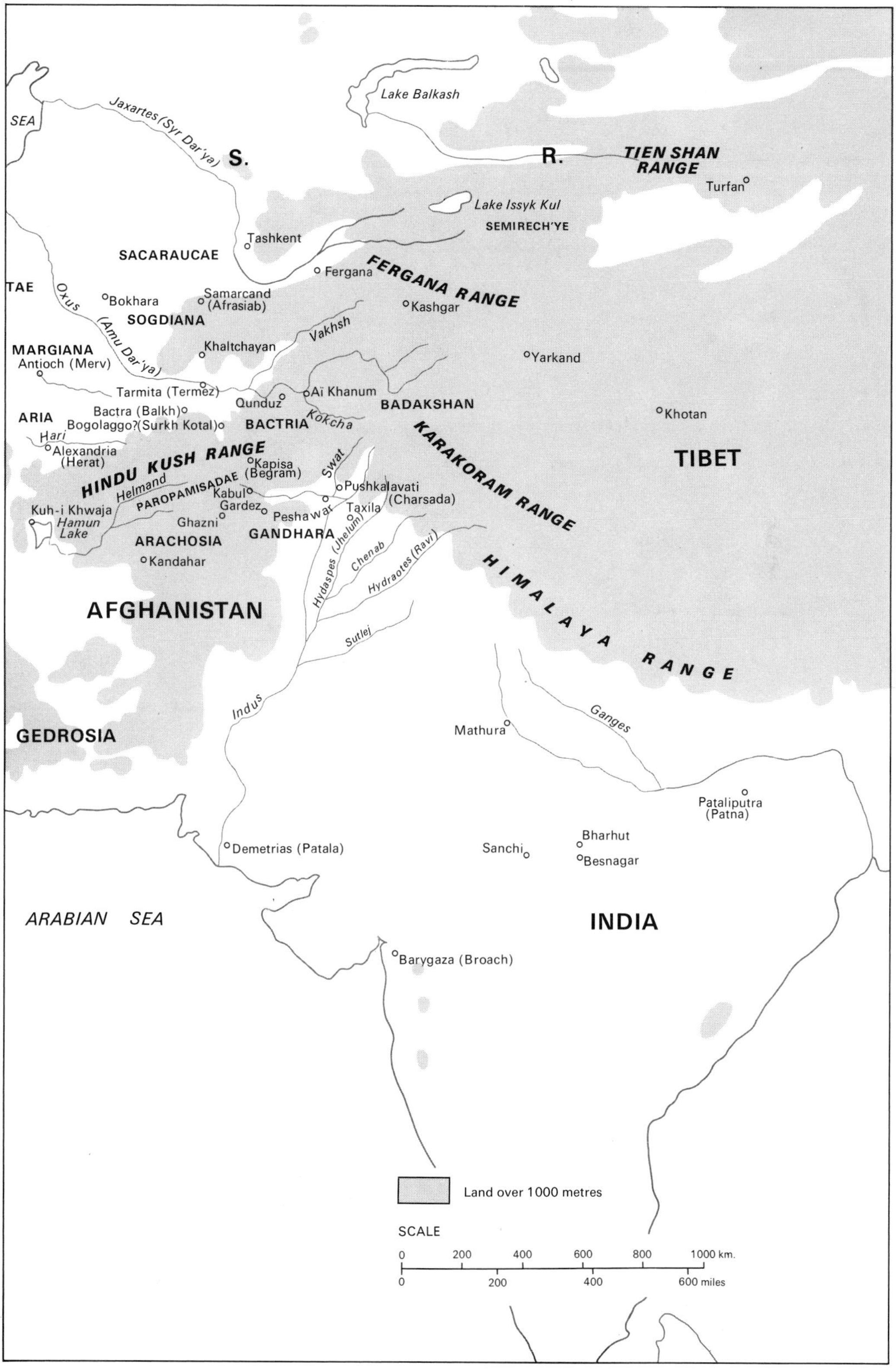

SEA
Jaxartes (Syr Dar'ya)
S.
Lake Balkash
R.
TIEN SHAN RANGE
Turfan
Lake Issyk Kul
SEMIRECH'YE
Tashkent
SACARAUCAE
Fergana
FERGANA RANGE
TAE
Oxus (Amu Dar'ya)
Bokhara
Samarcand (Afrasiab)
SOGDIANA
Kashgar
Vakhsh
MARGIANA
Antioch (Merv)
Khaltchayan
Yarkand
Tarmita (Termez)
Aï Khanum
Qunduz
BADAKSHAN
ARIA
Bactra (Balkh)
Bogolaggo?(Surkh Kotal)
BACTRIA
Kokcha
Khotan
Hari
Alexandria (Herat)
HINDU KUSH RANGE
KARAKORAM RANGE
TIBET
Kapisa (Begram)
Swat
Helmand
PAROPAMISADAE
Kabul
Pushkalavati (Charsada)
Gardez
Taxila
Kuh-i Khwaja
Hamun Lake
Ghazni
Peshawar
ARACHOSIA
GANDHARA
Hydaspes (Jhelum)
Chenab
Hydraotes (Ravi)
Kandahar
HIMALAYA RANGE
AFGHANISTAN
Sutlej
Indus
Ganges
GEDROSIA
Mathura
Pataliputra (Patna)
Bharhut
Demetrias (Patala)
Sanchi
Besnagar
ARABIAN SEA
INDIA
Barygaza (Broach)
Land over 1000 metres
SCALE
0 200 400 600 800 1000 km.
0 200 400 600 miles

16

17

16. Air view of the site of the Seleucid capital of Antioch on the Orontes, founded by Seleucus I in north-west Syria, with modern dwellings. The line of its once famous main street is clearly visible, running south west to north east along the plain, following an earlier track. By the second century B.C. there were rectangular buildings aligned along it, and stone surfacing. The city expanded west–east, and then south–north. Soon the street was enlarged to the monumental width of 29.40 m, probably by Antiochus IV (175–163 B.C.). Later, King Herod paved it, and the Roman emperor Tiberius flanked it with porticoes.

See J. Lassus, *Les Portiques d'Antioche* (*Antioch-on-the-Orontes* v) (1972).

17. View of the main administrative and residential areas of the Seleucid and Graeco-Bactrian city of Aï Khanum (ancient name unknown; founded by Alexander?) on the left bank of the river Oxus in northern Afghanistan, seen from the acropolis before excavation. In the left foreground the hollow of the theatre is visible in the hillside, with the main street passing below it. In the middle-distance the rectangular enclosures of the palace may be seen. Beyond this the Oxus river runs leftwards; to the top left is its confluence with its tributary, the Kokcha. Excavation here has enormously enriched our knowledge of eastern Greek colonial culture.

P. Bernard, *Fouilles d'Aï Khanoum* (1973); *id. CRAI* (1967) 306–24; (1968) 263–80; (1969) 313–55; (1970) 301–49; (1971) 385–452; (1972) 605–32; (1974) 280–308; (1975) 167–97; (1976) 287–322; (1978) 421–63.

18. Ruins of one of two little rectangular ashlar temples within a fortified enclosure (*asylon*?) erected on the Persian Gulf island of Icarus, the modern Faïlaka, by a Seleucid king (Seleucus II?) around 250–240 B.C. This temple has two Ionic columns *in antis*, and in the background is its rectangular altar; the other temple was Doric. The finds made here were remarkable for their cultural variety. Inscriptions, coins, pottery and some moulds were of normal Greek kinds, while certain figurines were more eastern and the architecture in particular mixed both Greek and oriental (especially Iranian) traditions, with such hybrid forms as the Ionic capital and palmette visible here.

E. Albrectsen, *ILN* (27 August 1960) 351–3; K. Jeppesen, *Kuml* (1960) 153–99; K. Jeppesen, in *Huitième congrès international d'archéologie classique* (1965) 541–4, pl. 136.

19. Fragment of a slightly under-life-size bronze head found in the ruins of the Hellenistic

18

19

Greek and Parthian-period shrine at Shami, in the Bakhtiari mountains of west Iran. To judge by the apparently royal character of most of the shattered marble and bronze sculpture found here, this little temple may have functioned as a dynastic shrine. This bronze head, in excellent Greek style and shown wearing the Hellenistic royal diadem, may have represented Alexander the Great, or possibly a Seleucid ruler (the religiously energetic Antiochus IV, who reigned 175–164 B.C.?).

(Teheran, Iran-e Bastan Museum 2477. Height 26.7 cm.)

F. Cumont, *Syria* 20 (1939) 167–8, fig. 2; M. A. Stein, *Old Routes of Western Iran* (1940) 150–1, pl. IV; R. Ghirshman, *Iran, Parthians and Sassanians* (1962) 20–1, figs. 26–7; M. A. R. Colledge, *Parthian Art* (1977) 82, pl. 8b.

20. Fragments of a large bowl or circular altar of greyish stone with relief busts of Satyrs and Sileni, found in the area of Denavar, near Kermanshah, west Iran. The stone resembles that used for the Achaemenid Persian sculptures at Persepolis. The sculptor has worked in a Greek style, however, and used Hellenistic tools and techniques: a fine claw chisel and flat chisels for the background, flat chisels, rasps and abrasives for the figures, and narrow drills sparingly in hair, ears, tear ducts, mouths and leaves. Such employment of Greek techniques on local materials is typical of Seleucid Asia.

(Teheran, Iran-e Bastan Museum 2402. Height 33 cm.)

For bibliography see B. Rowland, *Art Quarterly* 18 (1955) 171–4; also R. Ghirshman, *Iran, Parthians and Sassanians* (1962) 18, pl. 21; D. Schlumberger, *L'Orient hellénisé* (1970) 31; M. A. R. Colledge, *Parthian Art* (1977) 114, pl. 31a; id. in *East and West* 29 (Rome, 1979) 227–8.

20

21

21. Mould-made terracotta figurine of a dwarf from the area of the Seleucid capital of Seleucia on the Tigris, founded by Seleucus I (306–281 B.C.) in Babylonia. Under Persian domination horsemen and a nude goddess had been the commonest subjects for terracottas in this area. The Greeks greatly stimulated production, and introduced both Greek style and a wide range of subjects mostly imported from their Mediterranean homeland, such as deities, women, children, dwarfs (as here), grotesques and masks. But at Seleucia and elsewhere, at the same time, many artists were also producing figurines in oriental styles.

(Baghdad, Iraq Museum 8883. Height 13 cm.)

See W. Van Ingen, *Figurines from Seleucia on the Tigris* (1939); M. A. R. Colledge, *Parthian Art* (1977) 88.

22

a

b

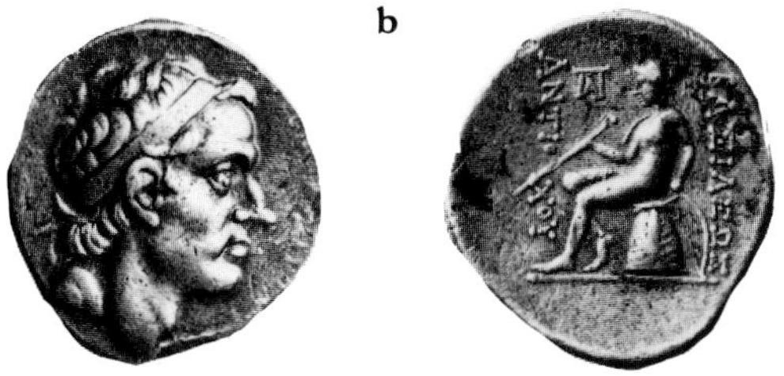

23

24

22. Seleucid coins.

(**a**) Silver tetradrachm minted at Persepolis with the beardless helmeted portrait head almost certainly of Seleucus I (named on the reverse) in right profile. Seleucus' coinage, like subsequent Seleucid issues, was based in fabric, design and technique on the Attic-standard coinage of Alexander the Great. The earliest Hellenistic monarchs, however, introduced an important innovation: the ruler's realistic portrait head on the obverse, as here, with the features remarkably individualized. Reverses usually showed a deity such as Zeus or Apollo standing or seated; here Victory crowns a trophy. These named royal Hellenistic coin portraits are sometimes used as evidence in attempts to identify unlabelled portrait sculpture (cf. **23**).

(Cambridge, Fitzwilliam Museum. Approximately actual size.)

McClean III, 325 no. 9244, pl. 335.8; E. T. Newell, *The Coinage of the Eastern Seleucid Mints* (*Numismatic Studies* I) (1938) 154f. no. 417, pl. XXXII.9; cf. Davis and Kraay, pls. 48, 49, 52.

(**b**) Silver tetradrachm minted at Nisibis with the beardless diademed portrait head of Antiochus III (named on the reverse; reigned 223–187 B.C.) in right profile. This fine piece is typical of the high standards of portraiture achieved by the Seleucid royal coin die-engravers. The ruler is shown wearing the commonest headgear to appear on coins, the royal diadem. The lean features and tumbled locks of Antiochus III, seen here, have led many to identify an unlabelled marble head as another portrait of him (**24**). On the reverse, seated Apollo.

(Cambridge, Fitzwilliam Museum. Approximately actual size.)

SNG IV, no. 5578; E. T. Newell, *The Coinage of the Western Seleucid Mints* (*Numismatic Studies* 4) (1941) 78 no. 877; cf. Davis and Kraay, pls. 72, 73, 76 (Antioch mint).

23. Head of a bronze portrait bust found with other bronzes in the Villa 'of the Pisones' or 'Papyri' at Herculaneum, central Italy, showing an unnamed beardless man wearing the diadem of a Hellenistic monarch. The inlaid eyes are original. Through comparison with the labelled profile portrait heads of Hellenistic kings shown on coins, many scholars believe this to represent Seleucus I (**22a**), who is recorded as having commissioned portraits from the sculptors Lysippus, Bryaxis and Aristodemus. The coin portraits, however, are small and their subjects tend to resemble Alexander the Great, so the identification is uncertain.

(Naples, National Museum 5590. Height of bust 56 cm, of head 25.5 cm.)

For bibliography see Richter, *Portraits* 270, figs. 1867–8.

24. Marble head of an unnamed beardless man wearing a fillet, found in Italy; it was intended for insertion into a separate statue. The style, sensitivity of carving and subject-matter all suggest a Hellenistic portrait, and the fillet a ruler. The evidence of Hellenistic royal coin portraits has been sifted, and many think as a result that this shows Antiochus III (**22b**). But the identification is no more sure than that of the bronze head of 'Seleucus I' (**23**).

(Paris, Louvre Museum MA 1204. Full height 35 cm; of head, 23 cm.)

For bibliography see Richter, *Portraits* 271, figs. 1878–9.

25

25. Rock relief of Heracles reclining ('Cubans'), overlooking an ancient highway at Bisutun, west Iran. The god (whose head survives and has now been put back) wears his characteristic lion skin and holds a cup; his club and quiver hang behind, and he has been placed on the back of an earlier lion. In genre, style and technique this is a hybrid, Graeco-oriental work. A completed Greek text records its dedication on behalf of the governor Cleomenes in June (Panemus) 148 B.C.; an Aramaic inscription is incomplete, suggesting an interruption of work (because of the advance of the Parthians?).

(*In situ.* Height *c.* 1.90 m; width *c.* 2.10 m.)

R. N. Frye, *The Heritage of Persia* (1962) 156, figs. 69–70; L. Robert, *Gnomon* 35 (1963) 76 (Greek inscription); S. B. Downey, *The Heracles Sculpture* (*The Excavations at Dura-Europos, Final Report* III.I.I) (1969) I, pl. I; W. Kleiss, *Archäologische Mitteilungen aus Iran*, n.s. 3 (1970) 145, pl. 66; S. A. Matheson, *Persia: an Archaeological Guide* (1972) 126, pl. 28; M. A. R. Colledge, *Parthian Art* (1977) 90, fig. 39A; id. in *East and West* 29 (Rome, 1979). 228–9, figs. 8–10.

3. THE GREEK KINGDOMS IN BACTRIA AND INDIA

M. A. R. COLLEDGE

The Graeco-Bactrian phase in Bactria, known mainly through coins and some excavation at the capital Bactra (Balkh), Kapisa (Begram) and especially Aï Khanum on the Oxus, shows various facets. Economic energy is illustrated by the Aï Khanum palace treasury of *c.* 150 B.C., with its coins, semi-precious stones and potsherds labelled in cursive Greek script. Culturally, to some degree Hellenistic Greek forms were maintained, often in local materials: in town walling, colonnades and peristyles in the houses and palace of Aï Khanum, the Aï Khanum gymnasium and library, sculpture, relief, figurines, pebble mosaics (**26**), pottery, and also at Aï Khanum in papyrus traces (**27**) and an inkpot. Coinage, on the Attic Greek standard, carried rulers' portrait heads of astonishing quality (**28**). Through contacts with Mediterranean Greeks (across Parthia), the Aï Khanum Doric and Corinthian orders and theatre (built *c.* 225–150 B.C.) remained up-to-date, plaster casts for metal wares were imported, and perhaps what seems to be Graeco-Bactrian portrait statuary was commissioned (**29**). Conversely oriental forms were also absorbed, Semitic in the 'indented' temples of Aï Khanum, and Iranian and central Asiatic at Aï Khanum in the palace treasury plan, corridors in buildings, and perhaps religious platforms. Blending between Greek and eastern traditions occurred, for instance at Aï Khanum in the regularized palace layout, a somewhat stylized statuette (**30**), and pottery. Cultural inventiveness, visible again at Aï Khanum, created an unusual architectural rotunda, a *pyxis* form, and figured architectural wall reliefs in wood, clay and plaster (**31**), doubtless echoing developments at the capital; Bactrian expertise may also have produced a fine series of mostly silver relief bowls from unrecorded contexts in the central Asian area (**32**). Graeco-Bactrian cultural influence can be seen in much early Parthian and Kushan work in central Asia.

The Indo-Greek (or 'Indo-Bactrian') expansion into north-west India is documented mainly by coins and by excavation primarily at two sites, Pushkalavati (Charsada) and the capital, Taxila, where new townships arose on 'Hippodamian' grid-plan lines, defended by walling, with standard housing (**33**). Greek types of pottery, figurine, jewellery and stone bowl-shaped cosmetic palette ('toilet tray', **34**), coexisted or coalesced with local kinds. Coins, upon which knowledge of the sequences of Indo-Greek kings primarily depends, were of good quality but considerably Indianized: few were on the Attic standard (**35**), while most had a lighter Indian weight, an Indian language reverse legend, and sometimes a square Indian shape (**36**). Indian languages were also used in contemporary texts mentioning the kings Menander and Antialcidas (**37**). This mixed civilization subsequently influenced Indo-Scythian, Indo-Parthian and Kushan cultures.

26

27

26. Figured mosaic of large pebbles set in rose-coloured cement, executed towards 150 B.C. in the bath block dressing-room of the palace at Aï Khanum, Afghanistan. The motifs, in white or greyish-white on a brownish-red ground, comprise a central rosette, palmettes, and dolphins, crabs and sea-monsters. Techniques, motifs and composition are almost all derived directly from earlier Mediterranean Greek pebble mosaic (cf. **139**), but this is a late, provincial example: by this time, in Greece itself, the cut stone cube (*tessera*) had become normal. The apparent restriction of mosaic to bathrooms at Aï Khanum may indicate an (oriental) preference for carpets in living rooms.

(*In situ.*)
P. Bernard, *CRAI* (1975) 173–80, figs. 4, 6–8.

27. Imprint from a Greek papyrus of *c.* 300–260 B.C., found on the floor of what may have been a library (room 107) added around 150 B.C. to the palace of Aï Khanum. The papyrus had perished, leaving only traces of ink. The remains of three columns of text may be seen, imprinted in reverse, written in a careful hand and divided into paragraphs; identifiable words suggest a work of philosophical, and somewhat Aristotelian, character. Adjoining the room was a large, contemporary court ringed with colonnades in the Doric order. This immensely significant find illuminates the high degree of Greek culture obtaining in the later Graeco-Bactrian kingdom.

(Kabul Museum. Approximately half size.)
P. Bernard, *CRAI* (1978) 456–60, fig. 20.

28. Gold stater of King Diodotus I or II of Bactria, minted in the later third century B.C.; on the obverse the portrait head of the king in right profile. Modelled on Seleucid coins and similarly struck on the Attic Greek standard, this piece is typical of the high quality of design and execution maintained by the Graeco-Bactrian rulers, and its material illustrates their wealth. On the reverse is Zeus throwing the thunderbolt and a Greek legend giving Diodotus' name and his status as king: so this belongs to the period after the Graeco-Bactrians had broken away from Seleucid control.

(Cambridge, Fitzwilliam Museum T.45-1918. Approximately actual size.)

28

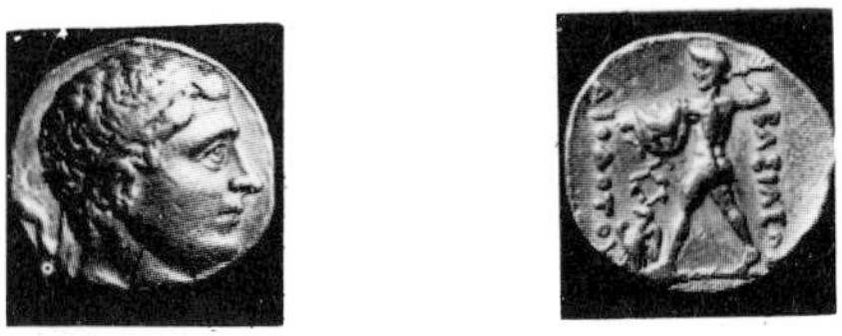

29

Cf. P. Gardner, *The Coins of the Greek and Scythic Kings of Bactria and India* (1886) 3 nos. 1–2, pl. I.4–5; A. N. Lahiri, *Corpus of Indo-Greek Coins* (1965) 113 no. 5, pl. XIII.8.

29. Marble portrait head of a man wearing the Greek *kausia* headdress. On the basis of the profile portrait heads of rulers on the obverses of Hellenistic royal coins this has been tentatively identified as one of the Graeco-Bactrian monarchs, who were often represented on coins in this headgear, and possibly Euthydemus I (around 200 B.C.). This head is presumably a copy of a powerful original created either in the ruler's kingdom, or (if correctly identified) in Asia Minor, with which Euthydemus had connexions. Whomsoever it represents, the head reflects the finest traditions of Hellenistic portraiture; this received its greatest stimulus in royal circles, for propaganda purposes.

(Rome, Torlonia collection, in the Villa Albani. Height 33 cm.)
For bibliography see Richter, *Portraits* 278, figs. 1970–1.

30 

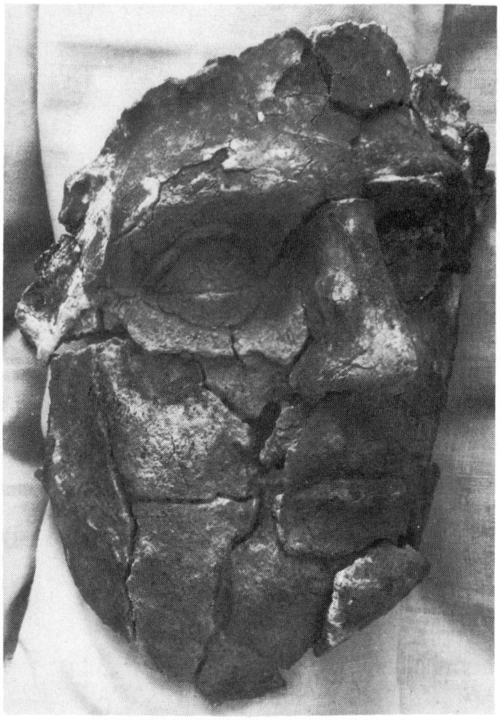 31

32 

30. Limestone statuette representing a female standing against a pillar which has an Ionic capital, found in the sanctuary of the Indented Temple ('à redans') at Aï Khanum. The piece is Hellenistic Greek in its conception and iconography, with its female proportions following the 'elongated' canon, its tunic (*chiton*) bound high beneath the breasts, and the drapery of the cloak (*himation*) held by the left hand at her hip. But the dry, linear quality of the largely flat-chisel execution indicates a hybrid, Graeco-oriental style, which suggests a date fairly late in Graeco-Bactrian history (around 150 B.C.?).

(Kabul Museum. Height *c.* 1 m.)

P. Bernard, *CRAI* (1972) 628–9, fig. 15; M. A. R. Colledge, *Parthian Art* (1977) 85, pl. 7.

31. Beardless male head in Greek style of clay and stucco, originally covered in gold leaf, which formed part of the architectural relief decoration of the Indented Temple ('à redans') at Aï Khanum, probably in the third century B.C. The Bactrian Greeks pioneered a special technique for making such reliefs from clay and stucco mounted on wooden framing for sacred and

33

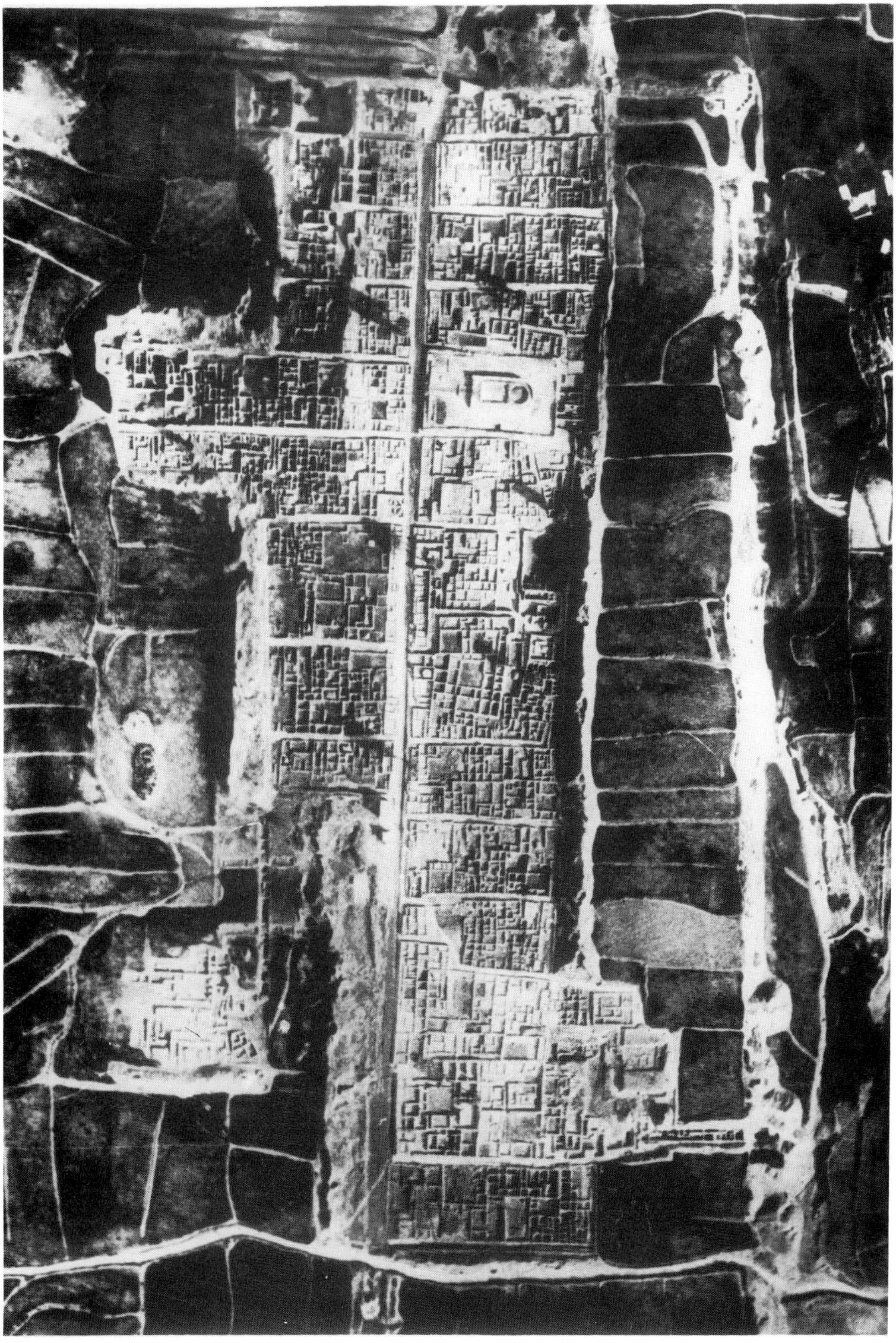

secular buildings, doubtless as a cheap local substitute for the stones commonly so used in the Greek homeland. This technique was adopted in the Parthian and Kushan empires, becoming immensely popular in central Asia, Afghanistan and north India, especially for Buddhist sculpture.

(Kabul Museum. Height *c.* 20 cm.)

P. Bernard, *CRAI* (1969) 344, fig. 20; Colledge, *op. cit.* 96, pl. 25*a*.

32. One of two very similar dishes of partly gilded silver with figures in relief (repoussé) of warriors on an elephant, one of whom wears the Greek *kausia*. This is one of a large group of plates, bowls and other utensils in silver (or sometimes gold) bearing Greek and Asiatic subjects in more or less Hellenistic styles whose precise provenances are unknown, but whose central Asiatic connexions have suggested to many a possibly Graeco-Bactrian origin for some at least, such as this. Stylistically this piece could belong to the third or second century B.C.

(Leningrad, Hermitage Museum. Diameter 24.7 cm.)

K. V. Trever, *Pamiatniki Greko-Baktriiskogo Isskustva* (1940) 45–8 no. 1, pl. 1; V. G. Lukonin, *Persia* II (1967) pl. 38 (colour); Colledge, *op. cit.* 115, pl. 46*a*.

33. Air view of the Sirkap mound, Taxila, Pakistan, occupied between its settlement probably by the Indo-Greeks ('Indo-Bactrians') in the mid-second century B.C., and its abandonment under the Kushan rulers around A.D. 100 in favour of a nearby site. Although most (if not all) of what is visible here represents the post-Greek occupation, the main outlines of the probably originally Indo-Greek settlement are clear with its 'Hippodamian' grid-plan of streets crossing at right angles and its rectangular areas between these streets with eight houses per block (as at the Seleucid capital, Seleucia on the Tigris).

J. Marshall, *Taxila* (1951); R. E. M. Wheeler, *Flames over Persepolis* (1968) 112ff.

34. Palette (or 'toilet tray') of black schist for women's cosmetics found in a house in 'Greek' level V at Taxila, Pakistan. It bears a relief in a hybrid Graeco-oriental style of a male banqueter reclining on a couch (*kline*) and holding a cup, attended by two females, one of whom holds out a wreath. Such palettes, although known elsewhere in the Hellenistic world, were particularly popular in post-Greek Gandhâra, of which Taxila was the capital, and exhibit there a wide range of Greek and oriental styles and subject-matter.

(Karachi Museum 195/1932–33. Diameter 13.5 cm.)

Marshall, *op. cit.* 494f. no. 63, pl. 144.63; for bibliography see H. P. Francfort, *Les palettes du Gandhâra* (Mémoires de la Délégation Archéologique Française en Afghanistan 23) (1979) 32–3 no. 27, pl. XIV.27.

35. Silver double decadrachm coin with the profile portrait bust of the Indo-Greek ('Indo-Bactrian') king Amyntas in a Greek *kausia* helmet, struck probably towards 120 B.C. on the Attic Greek standard. On the reverse is the king's name and rank, a seated Zeus and a monogram probably indicating the mint at Alexandria ad Caucasum (Kapisa, Begram) in Afghanistan. This unique issue, the largest silver coin of antiquity, with its fine Greek style, proclaims Amyntas' wealth. Its Attic standard is unusual for the Indo-Greek series, which normally adhere to a lighter Indian standard.

(Kabul Museum (Qunduz hoard). Approximately actual size.)

A. K. Narain, *The Indo-Greeks* (1957) pl. V.1; for bibliography see A. N. Lahiri, *Corpus of Indo-Greek Coins* (1965) 78f. nos. 1–2 and pl. III.1–2; R. Curiel and G. Fussman, *Le trésor monétaire de Qunduz* (Mémoires de la Délégation Archéologique Française en Afghanistan 20) (1965).

36. Square bronze coin of the Indo-Greek king Menander I Soter. The obverse bears his name in Greek, and the profile helmeted bust of either the king or the goddess Athena. Struck probably around 150 B.C. it typifies the degree of Indianization of many Indo-Greek coins, especially the bronze: it has a light Indian weight (as do most circular Indo-Greek coins also), the square shape of pre-existing Indian currency, and a legend in Indian Kharosthî script round the shield on the reverse. In such ways the Indo-Greek monarchs sought to reconcile their Asiatic subjects, and especially the merchants, to their rule.

(Cambridge, Fitzwilliam Museum. Approximately actual size.)

Cf. P. Gardner, *The Coins of the Greek and Scythic Kings of Bactria and India* (1886) 49 no. 59, pl. XII.2; for bibliography see Lahiri, *op. cit.* 155f. no. 17, pl. XXV.6–7.

34

36

35

37. Pillar of Indian type with a text in the Indian Brahmi script erected at Besnagar, near Bhilsa in the Vidishâ region of central north India, on the orders of the Indo-Greek king Antialcidas to commemorate a visit by his ambassador to the Indian king Kosiputra (or Kasiputra) of the Sunga dynasty towards 100 B.C. The text runs as follows: 'This Garuda pillar of Vâsudeva, the god of gods, was erected by Heliodorus, a Bhâgavata (i.e. a worshipper of Vishnu), the son of Dion, and an inhabitant of Taxila, who came as Greek ambassador from the

37

Great King Antialcidas to King Kosiputra (Kasiputra) Bhâgabhadra, the Saviour, then reigning prosperously in the fourteenth year of his kingship. Three immortal precepts when practised lead to heaven – self-restraint, charity, conscientiousness.' Unfortunately Sunga dynastic dates are as yet insufficiently accurately known for this to be more than roughly datable from the reference to a particular year of a certain reign. This practice of commissioning a monument from local craftsmen, however, in a place outside the monarch's own realm for political purposes, was common in the western Hellenistic kingdoms; so although the execution of this monument was Indian, its conception and purpose remained at least partly Greek.

(Besnagar, India. Height *c.* 8 m.)

For bibliography see A. K. Narain, *The Indo-Greeks* (1957) 42 n. 3, pl. VI.3.

4. ASIA MINOR

SUSAN M. SHERWIN-WHITE

The material record for the Greek cities of Asia Minor and the offshore islands is much richer in the Hellenistic period than for earlier periods. This greater volume of evidence in part reflects new developments, the growing prosperity of Greek cities which began to build more extensively than before, and also the activity of the Hellenistic kings both in founding new cities and in their patronage and refounding of old cities. The Seleucids in particular dotted new foundations along the old communication routes linking Asia Minor and the East. In addition some old non-Greek cities and towns are given a Greek plan, as Sardis was under the Seleucids (**38**), so hellenizing their physical appearance. The new cities and the settlement of military colonies of Macedonians, Greeks and Greek-speaking peoples in non-Greek areas of the countryside of old Achaemenid satrapies (e.g. in Lydia and Phrygia) inevitably injected centres of Greek culture into non-Greek areas. Urbanization on the Greek model increases in Asia Minor during this period. The partially hellenized kingdoms of Pontus and Cappadocia (**65**) emerged out of areas of the old Achaemenid empire never subdued by Alexander.

The old Greek cities of the islands and of the littorals of Asia Minor continue to function, as before, as administrative, cultural and cult centres, and, to a varying extent, as power units, in the ongoing struggle to secure the best conditions of co-existence possible from the Hellenistic kings (**39–45**). Priene provides a paradigm of a small Hellenistic Greek town, just as Old Smyrna does for the Geometric period (**46–8**; cf. **41**). New, grander sanctuaries are built, where the advances of Hellenistic architectural planning are exploited. Greater importance is now given to the overall architectural scheme than to individual buildings. This change of emphasis produces spectacular sites spread over several terraces which are integrated into the architectural plan (**49–50**). Old sanctuaries are embellished with new buildings and monuments (**51–3**). In addition to the building activity of the Greek cities themselves, the Hellenistic kings were active patrons of these cities, founding and funding individual fine buildings and costly monuments, civil and sacred, adding in many places to the architectural record of the period (**54**, cf. **85–6**). An enormous volume of minor artefacts attests different facets of social and cultural history (**43–4**). The 'Apotheosis of Homer' by Archelaus of Priene reflects contemporary intellectual trends and provides an important surviving example of an approach at allegory in small scale relief sculpture (**55**).

Pergamum, the royal capital of the Attalid dynasty (**56**), has a special importance because, of all the capitals of the new Hellenistic kingdoms, it is the only one that survives to any significant extent. The physical remains allow a glimpse of the visual appearance and majesty of a Hellenistic royal capital, while the Attalids' presentation of their kingship to the world can be studied in the victory monuments, buildings and sculpture especially of Eumenes II (**59–64**).

As is not unusual, country and village life in Hellenistic Asia Minor is less well explored and more poorly attested in the archaeological remains than town life, and needs to be better known. On the Greek islands, however, notably on Cos and on Rhodes, the settlements and pattern of life in the country, in the old towns and demes, is more familiar. Self-contained communities, with typical institutions (theatres, temples, festivals and local municipal organizations) reflect the continuing importance of life outside the world of the city (**41**, **50**).

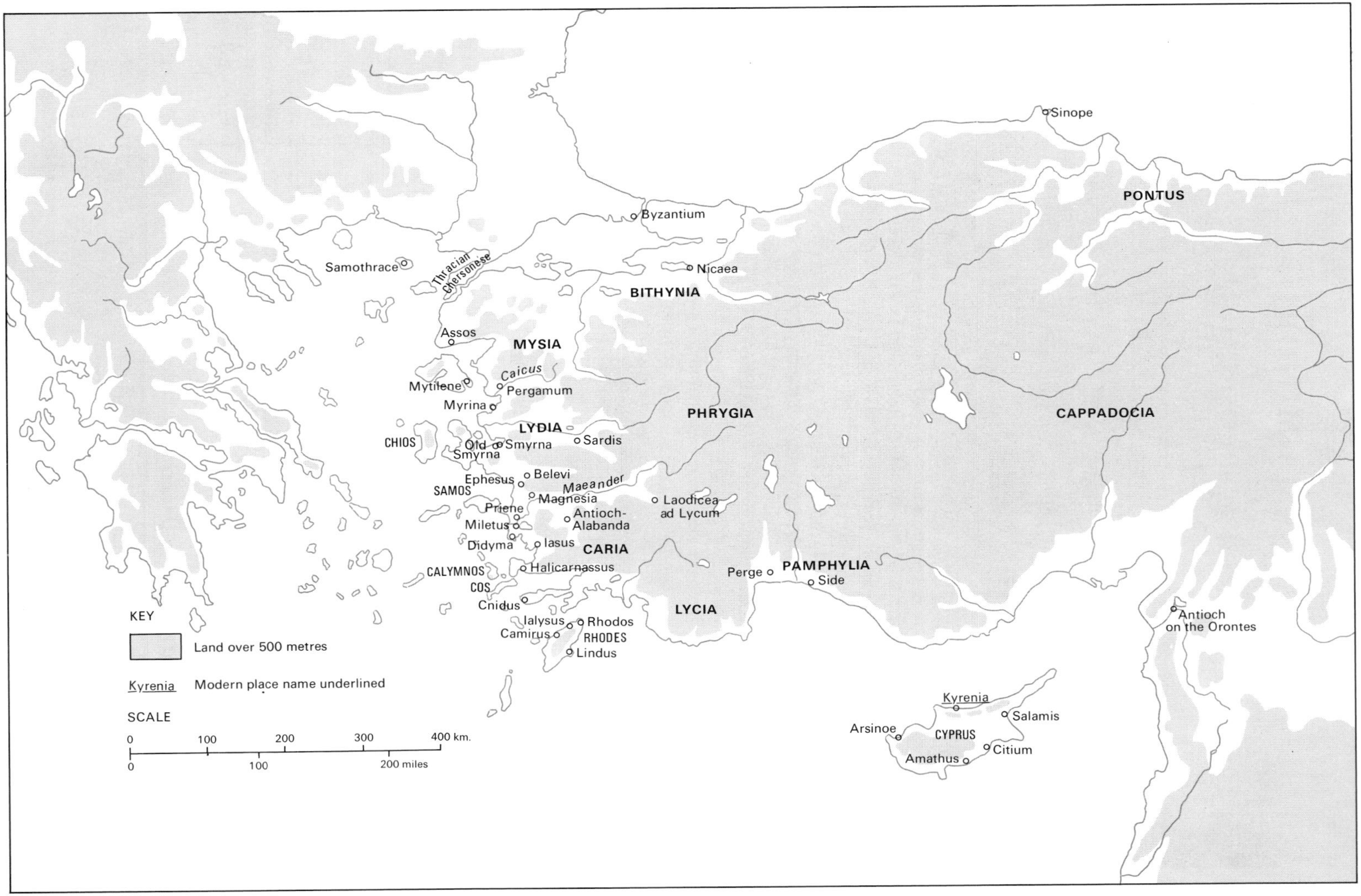
Sinope
PONTUS
Byzantium
Nicaea
BITHYNIA
Samothrace
Thracian Chersonese
Assos
MYSIA
Caicus
Mytilene
Pergamum
Myrina
PHRYGIA
CAPPADOCIA
LYDIA
CHIOS
Old Smyrna
Smyrna
Sardis
Ephesus
Belevi
Maeander
SAMOS
Magnesia
Priene
Laodicea ad Lycum
Miletus
Antioch-Alabanda
Didyma
Iasus
CARIA
CALYMNOS
Halicarnassus
Perge
PAMPHYLIA
Side
COS
Cnidus
LYCIA
Ialysus
Rhodos
RHODES
Camirus
Lindus
Antioch on the Orontes
Kyrenia
Salamis
Arsinoe
CYPRUS
Citium
Amathus
KEY
Land over 500 metres
Kyrenia
Modern place name underlined
SCALE
0
100
200
300
400 km.
0
100
200 miles

3. Asia Minor

38. Ionic temple of Artemis at Sardis. This large Hellenistic temple (*c.* 230 m × 200 m) is now thought to have been built in the later third century B.C. (*c.* 220–190 B.C.), and was perhaps preceded by an earlier Hellenistic temple (*c.* 270–220 B.C.). It was restored in the Imperial period. Sardis, capital of the Seleucid satrapy of Lydia, acquired other typical Greek public buildings during the third century (e.g. a stadium, theatre, gymnasium and city wall), and extensive re-planning of the haphazard old Lydian city was undertaken in the re-building after Antiochus III's siege of Achaeus in 213 B.C. The architectural development of the site furnishes an important illustration of the material hellenization of one of the non-Greek cities of Asia Minor during the Hellenistic period.

Sardis II: *Architecture* I: H. C. Butler, *The Temple of Artemis* (1925); G. Gruben, *Ath. Mitt.* 76 (1961) 155–96; Berve and Gruben 470–3. Generally on Sardis G. Hanfmann and J. C. Waldbaum, *A Survey of Sardis and the Major Monuments outside the City Walls* (Archaeological Exploration of Sardis Report I) (1975), esp. chs. 1–2, 4–5; *PECS* s.v.; see also Akurgal 124–31; Bean, *AT* 222–7, pls. 74–6.

39. Public decree of Cos, referring to the building of warships and to arrangements for their deployment 'to protect the sanctuaries, the *polis* and the *chora*'. Inscribed in fine lettering, the inscription relates to preparations for the naval wars of *c.* 205–200 B.C., when the Coan navy fought with the Rhodian navy and other allies, first against the Cretan pirates (First Cretan War, *c.* 205–*c.* 202 B.C.), and then against Philip V of Macedon.

(Cos, Castle Museum, in store. Marble, broken at bottom and at top left corner. Height 36 cm; width 35 cm; thickness 18 cm.)

M. Segre, *Rivista di filologia e di istruzione classica* n.s. 11 (1933) 365–78.

40. Decree from Iasus honouring Antiochus III (223–187 B.C.) and his wife and queen, Laodice III. The decree, dating between *c.* 197 and 193 B.C., belongs to a growing dossier of documents attesting Antiochus' dominance over the Greek cities of Asia Minor before his war with Rome. It reveals the king's intervention to establish 'democracy', 'autonomy' and 'concord' at Iasus and his propaganda as 'benefactor of the Greeks'. He is styled 'Great King', the title accorded to him after his successful *anabasis*.

(London, British Museum 1872.6–10.46. Grey marble, broken above and below. Height 25 cm; width 56 cm.)

GIBM no. 442; *OGIS* no. 237. Cf. G. Pugliese Carratelli, *ASAtene* 45–6 (1967–8) 445–53; L. Robert, *REG* 84 (1971) 502–9 no. 621.

39

41. General view over the site of Camirus, one of the three 'old' cities of Rhodes. All survived the synoecism of 408 B.C. to flourish as local townships in the Hellenistic period. Camirus lies on the slopes of a hillside, overlooking the sea, about 37 km south west of the modern capital (ancient Rhodos). There was considerable reorganization and new building in the Hellenistic period at dates difficult to fix accurately. The town was built over three levels. The lowermost contained public buildings and sanctuaries (back, right), the residential sector occupied the middle level (foreground), and on the top level, at 120 m above sea level, a Hellenistic stoa (*c.* 200 m long) was built across the plateau to crown the site. A main street (*c.* 8 m wide), running north–south, linked the levels, and alleys perpendicular to it divided the area into rectangular blocks. The site is a good example of the layout of a small Hellenistic town.

G. Konstantinopoulos, *Philerimo–Ialysos–Kamiros* (1971) 40–63; *PECS* 757.

42. Head of Helius (?) found in Rhodes, from a colossal statue of Parian (?) marble. First half of the second century B.C. The identification with Helius, the chief god of Rhodes after the synoecism (408/7 B.C.), is largely based on the identification of fifteen cuttings round the crown of the head as sockets for metal rays. A recent study has, however, established that the head could not have worn a crown of uniform rays

40

41

42

because of the uneven size and distribution of the holes. The head does bear a resemblance to portraits of Alexander, who could be represented wearing a headdress. The Colossus, the gigantic bronze statue by Chares of Lindus, was the most famous Rhodian celebration of Helius, erected after Demetrius I's unsuccessful siege of the city.

(Rhodes, Archaeological Museum. Found in a medieval wall (1938). Height 55 cm.)

L. Laurenzi, *Memorie pubblicate a cura dell'Istituto Storico-Archeologico... Rodi* 3 (1938) 19–26, pls. 23–5; G. S. Merker, *The Hellenistic Sculpture of Rhodes* (Studies in Mediterranean Archaeology XL) (1973) 29–30, no. 64, figs. 42–4; Lullies 130, pl. 261.

43. Tomb-relief of a rider in the Cova necropolis, Rhodes. On the left, a person pouring a libation into a *cantharus* with a funerary altar below; on the right, a snake relief. The main necropoleis of Rhodes extend south of the city from the south-west side of the acropolis (Monte Smith) to the coastal area of Cova on the east. The majority of tombs and tombstones are of the later Hellenistic period (after the earthquake of *c.* 225 B.C.). They provide rich information on the social history and the composition of the

43

44

population of Rhodes in a period of Rhodian prosperity.

Fraser 4, figs. 9–10 and *passim*.

44. Marble relief from Rhodes of a warrior leaning on his reversed spear before a funerary pillar. Late second or first century B.C. The warrior wears a 'Corinthian' helmet, with flowing crest and plume, and a breast-plate. A snake coils decoratively at the foot of the pillar, a symbol of the soul of the dead, as is common in Hellenistic funerary art (cf. **239**, **265**). This relief, and other warrior reliefs from Rhodes of the Hellenistic period, reflect the warfare in which Rhodes was almost continuously occupied at this time.

(London, British Museum 1905.10–23.1. Broken at top, left and bottom. Height 75.5 cm; width 33 cm.)
A. H. Smith, *JHS* 36 (1916) 81f., fig. 12; cf. 82–5.

45. Civic coins.

(**a**) Silver tetradrachm of Rhodes between 304 B.C. and 166 B.C. *Obv.* Head of Helius, with snaky locks. *Rev.* Centre, Rhodian rose, bud on the right and on the left a prow, a symbol of Rhodian naval power. Above, the Rhodian ethnic ΡΟΔΙΩΝ; below, name of magistrate. For Rhodian Heilus cf. **42**.

45

a

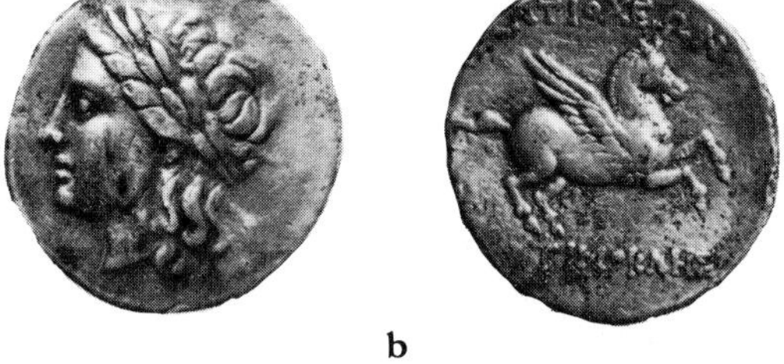

b

(Cambridge, Fitzwilliam Museum. Actual size.)
SNG IV, no. 4788.

(**b**) Silver tetradrachm of Antioch–Alabanda, Caria, between *c.* 250 and 189 B.C. *Obv.* Head of Apollo, facing left, wreathed. *Rev.* Pegasus, flying; above, city-ethnic ANTIOXEΩN; below, name of magistrate. The adhesion of the city of Alabanda to the Seleucids was symbolized by a metonomy characteristic of the period. From a date now known to be as early as the reign of Antiochus II, at some point between 260 and 250 B.C., Alabanda was renamed Antioch and retained this dynastic name until the collapse of Seleucid rule in Asia Minor. The Pegasus on the reverse is probably the emblem of the Chrysaorian league which centred on Alabanda.

(London, British Museum (electrotype). Actual size.)
BM Coins Caria, Cos, Rhodes, etc. (1897) 1 no. 1, pl. I.1. Cf. E. Babélon, *RN* 3.8 (1890) 417–34; M. Holleaux, *Études d'épigraphie et d'histoire grècques* III (1942) 141–57; L. Robert, *Études déliennes* (*BCH* suppl. I) (1973) 435–66.

46. View of the site of Priene (modern Turunçlar), which was re-founded in the mid-fourth century on the steep slopes of a great cliff of the mountain range of Mycale. The summit (Teloneia), accessible from the north, was walled and garrisoned by the Prienians for security. To the south (foreground) lies the fertile plain of the Maeander.

For bibliography see **47**.

47. Reconstruction, viewed from the south, of the central area of Priene. Among the principal public monuments are: (foreground) the second-century B.C. stadium, running parallel to the south wall, and the adjacent gymnasium (**176**); (top left) the Temple of Athena dedicated by Alexander the Great; (top centre) the fourth-century theatre (**193**); (centre) the third-century agora, the second-century Sacred Stoa (along the north side of the agora) and the *bouleuterion* (immediately behind the Sacred Stoa at its east

46

47

48

end). A regular and rectangular plan has the main streets orientated east–west, intersected by lanes running north–south to form blocks, generally with four houses (cf. **136**). The perimeter fortification wall, shown here only on the south side, dates from the foundation of the city. It had towers at intervals in its course. Stretches of curtain wall, joined by shorter return walls set at right-angles ('jogs'), allow the line of walling to be adapted to the hilly terrain.

(Berlin, Pergamon Museum (model by H. Schleif).)

T. Wiegand and H. Schrader, *Priene* (1904); Rostovtzeff 175–81; M. Schede, *Die Ruinen von Priene*, 2nd ed. (1964); *PECS* s.v.; Akurgal 185–206; Bean, *AT* 161–78, pls. 50–5.

48. The *bouleuterion* of Priene (second century B.C.) from the north west. The building is approximately square (20 m × 21 m) with rows of seats on three sides, west, east and north (capacity 640). It was originally covered by a wooden roof supported on pillars. The south side has two entrances flanking a rectangular recess with stone benches. Steps in the north-west and north-east corners led to entrances in the back and west. A decorated altar is centrally placed for the sacred rites normal before public business began. The building is usually identified because of its size as a *bouleuterion*, not as an *ekklesiasterion*, though the latter identification is not absolutely ruled out, given the comparatively small size of ancient Priene.

Wiegand and Schrader, *op. cit.* 219–30, figs. 209–23.

49. Temple of Asclepius on Cos. The temple, built of limestone, is of the Ionic order. It was not large, the stylobate (8.78 m × 15.07 m) being considerably smaller than that of the fourth-century temple of Asclepius at Epidaurus (11.76 m × 23.06 m). It was built between *c.* 300 and 250 B.C., in the first of the four main building phases of the Asclepium. A building with two rooms (foreground), lying between the temple and the retaining wall of the middle terrace, may have been an *abaton*, where pilgrims stayed

49

50

51

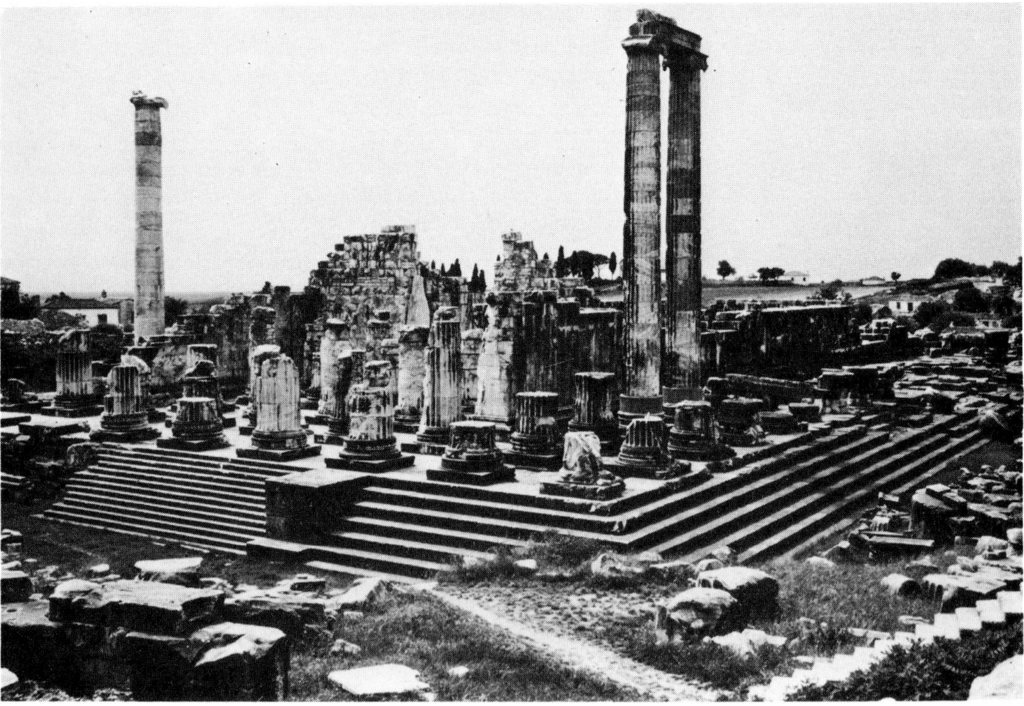

overnight to be visited by the god of medicine, Asclepius (cf. **214**). In the first building phase the sanctuary already extended over three terraces, the buildings of each terrace integrated within an overall scheme.

Kos I: R. Herzog and P. Schazmann, *Asklepieion* (1932); J. D. Kondis, *Hai hellinistikai diamorphiseis tou Asklipieiou tis Ko* (1956); M. Lyttelton, *Baroque Architecture in Classical Antiquity* (1974) 205–8, fig. 30; S. M. Sherwin-White, *Ancient Cos* (1978) 334–46.

50. Monumental stairway leading to the Propylaea of the temple of Athena at Lindus (Rhodes). The Propylaea was built about the early third century B.C. The splendid Doric stoa was added later, probably towards the end of the third century. Axial planning, a characteristic development of Hellenistic architecture (cf. the Coan Asclepium), was used to unite the stoa and the Propylaea into a coherent framework for the processional way which led up the staircase.

Lindos, fouilles de l'Acropole 1902–1914 et 1952 III: E. Dyggve, *Le sanctuaire d'Athana Lindia et l'architecture lindienne* (1960); J. J. Coulton, *The Architectural Development of the Greek Stoa* (1976) 61, 169f., 172, 251f., figs. 23, 79, pl. 4; *PECS* 756f.

51. North-east corner of the huge temple of Apollo at Didyma, near Miletus (stylobate 51.14 m × 109.39 m), one of the finest examples of the new religious buildings inaugurated in Hellenistic times in the old sanctuaries of Asia Minor.

For bibliography see **210** and *PECS* s.v. Cf. Dinsmoor 229–33; Bean, *AT* 192–203.

52. Statue of Victory (Nike) from the sanctuary of the Great Gods on Samothrace (cf. **217**, **218**). End of the third or first half of the second century B.C. Nike, with plumed wings raised, alights on the prow of a naval vessel (cf. **117**). This composition was part of a fountain set in a walled enclosure of limestone overlooking the sanctuary and facing seawards to the north. The combination of Victory and warship prow as symbol of naval might, or in commemoration of naval victory, was common in the Hellenistic period (e.g. on the coins of Demetrius Poliorcetes (cf. **70b**) and Antigonus Gonatas), and its use here has been attributed to the Rhodians as

52

celebration of their victory over the Seleucid fleet at Side in 190 B.C.; but this idea is based partly on the discovery at the site of a fragmentary inscription of the second-century sculptor Pythocritus of Rhodes, which does not belong to the monument.

(Paris, Louvre Museum 2369. Parian marble. Height 2.45 m.)

H. Thiersch, *Nachrichten von der Gesellschaft der Wissenschaften zu Göttingen, Philologisch-historische Klasse* (1931) 336–78; Bieber, *Sculpture* 125f., figs. 493–6; Robertson 535, 720f. n. 85, pl. 171a; Lullies 129f., pl. 260 (with further bibliography). For the site see *PECS* s.v. Samothrace.

53. Detail of the frieze from the late-second-century B.C. temple of Artemis Leucophryene at Magnesia on the Maeander. The subject, the battle of the Greeks and Amazons, goes back to temple-sculptures of the fifth century B.C., and the style is similarly classicizing. The original length was about 174.50 m and the height is 82 cm.

(Istanbul, Archaeological Museum (other sections in Paris and Berlin).)

M. Herkenrath, *Der Fries des Artemisions von Magnesia am Maeander* (1902); C. Humann, J. Kohte and C. Watzinger, *Magnesia am Maeander* (1904) 184f., pls. v, xii, xiii; G. Mendel, *Catalogue des sculptures grecques, romaines et byzantines* (Musées Impériaux Ottomans) i (1912) 369–419, nos. 148–87; Bieber, *Sculpture* 164f., figs. 702–3.

53

54. Stoa of the Hellenistic gymnasium in Cos. The Doric colonnade (originally about 180 m long and 7.0 m deep) was part of the *xystus* (covered running track) which lay on the east side of an enormous gymnasium. Seventeen marble columns of the Doric colonnade have been restored. The gymnasium buildings are unexcavated. The *xystus* is dated to the first half of the second century B.C. on architectural style. The evidence of widespread patronage of the Coan gymnasium by Hellenistic kings in the second century reflects typical royal role-playing.

L. Morricone, *BdA* 35 (1950) 224–7, figs. 33–6; J. Delorme, *Gymnasion* (1960) 119–21; J. J. Coulton, *The Architectural Development of the Greek Stoa* (1976) 248; S. M. Sherwin-White, *Ancient Cos* (1978) 135f., 138.

55. Marble relief representing the apotheosis of Homer, found at Bovillae near Rome: a splendid later Hellenistic work by a sculptor of Priene, Archelaus, perhaps to commemorate the dedicator's victory in a poetic contest. The setting of the three upper registers is a mountain. At the top Zeus reclines with sceptre and eagle. In the second tier: five Muses, one of whom

54

55

a

56

b

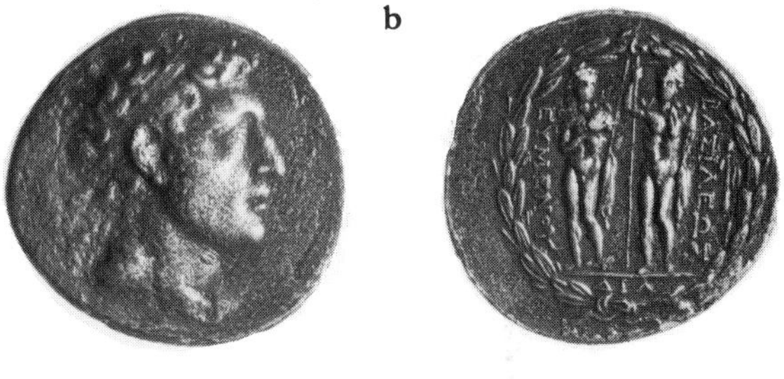

points with a double pipe at Archelaus' signature, and Mnemosyne (Memory), mother of the Muses. Third tier (left to right): three more Muses, Apollo, with large lyre, standing in a cave with the last Muse, and a statue of the dedicator on a pedestal with a tripod in the background. Bottom tier (left to right): the Inhabited World (Oecumene) crowning Homer, who is seated and flanked by kneeling figures of the Iliad holding a sword and the Odyssey holding an *aphlaston* (stern ornament of a ship); a small boy (Myth) and History/Enquiry (Historia), preparing an altar; figures of Poetry holding two torches and Tragedy and Comedy with right arms raised in salutation; and an attendant group of Nature (Physis) as a small child, Virtue (Arete), Remembrance (Mneme), Trust (Pistis) and Wisdom (Sophia). The figures of this tier are all identified by inscriptions cut below on the relief's lower edge. The relief is dated, on stylistic and epigraphic grounds, generally to the second century B.C., perhaps the second half. Its subject may refer back to Ptolemy IV's dedication of the Temple of Homer in Alexandria, for the features of Time (Chronus), standing beside Oecumene, have been identified as those of the Egyptian king. The relief is a fascinating example of Hellenistic development of the personification of abstracts.

(London, British Museum 1819.8-12.1. Parian marble. Height 1.15 m; width (at base) 81 cm.)

A. H. Smith, *A Catalogue of Sculpture in the Department of Greek and Roman Antiquities, British Museum* III (1904) 244–54 no. 2191; *GIBM* IV, no. 1098; Bieber, *Sculpture* 127–30; D. Pinkwart, *Das Relief des Archelaos und die 'Musen des Philiskos'* (1965); *Antike Plastik* 4 (1965) 55–65, pls. 28–33; D. B. Thompson, *Ptolemaic Oinochoai and Portraits in Faience, Aspects of Ruler Cult* (1973) 90, 114; Robertson 562f., 728 n. 155, pl. 172*c*; Lullies 138, pl. 283.

56. Coins of the kings of Pergamum.

(**a**) Silver tetradrachm of Attalus I (241–197 B.C.). *Obv.* Wreathed head of Philetaerus (282–263 B.C.), facing right, founder of the Attalid dynasty: a realistic portrait regularly used by Philetaerus' successors for the obverses of their coins. *Rev.* Helmeted Athena, patron goddess of the Attalids, seated and armed with a spear, crowning with a wreath the legend ΦΙΛΕΤΑΙΡΟΥ; right, a strung bow.

(Cambridge, Fitzwilliam Museum. Actual size.)

McClean III, 61 no. 7674, pl. 263.23; U. Westermark, *Das Bildnis des Philetairos von Pergamon* (1960) 60 no. V.XLIV: B, pl. 4. Cf. Davis and Kraay, pls. 180–1, 184.

(**b**) Silver tetradrachm of Eumenes II

57

58

(197–159 B.C.). *Obv.* Head of Eumenes, diademed, facing right. *Rev.* Dioscuri standing frontally, holding spears, and enclosed within wreath; to right and left, ΒΑΣΙΛΕΩΣ ΕΥΜΕΝΟΥ. This unique issue may celebrate Pergamum's alliance with Rome, whose *denarii* also carried a reverse type of the Dioscuri.

(London, British Museum. Actual size.)

BM Coins Mysia (1892) 117 no. 47, pl. XXIV.5; Davis and Kraay, pls. 182–3, 185.

57. A general view from the acropolis of Pergamum along the fertile Caicus valley, illustrating the strategic importance of the site. The citadel dominates the entrance to the Caicus plain, rising to a height of some 355 m above it. Tributaries of the Caicus on west and east and the steepness of the slopes on north, east and west add strong natural protection to the fortifications of the Attalids.

For the topography and communications of Pergamum see *Altertümer von Pergamon* I: A. Conze, *Stadt und Landschaft* (1912–13); E. V. Hansen, *The Attalids of Pergamon*, 2nd ed. (1971) 1–4. For the Attalid development of the city see R. Martin, *L'Urbanisme dans la Grèce antique* (1956) 127–51; Berve and Gruben 481–91; Hansen, *op. cit.* 234–84; *PECS* s.v.; Akurgal 69ff.; Bean, *AT* 45–57, pls. 10, 13–15.

58. The sanctuary of Demeter at Pergamum, founded by Philetaerus (283–263 B.C.) and his brother Eumenes. The sanctuary occupies a south-facing terrace in the middle city, on the route from the gymnasium to the upper city (acropolis). According to an inscription from the propylon, the colonnades and the *oikoi* were commissioned by Apollonis, the wife of Attalus I (247–197 B.C.). The masonry of the buttressed retaining wall (left) is typical of Attalid construction.

W. Dörpfeld, *Ath. Mitt.* 35 (1910) 355–84, pls. XV–XXI.

59. Propylon of the sanctuary of Athena Nicephorus (Bringer of Victory) at Pergamum. The temple of Athena Nicephorus, built in the late fourth century B.C., lay on the second highest terrace of the acropolis. Eumenes II (197–159 B.C.) enclosed the sanctuary precinct with two-storeyed stoas on the north and east and built this monumental entrance. The frieze below the crowning gable contains motifs of garlands of oak and olive leaves looped alternately over *bucrania* and eagles, while over the garlands owls alternate with *phialai*. The symbols and attributes recall Athena and Zeus, as do the dedications in the sanctuary. The balustrade of the second storey is carved with armour and weaponry captured in wars, including (right) a very rare representation from Greek antiquity of the spring frame of a *ballista* (cf. **111**, **112**). Fragments surviving from the inscription on the epistyle give the dedication, 'King Eumenes to Athena Nikephoros'. The military theme broadcasts the power and the successes of the Attalid kings under the auspices of their patron goddess.

(Berlin, Pergamon Museum (reconstruction).)

Altertümer von Pergamon II: R. Bohn, *Das Heiligtum der Athena Polias Nikephoros* (1885).

60. Statue of a dying Gaul, probably a copy of a bronze work from a monument of the late third century B.C. set up by Attalus I at Pergamum in commemoration of his victory over the Galatians. This monument, which stood in the sanctuary of Athena, probably included the group of a Gaulish chieftain killing himself and his wife of which a famous replica survives in the Terme Museum, Rome (the so-called Ludovisi Gaul). Pliny (*NH* XXXIV.84) names four artists, Isigonus (a mistake for Epigonus?), Phyromachus, Stratonicus and Antigonus, who 'represented the battles of Attalus and Eumenes against the Gauls'.

(Rome, Capitoline Museum 747. Greek marble; details, including right arm and left part of plinth, restored. Height (including plinth) 93 cm; length of plinth 1.86 m; width 89 cm.)

H. Stuart Jones, ed., *A Catalogue of the Ancient Sculptures Preserved in the Municipal Collections of Rome. The Sculptures of the Museo Capitolino* (1912) 338–40, no. 1, pl. 85; W. Helbig, *Führer durch die öffentlichen Sammlungen klassischer Altertümer in Rom*, 4th ed. II (1966) 240–2 no. 1436; E. V. Hansen, *The Attalids of Pergamon*, 2nd ed. (1971) 301–5; Robertson 531–3, 719 n. 71, pls. 167*c*, 168*b*; Lullies 128, pls. 256–7.

61. Façade of the Great Altar of Pergamum, as reconstructed. Built of bluish white marble, this enormous altar (*c.* 36.44 m × 34.20 m at base) was raised on a nearly square, colonnaded plat-

59

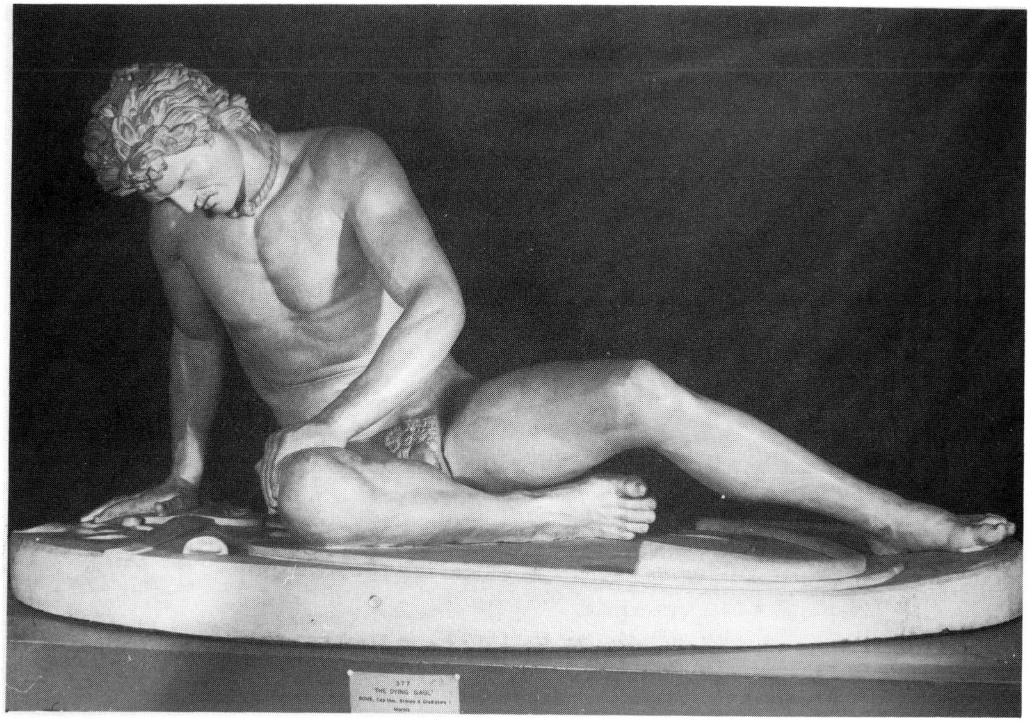

60

61

62

form and approached by a monumental staircase, like other Hellenistic altars (e.g. at Priene and Magnesia). It was set on a terrace above the agora of the citadel and below the precinct of Athena (**59**). It probably dates to the reign of Eumenes II. The frieze in high relief which ran round the podium (2.29 m high and *c.* 120 m long) depicts the war of the gods and the giants, the mythical counterpart claimed for the great struggle of the Attalids against the Galatians, which culminated in Eumenes' successful suppression of a Gaulish rebellion in 168 B.C.

(Berlin, Pergamon Museum (reconstruction).)

Altertümer von Pergamon III.1: J. Schrammen, *Der grosse Altar, der obere Markt* (1906) 3–82; III.2: H. Winnefeld, *Die Friese des grossen Altars* (1910); H. Kähler, *Der grosse Fries von Pergamon* (1948); E. Rohde, *Pergamon, Burgberg und Altar* (1961); E. Schmidt, *The Great Altar of Pergamon* (1962); Hansen, *op. cit.* 264–7, 319–48; Robertson 538–44, 721f. nn. 89ff., pl. 170*d*; Lullies 131–3, pls. 263–71.

62. Detail of the east frieze of the Pergamum altar; the three-bodied Hecate strikes at a bearded giant with serpent-legs (Clytius). On Hecate's left the giant Otus, with plumed helmet, faces the attack of Artemis, who treads on a prostrate giant.

(Berlin, Pergamon Museum.)

For bibliography see **61**.

63. Relief from the second and smaller frieze of the Great Altar: King Teuthras of Mysia and his train meeting the mother of Telephus, Auge, as she lands in Mysia, a refugee from her home in Arcadia. The frieze ran round the interior of the altar. It contained scenes from the legend of Telephus, son of Heracles, mythical founder of Pergamum, and an ancestor of the Attalid dynasty. The story is presented as a continuous narrative, with many of the same figures appearing several times.

(Berlin, Pergamon Museum. Marble. 1.58 m high.)

For bibliography see **61**, esp. Winnefeld, *op. cit.* 155–228, pls. XXXI–XXXVI. See also C. Bauchhenss-Thüriedl, *Der Mythos von Telephos in der antiken Bildkunst* (1971) 40–74 and end-folders.

64. The theatre at Pergamum, built into the steep west slope of the acropolis, below the sanctuary of Athena (**59**). It is one of the largest of the Hellenistic theatres, with a capacity of about 10,000 spectators, and replaced an older theatre dated early in the Attalid dynasty. The present structure is usually attributed to the building programme of Eumenes II, though

63

modifications took place in the Imperial period. Cf. **198**. The site of the Great Altar is marked by the two trees in the background.

Bieber, *Denkmäler* 37f., fig. 39, pls. 14–18; Hansen, *op. cit.* 240–1, 276–7; D. De Bernardi Ferrero, *Teatri classici in Asia Minore* III (1970) 24–34 (with further bibliography).

65. Coins of the kingdoms in eastern Asia Minor.

(**a**) Silver drachm of Ariarathes (404–322 B.C.), satrap and eponym of the Cappadocian dynasty, minted at Sinope, *c.* 333–322 B.C. *Obv.* Head of nymph Sinope (barbarous style) in a border of dots. *Rev.* Eagle with wings aloft on dolphin. Below, instead of ethnic ΣΙΝΩ, part of Ariarathes' name in Aramaic (Ariorath).

(Cambridge, Fitzwilliam Museum. Actual size.)
McClean III, 18 no. 7424, pl. 253.2.

(**b**) Silver drachm of Ariarathes IV (220–163 B.C.). *Obv.* Diademed portrait of Ariarathes, facing right. *Rev.* Athena standing, facing left, spear in left hand and Nike in right; legend, ΒΑΣΙΛΕΩΣ ΑΡΙΑΡΑΘΟΥ ΕΥΣΕΒΟΥΣ. The coins of the Ariarathid dynasty provide a good source by which to monitor the rulers' gradual adoption of a Greek image.

64

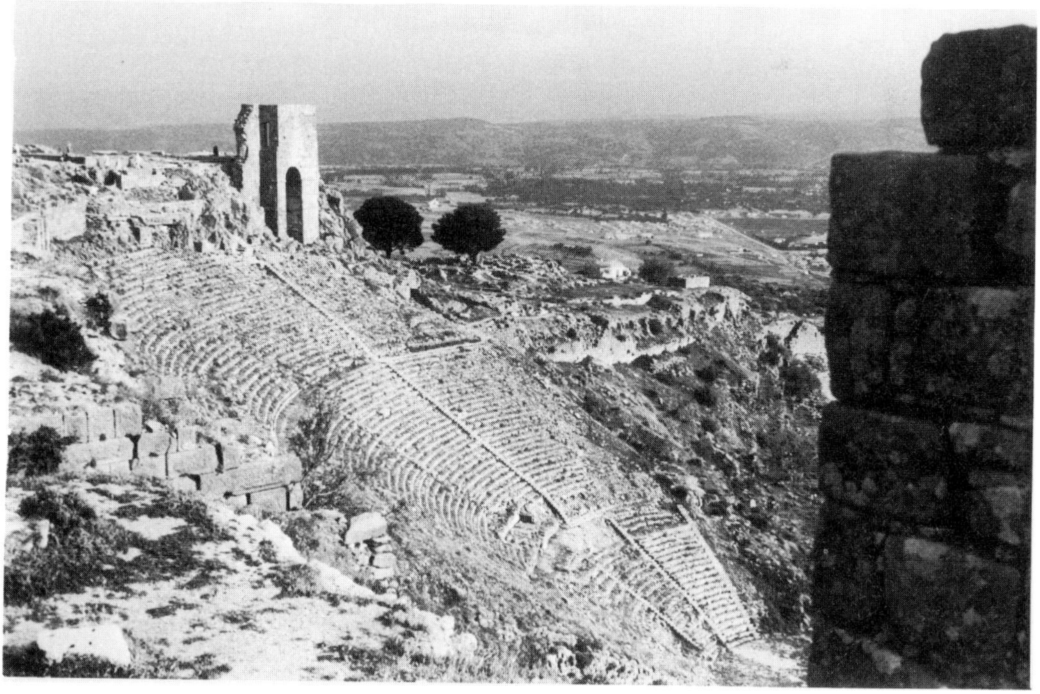

65

a

b

c

d

(Cambridge, Fitzwilliam Museum. Actual size.)

SNG IV, no. 5405. On the problems of attribution in Ariarathid coinage see T. Reinach, *Trois royaumes de l'Asie Mineure* (1888) 1–87; B. Simonetta, *NC* 7.1 (1961) 9–50; O. Mørkholm, *NC* 7.2 (1962) 407–11; 7.4 (1964) 21–5; Simonetta, *ibid.* 83–91; *id. Rivista italiana di numismatica* 76 (1974) 95–105; *id. The Coins of the Cappadocian Kings* (*Typos* II) (1977).

(**c**) Silver tetradrachm of Mithradates III of Pontus (*c.* 220–*c.* 185 B.C.). *Obv.* Realistic portrait of king, with diadem, facing right. *Rev.* Seated Zeus, facing left, holding eagle in outstretched right hand; legend, ΒΑΣΙΛΕΩΣ ΜΙΘΡΑΔΑΤΟΥ. In field a star and crescent, and a monogram. The astral emblems (cf. **121b**) perhaps allude to the regionally important cult of Ma, or may relate more generally to the religion of Persia from the Achaemenid rulers of which the Pontic dynasty claimed descent.

(London, British Museum. Actual size.)

PCG 58 no. V.A.1, pl. 32.1; Davis and Kraay, pls. 198–9, 202.

(**d**) Silver tetradrachm of Mithradates VI Eupator of Pontus (121/20–63 B.C.): 76/5 B.C. *Obv.* Idealized head, facing right, with diadem buried in a curling mass of flowing hair. This portrait may represent Mithradates VI, who took the surname Dionysus, as the god. *Rev.* In centre, grazing stag. Pontic era date to right (ΒΚΣ: 222 = 76/5 B.C.). To left, star and crescent symbols, as on earlier Pontic coins (cf. **65c**). Legend ΒΑΣΙΛΕΩΣ ΜΙΘΡΑΔΑΤΟΥ ΕΥΠΑΤΟΡΟΣ and monograms. All in a leaf and berry wreath.

(Cambridge, Fitzwilliam Museum. Actual size.)

SNG IV, no. 4055. On the coinage and history of the kingdom of Pontus see T. Reinach, *RN* 3.5 (1887) 97–108; *id. Trois royaumes de l'Asie Mineure* (1888) 153–204; G. Kleiner, *Istanbuler Mitteilungen* 6 (1955) 1–21; M. J. Price, *NC* 7.8 (1968) 1–12.

5. MACEDONIA, GREECE AND THE CYCLADES

R. A. TOMLINSON

By the time of Alexander's death in 323 B.C. the cities and sanctuaries of mainland Greece and the Cycladic islands had created most of their important buildings and other monuments. Economic difficulties in the fourth century, as well as political uncertainties, had already restricted the number of new buildings, though the dedication of statues and similar monuments seems to have continued unabated. The Macedonian conquest of Greece had initiated a few new buildings, the result of political change and new patronage, but this impetus was of limited effect. Macedonia itself, on the other hand, had experienced the great upsurge in wealth which had resulted from the unprecedented extension of her power; and this gave an impetus which continued into the Hellenistic age, leading to the spacious and finely built houses of Pella (**66**), while the wealthy dead were placed in the buried architectural splendours of chamber tombs, modelled on those of the last Argead kings at Vergina (**67**; cf. **247**), or at the least given rich grave goods such as those found in the simpler burials of the cemetery on the Langadas pass to the north of Thessalonica.

Undoubtedly the more troubled times at the end of the fourth century and the beginning of the third weakened this impetus, while the division of Alexander's empire reduced the wealth available to Macedon; but new cities continued to be founded, usually by the amalgamation of existing communities and some movement of population. It is difficult to assess the quality of their early construction on an archaeological basis; Cassandria has yet to be excavated, early Thessalonica (**68**) cannot reveal more than the approximate street plan, though its size and lasting success as a city demonstrates the importance of this Hellenistic development. The royal building or palace at Vergina (**69**) is large compared with classical Greek private houses, but relatively modest for a king; though, as Vitruvius reminds us, kings used not to be ashamed to build in mudbrick. Though the Hellenistic kings initially claimed to be successors to Alexander, and demonstrated this on their coins (cf. **70**), they soon asserted their individual power and prestige; the palace at Vergina was surely not equipped in a modest fashion, as the size of its dining-rooms and the impressive mosaic floors demonstrate.

The cities and sanctuaries of the Greek mainland continued to build in the Hellenistic age (**71–6**), modestly enough if they were dependent on their own restricted resources, even when they were members of the larger political units, the federal leagues. Certain statues (cf. **77**) and coinage (**78**) also testify to the independent activities of cities and leagues. Wealthy individuals might be responsible for ostentatious memorials beyond the more restrained limits general in the classical period (**79**; cf. **82**). In this respect, during his autocratic domination of Athens, Demetrius of Phalerum had to pass the sumptuary legislation which finally put an end to the series of Attic grave reliefs (cf. **231–2**). In contrast it must be remembered that parts of mainland and Aegean Greece were from time to time under the direct control of one or other of the Hellenistic kings (**81–2**). The Ptolemaic presence in Crete is now demonstrated by the Hadra vases (**83**) named after the Alexandrian cemetery where they have been found in abundance, but many of which are now known to have originated in Crete. In addition, the rivalries of the Hellenistic powers, greater and lesser, stimulated them to seek influence, or at least prestige, by gifts to the sanctuaries and cities of Greece even if they did not control them (**80**, **84–8**), and these became the usual source of major construction work and the erection of monuments, rather than the city-states themselves.

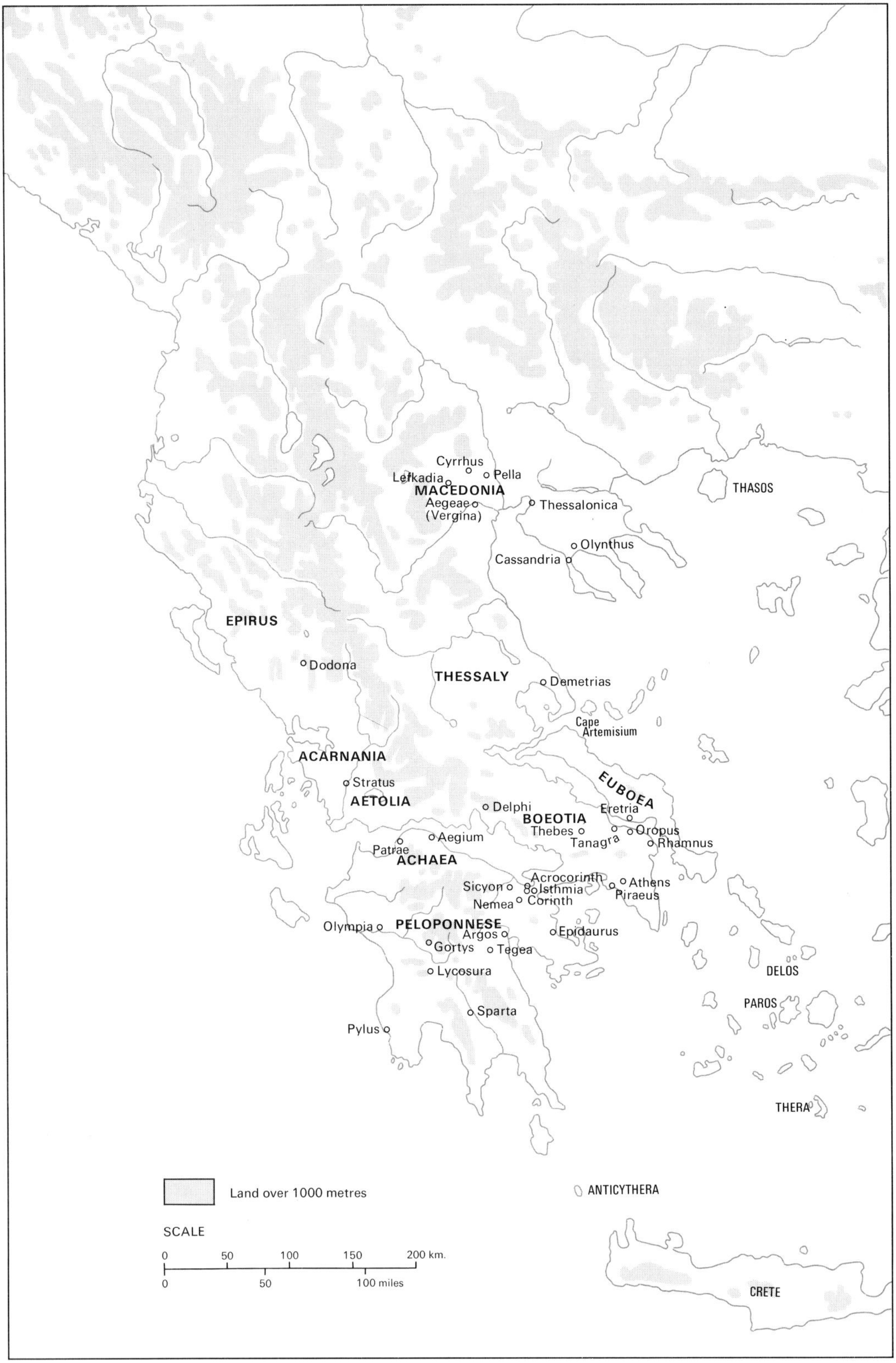

4. Macedonia, Greece and the Cyclades

66

66. Aerial view of the excavations at Pella, which seems to have replaced Aegeae (Vergina) as the centre of the Macedonian kingdom probably in the reign of Archelaus. The palace of Philip II was situated here, though Aegeae continued its traditional importance (see below, **69**). Philip's palace was on the low hill where the modern village is situated (off the picture to the right); recent excavations have now begun to reveal parts of it. The main area of excavations is at the southern limits of the town, and was originally adjacent to the sea, long since silted up and completely drained earlier in this century. This area of the town, at least, was laid out to a regular grid plan with wide streets. The houses of this quarter are particularly spacious and well built (in comparison with those of fourth-century Olynthus) with large colonnaded courtyards; the Ionic columns, typically of Macedonia, following the Peloponnesian rather than the Asiatic or Attic type, having only twenty flutes on the shafts, though the capitals retain the more normal double volute form, not the Peloponnesian form with four angled volutes. In the rooms are excellent pebble figured mosaics (cf. **139**), as well as floors with geometric patterns. These are probably private houses, and, if so, indicate for the end of the fourth century B.C. a high level of material wealth for the Macedonian city populations.

Ph. M. Petsas, *Archaeology* 17 (1964) 74–84; *id. Pella: Alexander the Great's Capital* (1978) (reprinting this and other articles).

67. Reconstruction drawing of the façade of the largest Macedonian tomb known, that excavated by Professor Ph. Petsas at Lefkadia, near Naoussa. In this two-storeyed façade (other Macedonian tombs with decorated façades have never more than one storey) the upper, Ionic order of engaged half columns does not coincide with the lower, Doric. Spaces between the Ionic half columns are filled with representations of window shutters (rather than doors). The painted decoration is developed from concepts used previously on the royal tomb at Aegeae (Vergina), and with decorative details, such as the maeander on the Doric taenia, remarkably similar. Painted figures between the Doric

67

half-columns represent the dead man (unfortunately unnamed), Hermes, Aeacus and Rhadamanthys (cf. **247**). The continuous frieze over the Doric entablature is moulded in stucco and painted. The tomb belongs to a cemetery with several imposing Macedonian tombs, presumably connected with a powerful family which must be distinguished from the Argead dynasty buried at Aegeae.

(Height approx. 8.20 m; width approx. 8.30 m.)
Ph. M. Petsas, *Ho taphos ton Leukadion* (1966).

68. Plan of Thessalonica (Thessaloniki). Continuous occupation since the city was founded by Cassander in *c.* 316 B.C. and important developments in the later Roman period when the emperor Galerius made it his capital have obscured the evidence for the early city, and have made the elucidation of the original Hellenistic plan difficult. The street grid, however, appears discernible in the line of streets as they were immediately prior to the great fire of 1917. The plan also shows the later Roman development, on the east side; of the Turkish period, on the slopes below the acropolis citadel (top); and of the nineteenth century on the south-western side, probably on the site of the ancient harbour which had silted up. Within this plan it is impossible to locate precisely the various public buildings of the original foundation. A major problem is the position of the agora; that in the centre of the plan is Roman, its architecture closely related to that of the Roman agora at

Smyrna, on an artificially levelled area some way above the sea, its stoas depending on vaulted substructures and terracing. The original Hellenistic agora may have been closer to the sea and the harbour.

M. H. Vickers, *JHS* 92 (1972) 156–70; *PECS* 912f. (with bibliography).

68

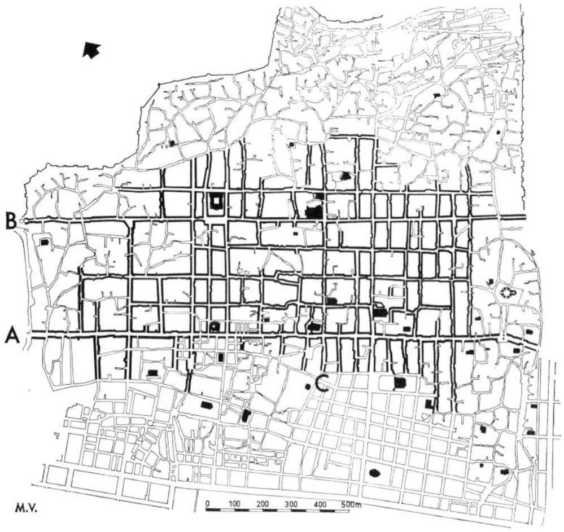

69. Plan of the Hellenistic palace at Vergina, now identified as the ancient Aegeae and therefore the original centre of the Macedonian kingdom; nearby is the extensive and important early iron age cemetery. Here are the graves of the last Argead kings, whose vaulted tombs were subsequently covered with the great burial mound, probably erected by Antigonus Gonatas after the plundering by Pyrrhus' Gallic mercenaries. Another vaulted tomb, with an Ionic façade whose order is modelled on that of the Philippeum at Olympia, is situated on the low ground below the palace. The palace itself was built of unbaked brick on a stone footing, but with stone columns, including some, at the entrance and a vestibule to two rooms on the south side (E and G), of white marble. The rooms are largely arranged as formal dining-rooms: the two on the south side approached through the vestibule are also distinguished by marble thresholds, and have floors decorated with high-quality pebble mosaic. These seem the most important rooms and were presumably used by the king. The eleven couches in these rooms were about 2.25 m long, larger than those in dining-rooms of the Greek cities. Other dining-rooms on the west side were larger –

69

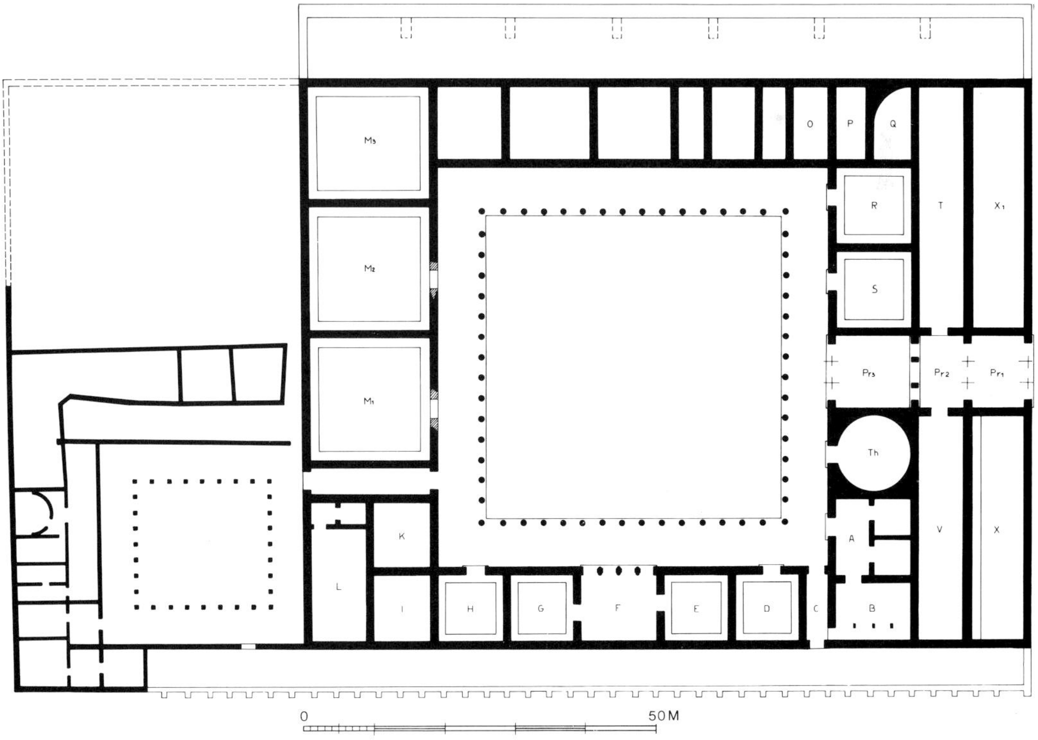

70

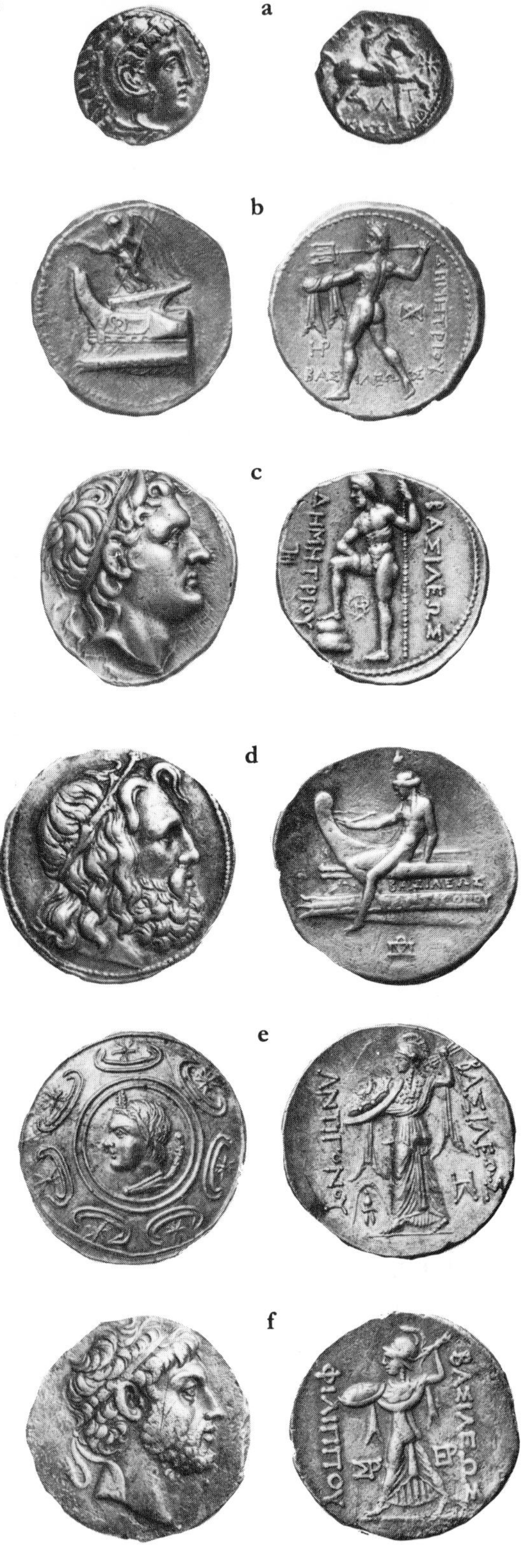

their roofs, at over 16 m, had the largest unsupported span known in Greek architecture – but had floors made from broken fragments of marble only. Perhaps the differing size and decoration of these rooms reflect different gradings of Hellenistic courtiers in their proximity to the king. The palace may date from the end of the fourth century B.C.

M. Andronikos and others, *To anaktoro tis Verginas* (1961); M. Andronikos, *Vergina, the Prehistoric Necropolis and the Hellenistic Palace* (1964); R. A. Tomlinson, in V. Laourdas and Ch. I. Makaronas, eds., *Archaia Makedonia* (1970) 313–15; D. Pandermalis, in P. Zanker, ed., *Hellenismus in Mittelitalien* (1976) 391–5.

70. Coins of the Macedonian kings (actual size).

(**a**) Cassander (316–297 B.C.), bronze (cf. **121**). *Obv.* head of Heracles; *rev.* jockey on horseback. The Heracles head is of the same type as that used on certain coins of Alexander.

(Cambridge, Fitzwilliam Museum.)
McClean II, 66 no. 3554, pl. 132.14.

(**b**) Demetrius Poliorcetes (306–283 B.C.). Silver tetradrachm. *Obv.* Nike on prow; *rev.* Posidon casting trident. An obvious reference to Demetrius' naval victory at Cypriot Salamis in 306 B.C.

(Cambridge, Fitzwilliam Museum.)
SNG IV, no. 2287.

(**c**) Demetrius Poliorcetes. Silver tetradrachm. *Obv.* portrait head of the king; *rev.* Posidon with foot resting on rock. Again Posidon emphasizes the naval victory. The portrait of Demetrius honours him as a king in his own right.

(Cambridge, Fitzwilliam Museum.)
SNG IV, no. 2299.

(**d**) Antigonus Gonatas (277–239 B.C.). Silver tetradrachm. *Obv.* head of Posidon; *rev.* Apollo seated on prow.

(Cambridge, Fitzwilliam Museum.)
SNG IV, no. 2309.

(**e**) Antigonus Gonatas. Silver tetradrachm. *Obv.* bust of Pan on shield; *rev.* Athena with shield and thunderbolt. A typical Macedonian shield, with sunburst symbols in peltae round the rim, recalling the sunbursts on the gold casket from the royal burial at Vergina. Pan recalls the panic inflicted on the Gauls at their defeat by Antigonus in 277, which confirmed him as king of Macedon.

(Cambridge, Fitzwilliam Museum.)
SNG IV, no. 2304.

(**f**) Philip V (221–178 B.C.). Silver tetradrachm. *Obv.* portrait head of Philip; *rev.* Athena as on coins of Gonatas.

(Cambridge, Fitzwilliam Museum.)
McClean II, 73 no. 3628, pl. 135.1; cf. Davis and Kraay, pls. 123–4, 127.

71. The vaulted passage leading to the stadium track at Nemea, where pro-Macedonian Argos had been confirmed in control of the Nemean games. The tunnel vault (here securely dated by the stratigraphy to *c.* 325 B.C.) represents a distinctly Macedonian contribution to the architecture of southern Greece; there are similar vaulted passages in the auditorium of the theatre at Sicyon, at the inland site to which the city was moved by Demetrius Poliorcetes who gave it his dynastic name.

S. G. Miller, *Hesperia* 47 (1978) 84–8; 48 (1979) 96–103; 49 (1980) 198–203; 50 (1981) 65–7.

72. Porticoes and *exedrae* of the Palaestra at Olympia. The political involvement of the Hellenistic powers is less marked at Olympia than one might expect. Macedonian influence can be seen in the dedication of the Philippeum, and perhaps, after the example at Nemea, in the vaulted passageway to the stadium (though this is generally described as Roman). There is a Ptolemaic stoa. Otherwise, the non-involvement of the great powers is a reflection of the established international character of the sanctuary, its geographical position, and above all the increasing exclusion of the kingdoms from influence by the federal leagues in those parts of Greece which they dominated. The Palaestra conforms well with Vitruvius' description (V.11) of the typical Greek form (cf. **182**). It consists of a large court 41.42 m × 41.52 m, each side having nineteen Doric columns. Rooms on all four sides are largely open through secondary colonnades to the peristyle. There is a large open room on the north side with a bench around its walls (Vitruvius' 'sedes, in quibus philosophi, rhetores, reliquique, qui studiis delectantur, sedentes disputare possint'). There are similar, slightly smaller rooms on the east and west sides. The Palaestra dates to the third century B.C., and

71

72

was presumably a gift to the sanctuary, though there is no evidence to associate it with one of the Hellenistic kings.

F. Adler and others, *Die Baudenkmäler von Olympia* (*Olympia, die Ergebnisse der vom dem Deutschen Reich veranstalteten Ausgrabung* II) (1892) 113–21, pls. LXXIII–LXXV; H. Schlief and R. Eilmann, *Ol. Bericht* IV (1940–41) 8–31; A. Mallwitz, *Olympia und seine Bauten* (1972) 278–84, figs. 231–4.

73. The Hellenistic temple of Despoina at Lycosura, in the mountains of Arcadia. The base in the *cella* (to the front of the photograph) supported the marble statue-group, a mid-second-century classicizing work by Damophon, of which there are significant fragments surviving. An unusual feature, but one found in other Arcadian temples, is the door in the side of the *cella*.

P. Kavvadias, *Fouilles de Lycosoura* (1893); E. Lévy, *BCH* 91 (1967) 518–45; *PECS* 537 (with further bibliography).

74. Remains of the temple of Zeus at Stratus in Acarnania. The construction in north-west Greece of buildings in the styles developed in the city-states (not, of course, without earlier precedent) emphasizes the much more direct involvement of this area in Hellenistic history and society. The temple of Zeus is in the simplified Doric form which evolved in the fourth century B.C. It has only six × eleven columns in its peristyle, and its plan omits the *opisthodomus* (false porch) behind the *cella*. It belongs to the turn of the fourth to the third century B.C., and was constructed while Stratus was the chief town of an independent Acarnania, not yet incorporated into the Aetolian league. It was never completed.

A. K. Orlandos, *Deltion* 8 (1923) 1–51; C. Picard and F. Courby, *Recherches archéologiques à Stratos d'Acarnanie* (1924).

75. The auditorium of the theatre at Dodona. The sanctuary of Zeus at Dodona had been of panhellenic importance since archaic times, though it had never acquired a conventional

73

74

75

76

temple. The construction of its great theatre reflects the political importance of the kingdom of Epirus in the third century B.C.; its function, as a structure in which the Epirotes could gather *en masse*, like that of theatres elsewhere, is not without political significance, and it should be remarked that it was considered more important to build this than a temple.

S. Dakaris, *Deltion* 16 (1960) 4–40, pls. 2–13; *BCH* 84 (1960) 746–50; *Neue Ausgrabungen in Griechenland* (*Ant. K.* suppl. 1) (1963) 36–49, pls. 19–22; *PECS* s.v. Dodona.

76. Detail of the Hellenistic agora of Thasos; in the background the north-west stoa (early third century), in the foreground the circular foundations of an early-fourth-century monument possibly set up in honour of the athlete Theogenes. Despite its proximity to Macedonian territory the island of Thasos managed to maintain its independence, which perhaps had been granted originally by Lysimachus. It was captured by Philip V in 202, plundered, and its population sold into slavery. After the defeat of Philip by the Romans the independence of Thasos was restored by the terms of the peace of 196. It then flourished (presumably the population was successfully liberated); its wine commanded a wide market and had a high reputation (cf. **128a**, **129**). The late Hellenistic prosperity of the island is reflected by the buildings of that period, particularly in the agora of Thasos town.

Études thasiennes: R. Martin, *L'Agora* I (1959); *Guide de Thasos* (1967) 24ff.

77. Statue of Demosthenes by Polyeuctus (the original does not survive, and the illustration is of a Roman copy) set up in the Athenian Agora at about 280 B.C., at the instigation of the orator's nephew Demochares. This memorial to the great opponent of Macedonian imperialism belongs to a moment when Antigonus Gonatas' control of Macedon, let alone southern Greece, was precarious. However, a Macedonian garrison remained in Piraeus, and Athens was still dominated by Macedon.

(Copenhagen, Ny Carlsberg Glyptothek. Marble; hands and minor details restored. Height 2.02 m (including plinth).)

Richter, *Portraits* 219 no. 32, figs. 1398–1402 (with bibliography).

77

78. Coins of the leagues and Athens (actual size).

(**a**) Aetolian League. Silver stater. *Obv.* male head; *rev.* Aetolus, the eponymous hero of the league, with *chlamys* on left arm, *kausia* at shoulder, scabbard at hip, leaning on spear with foot raised on rock.

(Cambridge, Fitzwilliam Museum.)

SNG IV, no. 2798.

(**b**) Aetolian League. Silver hemidrachm. *Obv.* head of (?)Atalanta wearing *kausia*; *rev.* boar, with spear-head in exergue.

78

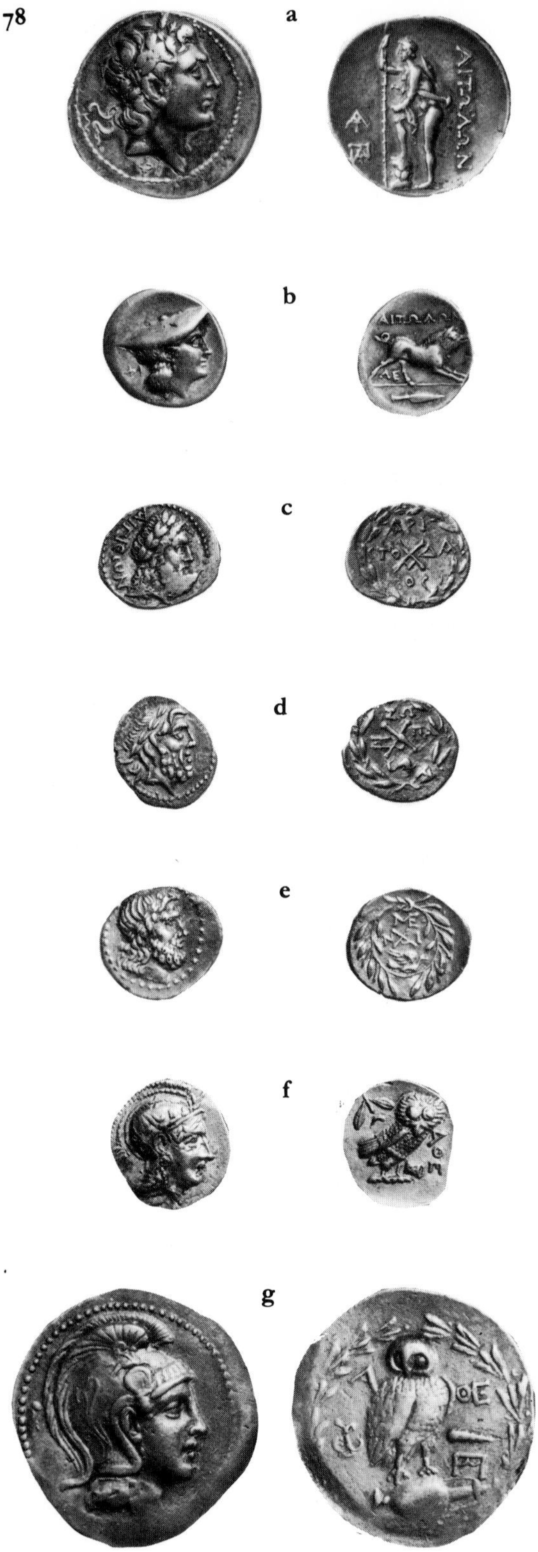

(Cambridge, Fitzwilliam Museum CM 79–1965.)
Unpublished.

(**c**)–(**e**) Achaean League. Silver hemidrachms. *Obv.* head of Zeus, the standard League type; *rev.* monogram (A+X) of the Achaean League, magistrates' names and city symbols: (**c**) Aegium, (**d**) Patrae, dolphin, (**e**) Sicyon, dove. Unlike the Aetolian League (which was not urban-based in the true sense) the Achaean League was a combination of cities, and this is reflected in the city issues of its coins.

(Cambridge, Fitzwilliam Museum.)
(a) *McClean* II, 412 no. 6374, pl. 221.21; (b) *SNG* IV, no. 3642; (c) *SNG* IV, no. 3647.

(**f**) Athens. Gold stater. *Obv.* Athena; *rev.* owl, with olive-sprig above and basket below. Period of Lachares (300–295 B.C.): the owl retains the traditional form.

(Cambridge, Fitzwilliam Museum.)
SNG IV, no. 3194A.

(**g**) Athens. Silver tetradrachm. *Obv.* Athena; *rev.* owl, within laurel wreath, with magistrates' monograms. An early example of the New Style coinage, introduced in the second century B.C. (cf. **121b**), the wreath possibly derived from Pergamene royal coinage.

(Cambridge, Fitzwilliam Museum.)
McClean II, 357 no. 5897, pl. 208.22.

79. Reconstruction drawing of the double-column monument of Aristaeneta, a wealthy Aetolian lady, put up near the north-east corner of the temple of Apollo in the sanctuary at Delphi. Third century B.C. On the left the front elevation, at the right the side elevation. Delphi was under Aetolian domination from about 300 B.C. onwards; the Hellenistic monuments therefore reflect Aetolian interests and alliances. This is one of several important examples.

(White marble. Height (as restored) 9.50 m.)
E. Bourguet, *BCH* 35 (1911) 472–81; *Fouilles de Delphes* II: F. Courby, *La terrasse du temple* (1927) 257–62, figs. 201–4.

80. The pillar monument of King Prusias of Bithynia (*c.* 180 B.C.), another Hellenistic dedication at Delphi. It takes the form of a tall pedestal with relief sculpture (a frieze of *bucrania* and garlands) and other decoration, originally surmounted by an equestrian statue.

79

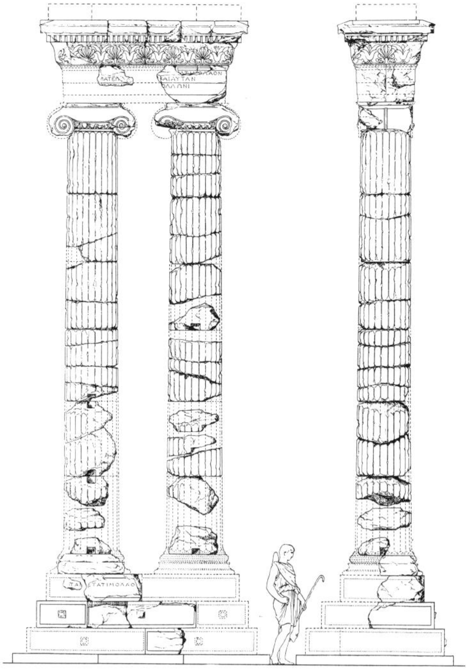

80

(Height 9.70 m.)
Courby, *op. cit.* 262–5, figs. 206–7.

81. The medieval gate of the fortress on Acrocorinth, incorporating (in the right-hand tower) a Hellenistic structure. The fortifications of Acrocorinth, one of the 'fetters of Greece', were strengthened for Demetrius Poliorcetes, and garrisoned by his son Antigonus Gonatas until the notorious surprise attack by night carried out in time of peace in 243 B.C. for the Achaean League at the instigation of Aratus of Sicyon.

Corinth III.2: Rhys Carpenter and A. Bon, *The Defences of Acrocorinth and the Lower Town* (1936).

82. Rock carvings in the precinct dedicated by Artemidorus of Perge, in the third century B.C., at the town site of Thera. There are connexions here with Ptolemaic Egypt. Thera in the third century B.C. served as the central Ptolemaic naval and military base in the Aegean, and Perge in Pamphylia was also a Ptolemaic possession, the birthplace of the mathematician Apollonius, who worked in the Museum at Alexandria.

F. Hiller von Gaertringen and P. Wilski, *Thera* IV: *Stadtgeschichte von Thera* (1904) 89–102, figs. 73–84.

83. A 'Hadra' vase of the late third century B.C. The modern name is the consequence of the discovery of many examples in the Hellenistic cemeteries of Hadra, a suburb on the east side of present-day Alexandria in Egypt. Excavations in Crete have, however, shown that many of them (notably those with decoration applied directly to the clay rather than over a white slip) were originally manufactured and painted there, at a date somewhat later than that which has been attributed to them in earlier studies. They present tangible evidence of the important interests the Ptolemies established in Crete.

(Brussels, Royal Museums A13, from Arsinoe in Cyprus. Height 37.5 cm.)
CVA Belgique, pl. 141 (no. 2); P. J. Callaghan, in *Studi in onore di A. Adriani* (in press).

81

82

83

84

84. Entablature of the Stoa of Antigonus, which forms the northern boundary of the sanctuary of Apollo, Delos. The bull's-head decoration on the triglyphs is possibly an echo of Achaemenid architectural forms. Delos was a free community from 314 to 166 B.C. Its position in the central Aegean, and the status of the sanctuary inevitably involved it in the rivalries of the Hellenistic powers, particularly the struggle for naval domination of the Aegean between the Ptolemies and the Antigonids. Both dynasties established festivals in their own honour. Antigonus Gonatas' success was expressed architecturally with his great stoa; earlier his father, Demetrius Poliorcetes, had dedicated his flagship, after the naval victory at Cypriot Salamis, in a long hall on the east side of the sanctuary, formerly identified as the Pythion (and so marked on older plans of the sanctuary) but better called the Neorion.

(Bluish marble. Total height about 1.26 m.)

Generally on the Stoa, *EAD* V: F. Courby, *Le portique d'Antigone ou du nord-est* (1912) 13–45, figs. 15–57; Bruneau and Ducat 92f. no. 29; cf. (for the Neorion) 90f. no. 24.

85. Back-wall of the Stoa of Eumenes in Athens. Even after Athens became independent and neutral in 229 B.C., Hellenistic monarchs continued to take a lively interest in her, though this was now in the more beneficent form of gifts, buildings and monuments intended to enhance the prestige of the donor as well as to win the favour of the Athenian populace. The kings of Pergamum were particularly generous, especially with their gifts of stoas in a distinctly Pergamene style of architecture which contrasts sharply with that of their classical neighbours. That of Eumenes II (197–159 B.C.) provided covered shelter in front of an extended terrace wall along the south side of the Acropolis from the vicinity of the theatre of Dionysus (it is identified from Vitruvius' reference, V.9.1).

U. Köhler, *Ath. Mitt.* 3 (1878) 147–54, pl. VII; J. Martha, *BCH* 2 (1878) 584–6; W. Dörpfeld, *Ath. Mitt.* 13 (1888) 100–2; Ph. Versakis, *Arch. Eph.* (1912) 173–82; J. Travlos, *Pictorial Dictionary of Ancient Athens* (1971) 523–6, figs. 660–4 (with bibliography).

86. South end of the Stoa of Attalus in Athens, rebuilt to form the museum and offices of the Agora Excavations. Built by Attalus II of Pergamum (159–138 B.C.), it is similar in its details to the Stoa of Eumenes and may well be by the same architect. It forms part of an extensive modernization of the Agora with extended stoas (Attalus' on the east, the middle stoa and south stoa II on the south, and various colonnades added to the buildings on the west side) which brought it more into conformity with the colonnaded square of the agoras in the grid-plan cities of Asia Minor. There were also

85

86

87

Pergamene gifts of statuary, copies of the victory monument over the Gauls on the Acropolis, an equestrian statue of Eumenes II by the Propylaea, erected in 178 B.C., whose base was later appropriated for a statue of Agrippa.

H. A. Thompson, *The Stoa of Attalos II in Athens* (APB II) (1959); Travlos, *op. cit.* 505–19, figs. 636–56; *The Athenian Agora* XIV: H. A. Thompson and R. E. Wycherley, *The Agora of Athens* (1972) 103–8.

87. Standing columns at the south-east corner of the temple of Olympian Zeus in Athens. Renewed work on this massive project, which had been abandoned in the late sixth century after the downfall of the Pisistratids, was the principal Seleucid gift to the city, made by Antiochus IV (176–165 B.C.). This should be linked to Antiochus' promotion of the cult of Zeus as a unifying factor in his reduced and troubled kingdom. No attempt was made (any more than was done by the Pergamene kings) to incorporate classical Athenian architectural forms, and the temple was designed in the florid Corinthian style which seems to have found favour, by the second century B.C., in the Seleucid area. The temple was completed to the Seleucid design by the Romans.

Travlos, *op. cit.* 402–11, figs. 522–31 (with bibliography).

88

88. Detail of the frieze from the monument of Aemilius Paullus at Delphi. The monument, which commemorated the Roman general's victory at Pydna in 168 B.C., was similar to that of Prusias (**80**), a pillar surmounted by an equestrian statue. The central figure in this part of the relief carries a Macedonian shield; the foreshortened horse to the right has an antecedent in the painted frieze of the great royal tomb of Vergina, over a century and a half earlier, thus linking the beginning with the end of Macedonian supremacy in Greece.

(White marble. Height 45 cm.)

For the monument *Fouilles de Delphes* II: F. Courby, *La terrasse du temple* (1927) 302–5, figs. 245–50. For the frieze A. J. Reinach, *BCH* 34 (1910) 433–68; P. Lévêque, *Rev. Arch.* 6.31–2 (1949) 633–43; D. E. Strong, *Roman Imperial Sculpture* (1961) 8f., fig. 13; H. Kähler, *Der Fries vom Reiterdenkmal des Aemilius Paullus in Delphi* (Monumenta Artis Romanae V) (1965).

6. SICILY AND MAGNA GRAECIA

J. C. CARTER

In the western Greek world the salient fact of the early Hellenistic period is the remarkable economic recovery of the whole of Sicily with the advent of Timoleon in the 340s (cf. **97**), and the general prosperity of Magna Graecia (cf. **89–92**) under the hegemony of Taras (Tarentum) and her imported *condottieri*, two of whom, Agathocles and Pyrrhus, personally and very visibly linked the history of the two regions. The limited resources of Greece – in particular the original mother-cities – were tapped for leaders and new colonists. Recent excavations attest the resurgence of the countryside. Farmhouses in great numbers rose fresh in the second half of the fourth century B.C., in the territories of Gela, Metapontum and other coastal cities, and in the interior (cf. **93**), after long periods of virtual abandonment. The new wealth, based in large part on agriculture, is manifest in the greatly expanded coinage of Metapontum, Syracuse, Neapolis and others (**94**). It is reflected in the vast artisan production (vases, terracottas) of declining quality, destined for a mass market (cf. **95–6**), but above all in great projects of urban renewal and fortification. The emphasis in Sicily (**97–8**), as in densely populated Asia Minor, was on refounding existing centres. In terms of material culture there is little to differentiate native and Greek centres (**96**). In this sense Sicily and Magna Graecia were Hellenistic long before Alexander or Timoleon.

Development throughout this period was conditioned by the pressure of external forces, namely the perennial hostility of Carthage, the influence of the more or less hellenized native populations of the interior, and the relentless expansion of Rome (cf. **94b–c**). The fall of Taras (275 B.C.) and Syracuse (212 B.C.) marks the end of autonomy and the beginning of a long economic and cultural decline only partially arrested by Roman administrators.

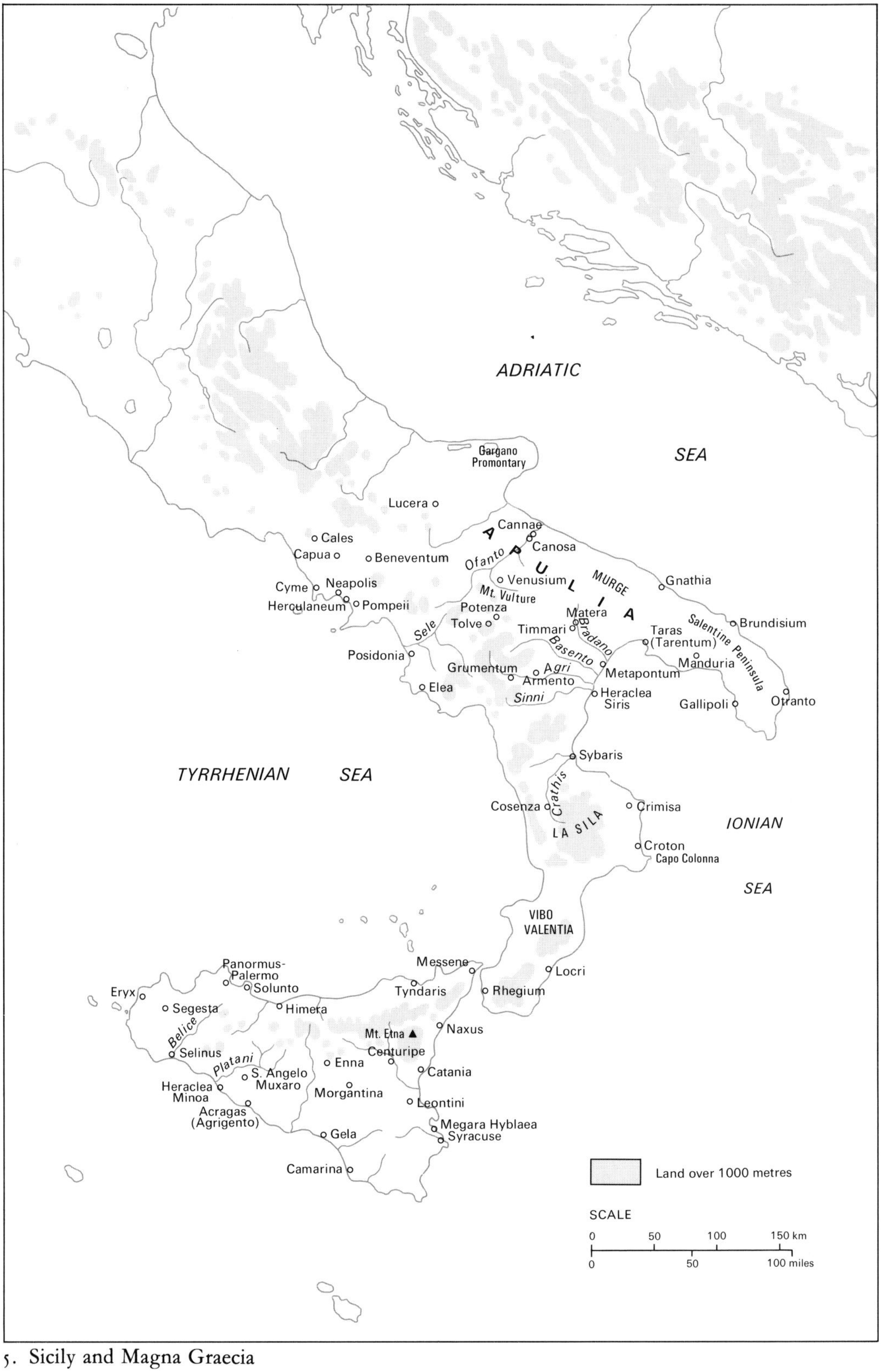

5. Sicily and Magna Graecia

89

89. Aerial view of Heraclea in Lucania. The grid plan of the capital of the Italiote League, discovered by aerial photography and partially excavated, occupies a ridge 1.7 km long. It is divided by a broad east–west street with intersecting alleys 36.8 m apart. The western end (excavated area, foreground) was residential; the insulae in the centre with numerous kilns for terracotta and iron production comprised an industrial quarter. Furnished with drains, and isolated within the city walls, it was in use from the fourth to the second centuries B.C. Its products were traded with the interior, as discoveries (for example, a Heraclean matrix at Grumentum) attest. Relations with the immediately surrounding territory are documented in the famous Heraclea bronze tablets of the time of Alexander the Molossian, or of Pyrrhus, who fought the Romans outside these walls in 280 B.C.

L. Quilici, *Siris-Heraclea* (Forma Italiae Reg. III. 1); B. Neutsch, *Herakleiastudien* (*Rom. Mitt.* Ergänzungsheft XI) (1967); D. Adamesteanu, *La Basilicata antica* (1974) 93–119; *PECS* 384.

90. Limestone relief from a Tarentine *naiskos*. The eastern part of Taras, Polybius noted, was

90

full of tombs, brightly painted, richly sculptured little funerary temples, reflections of the private opulence and taste of the early Hellenistic period. This metope-like panel and five others decorated the grandest surviving example. The mounted warrior, whose *gorgoneion* breastplate emblem, wild hair and powerful steed are clear allusions to Alexander, triumphs over a nude barbarian with pelta shield. The date, about 275 B.C., suggests that the tomb may have been occupied by a casualty of Pyrrhus' campaigns. The rude power of the figures and impressionistic treatment of form contrasts with the refinement of Tarentine jewellers, painters and terracotta-makers, and seems to anticipate in some respects sculptural developments in Asia Minor.

(Taranto, National Museum 113 768. Height 51.5 cm; width 49.5 cm; thickness 12 cm.)

J. C. Carter, *AJA* 74 (1970) 127f., fig. 4; *id. The Sculpture of Taras* (*Transactions of the American Philosophical Society* n.s. 65.7) (1975) 70–2 no. 202, pls. 33, 36c–d.

91. Bronze tablet from the archives of the temple of Olympian Zeus at Locri. This example (No. 12) and thirty-eight similar ones, found buried in a cylindrical stone box at Locri in 1959, record transactions of the temple treasury. The text contains (normally) the names of magistrates (preceded by a three-letter symbol for the deme), the object (loan, amount and period, or more rarely repayment), the uses to which the

91

92

money is to be put and its sources. They cover an exceptional period for the city. Most are loans for tower-building or contributions to King Pyrrhus. The mention of sources of income, often payments in kind, makes the tablets precious documents of social and economic history, comparable to those from Heraclea. Tablet 12 is unique in showing a sketch plan of a tower – the one surely for which the loan was made. It is strikingly similar to an extant tower foundation in the city wall.

(Reggio di Calabria, National Museum. Height 11 cm; width 17.2 cm; thickness 4 mm.)

A. De Franciscis, *Stato e società in Locroi epizefiri* (1972) (with earlier bibliography).

92. Detail from a painted chamber tomb in the Spinazzo necropolis at Paestum, one of a small group of early-third-century B.C. paintings which differs markedly in subject and style from the more familiar Lucanian painting of the second half of the fourth. The rectangular tomb was entered from a short end. Processional scenes on the sides converge opposite the entrance on a composition of an aristocratic woman, head veiled, reaching to clasp the hand of an elegantly dressed man with wizened cheeks and a bulbous nose. A black signet ring conspicuously displayed on his left hand proclaims his authority. With its elegant draftsmanship, modelling of facial contours and sensitive characterization, the Tomb of the Magistrate marks a return to traditions more in line with the broader currents of Hellenistic art – at the moment when a Roman colony was being established at Paestum.

(Paestum, Museum. Height of detail 34 cm.)

M. Napoli, *Atti del 12º Convegno di studi sulla Magna Grecia* (1973) 301f., pls. XII–XV; A. D. Trendall, *Archaeological Reports for 1972–73* (1973) 35, figs. 4–5.

93. Isolated farmhouse near Tolve, north east of Potenza. The well-preserved plan of this

94

a

b

c

d

e

f

third-century B.C. farmhouse illustrates both the hellenization of the interior of Lucania and the transition from the colonial farmhouse of the coastal cities to the autonomous *villa rustica*. Domestic activities, tool-room and stall (?) occupied the west wing (top). Divided by a courtyard, as in Metapontine farmhouses, the residential section (foreground) included the earliest known private bath in Italy. In the first of three interconnecting rooms is a tub with a seat, like those of the early-third-century baths of Gela – the earliest public baths in Italy and among the first anywhere to be heated by a hypocaust (cf. **183**). With the arrangement of its rooms in sequence the bath at Tolve foreshadows another important aspect of Roman public baths.

G. Tocco, *Atti del 13º Convegno di studi sulla Magna Grecia* (1974) 461–8, pls. CII–CV. For Gela, P. Orlandini, *Notizie degli Scavi* (1960) 181–202.

94. Coinage of southern Italy and Sicily.

(**a**) Obverse of a silver didrachm of Taras (Tarentum), about 325 B.C. A groom removes a stone from the horse's hoof, as on Ambracian coins exported to the west at the time of Timoleon's expedition.

(Diameter 23 mm.)

BM Coins Italy (1873) 184 no. 182. Cf. G. K. Jenkins, in O. Mørkholm and N. M. Waggoner, eds., *Greek Numismatics and Archaeology* (1979) 109–14.

(**b**) Reverse of a silver stater of Locri with the earliest known personification of Roma, crowned by Pistis. About the time of Pyrrhus.

(Diameter 20 mm.)

PCG 66 no. V.C. 14, pl. 37.14. Cf. E. Pozzi Paolini, in D. Musti, ed., *Le tavole di Locri* (1977) 139 no. 4, pl. I.12.

(**c**) Reverse of the earliest Roman bronze coin minted in Neapolis (some time after 326 B.C.) with the legend ΡΩΜΑΙΩΝ and a man-headed bull.

(Diameter 16 mm.)

M. H. Crawford, *Roman Republican Coinage* (1974) 131 no. 1.

(**d**) Obverse of a Siculo-Punic silver tetradrachm with head of Tanit-Artemis. About 320 B.C. or after.

(Diameter 25 mm.)

PCG 47 no. III.C.41, pl. 26.41. Cf. G. K. Jenkins, *Schweizerische numismatische Rundschau* (1977) 24–31, 62 no. 271, pl. 22.

95

(**e**) Reverse of a bronze pentonkion struck in Messene in the late third century B.C. Warrior advancing to right with helmet, lance and shield.

(Diameter 26 mm.)

BM Coins Sicily (1876) 111 nos. 26–8. Cf. M. Särström, *A Study in the Coinage of the Mamertines* (1940) 113f., 118, pl. XXXIII.

(**f**) Obverse of a gold stater of Syracuse with the head of Persephone minted in the name of Hicetas, during or after Pyrrhus' invasion of Sicily.

(Diameter 15 mm.)

BM Coins Sicily (1876) 201 nos. 433–5. Cf. T. V. Buttrey, *NC* 7.13 (1973) 1–17, pls. 1–2.

95. Apulian column-crater attributed to the workshop of the Patera Painter (about 320 B.C.). Native warriors, dressed in *chitoniskoi* with elaborate belts and conical hats, appear only on this shape in Apulian workshops until the third quarter of the fourth century, which would indicate that there was a special market. Favourite subjects are the pursuit of women, banquets, libations, boar-hunts and above all battles. The Patera Painter is one who also decorates small vessels with natives.

96 a

b

c

d

97

(Height 56 cm.)
Cf. A. D. Trendall, *Gli indigeni nella pittura italiota* (1971).

96. Selected votives. Votive images are eloquent testimony to the hellenization of the native centres of the interior of Sicily and Magna Graecia, and a reciprocal native influence especially on the popular arts of the colonial *poleis*.

(**a**) A bronze Heracles, with bow and lion-skin, from a sanctuary by a spring (?) in the interior of Camarina. Excellent work, probably Syracusan. Third century B.C.

(Syracuse, National Museum 63890. Height 22 cm.)
P. Pelagatti and G. Voza, eds., *Archeologia in Sicilia sud- orientale* (1973) 158 no. 464, pl. L.

(**b, c**) Terracotta votive busts from the sanctuary at Timmari, an important native settlement in the hinterland of Metapontum (near Matera). These contemporaneous images of the bejewelled divinity in her native and Hellenic aspects are from the same deposit.

(Matera, National Museum D. Ridola. (**b**) 5957. Height 34 cm. (**c**) 5918. Height 50.5 cm.)
D. Adamesteanu, *La Basilicata antica* (1974) 210–11.

(**d**) Mould-made terracotta bust of Hephaestus (holding patera and tongs), much elaborated with the stylus. *c.* 300 B.C. From the ironworking quarter of Heraclea.

(Policoro, National Museum 36603. Height 24.9 cm.)
Adamesteanu, *op. cit.* 105–6.

97. The Hellenistic agora of Morgantina (near Aidone) in Sicily. The grid and walls of this strategic town refounded by Timoleon were laid out *ex novo* on a long ridge to the south of the archaic acropolis (in the background) destroyed by Ducetius in 459 B.C. The agora developed in a hollow on two levels connected by an elegant, half-hexagonal stair. Enclosed on the east and west by stoas, and on the north by a gymnasium, it bears witness to the munificence of Agathocles and Hieron II. Syracusan workmanship and Corinthian inspiration have been seen in the unfinished Agathoclean west stoa. Just to the north of the stairs are the well preserved foundations of the second-century B.C. *macellum* – one of the few important works post-dating the sack of the city by the Romans in 211 B.C. To Hieron II's time has been assigned the granary on the lower level and the interesting villas on the hill behind. The 'House of Ganymede', in this prosperous provincial centre of mixed Hellenic and indigenous origins, contains the earliest surviving tessellated mosaic.

R. Stillwell and E. Sjöqvist, *AJA* 61 (1957) 151–9; 62 (1958) 158–62; 63 (1959) 167–71; 64 (1960) 125–33; 65 (1961) 275–81; 66 (1962) 135–40; 67 (1963) 163–71; 68 (1964) 137–47; 71 (1967) 245–50; H. L. Allen, *AJA* 74 (1970) 359–69; *PECS* 594f.

98

98. Interior of the theatre in Syracuse. Hieron II's urbanization of the Neapolis quarter of the city added much to the splendour of the most venerable of Hellenistic capitals. The theatre, built between 238 and 215 B.C., was the focal point. Its auditorium, hollowed from the living rock, was divided by a horizontal passage on whose walls still appear the names of gods and royalty to whom the sectors were dedicated. Olympian Zeus in the centre is flanked by Hieron and his queen. Cuttings honeycomb the area of the stage building (foreground), and have been variously interpreted by scholars. The two furthest to the right belong, with the tunnel exits, to a Roman remodelling. Several Hieronian stages have left traces (left). On the landscaped hill behind: a temple of Apollo Temenites, a Nymphaeum or Museum and stoas. Below the theatre Hieron built a monumental altar (198 m long) to Zeus Eleutherius, on which 450 oxen were annually slaughtered in thanksgiving for the overthrow of Thrasybulus in 466 B.C.

G. E. Rizzo, *Il teatro greco di Siracusa* (1923); L. Bernabò Brea, *Palladio* n.s. 17 (1967) 97–154; L. Polacco and C. Anti, *Il teatro antico di Siracusa* (1981).

7. HELLENISTIC WARFARE

P. CONNOLLY

The Hellenistic period began with an era of rapid development. Most significant was the evolution of the Macedonian pike phalanx. The recent discovery of the head and butt of a Macedonian pike (*sarissa*) at Vergina (**101**), which together weigh over 2 kg, give some idea of the formidable size of this weapon.

The main change in armour was the increasing use of iron. Several recent discoveries show that both cuirasses and helmets were being made of iron. The linen cuirass remained popular but during the period was gradually superseded by mail. Both the mail shirt shown on the Pergamene relief (**99**) and the plate iron cuirass found in the 'Tomb of Philip II' at Vergina are modelled on the linen cuirass. Although both Philip and Alexander appear to have worn plate iron cuirasses of this type, by the middle of the period the dress of senior officers assumed a standard form (**103**) which continued in use down through the Roman empire. The most popular helmet of the period was the Thracian type (**104**) which gradually developed into a sort of peaked cap (**105–6**). In the third century the long Celtic slashing sword stimulated the development of helmets with higher crowns (**100** right).

In tactics the great novelty of the period was the introduction of elephants which were mainly used against cavalry. For about 100 years they remained an important factor in Hellenistic warfare though they seldom influenced the course of battle and often caused as much damage to their friends as their enemies. The Egyptians and Carthaginians, unable to obtain Indian elephants (**110**), had to make do with the smaller North African forest type (**109**).

One of the main characteristics of the early period was the development and increasing use of gargantuan siege engines. This reached a climax at the end of the fourth century. Vast moveable towers (**113**), often more than 30 m high, raised the besiegers above the level of the walls. The lower floors of these towers were stocked with huge torsion catapults capable of hurling stones weighing over 100 kg. These were used to strip the battlements from the walls so that lighter bolt-shooting artillery (**111**) at the higher levels could be brought to bear on the defenders. Once the walls were cleared rams and borers could be brought into action.

A correspondingly rapid development took place in fortifications. The new strategy was to keep the enemy and his engines away from the walls. The old system of crenellated walls and towers was abandoned in favour of artillery emplacements. This is well illustrated by the defences of Perge (**114–15**). Here both towers and walls were specifically designed to house artillery.

Similar developments took place at sea. Although light vessels (**118**) still played an important part in naval warfare new heavily armoured vessels were designed with the hull completely enclosed (**117**). These were powered by oars at two or three levels each operated by several men. As a result they were much broader in the beam and capable of carrying heavy catapults and towers without turning turtle.

99

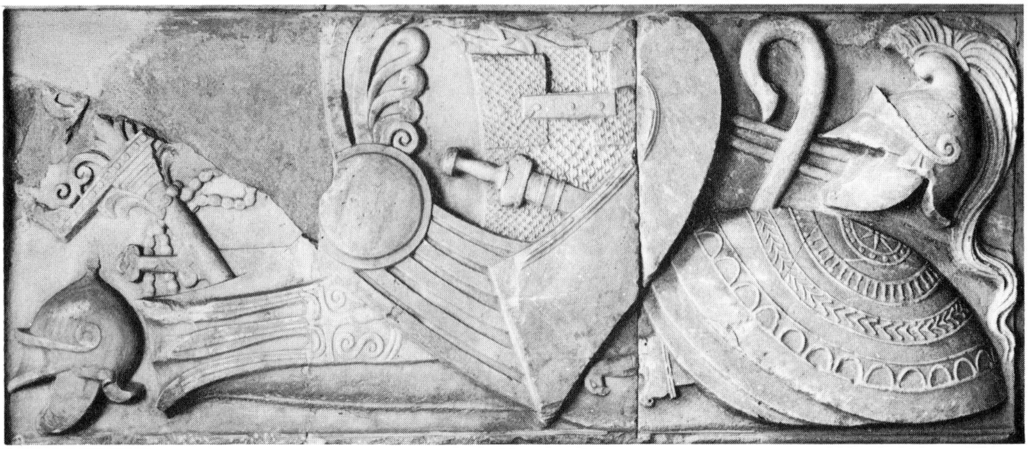

100

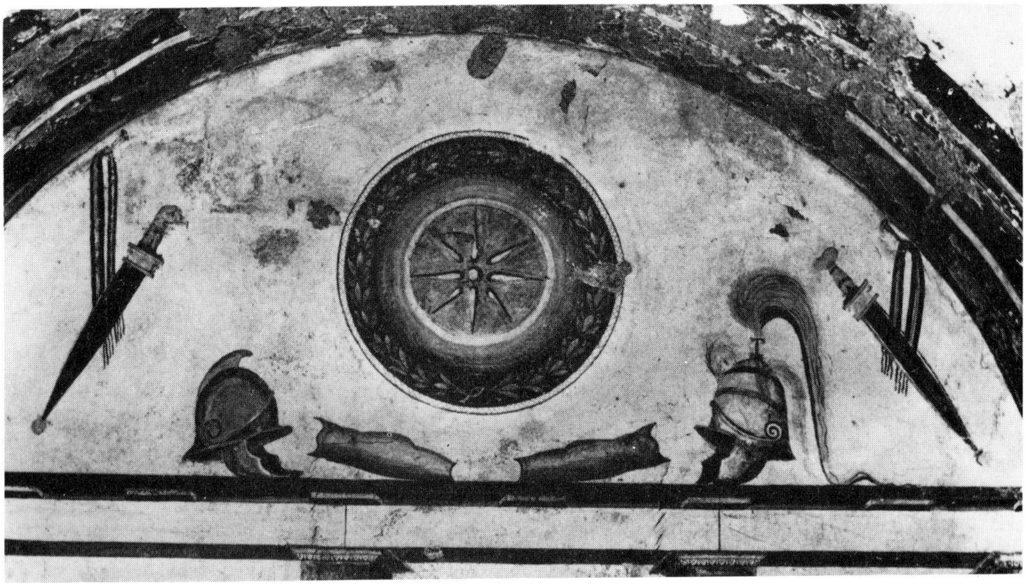

99. Relief of Hellenistic and Galatian trophies from the Sanctuary of Athena at Pergamum (*c.* 170 B.C.). On the right are a group of Macedonian type shields, with a *kopis* (cf. **102**) beneath them, and a Thracian helmet. In the centre are the sternposts (*aphlasta*) of two ships and the ram of another. Between the sternposts is a mail shirt and a Greek hoplite sword. This mail shirt, which is generally believed to be Celtic (Galatian), may be Greek as it is modelled on the linen cuirass. In the west Celtic shirts usually have shoulder capes. In the lower left corner is a helmet which, although clearly derived from the Celtic 'Montefortino' type, shows strong Hellenistic influences in the peak and brow band. A typical Celtic long sword can be seen behind the ship's ram.

(Berlin, Pergamon Museum. Approx. height 87 cm; width 2.06 m.)

H. Droysen, in *Altertümer von Pergamon* II: R. Bohn, *Das Heiligtum der Athena Polias Nikephoros* (1885) 93–138, pls. XLIII–L. Cf. **59**.

100. Painting of late-Macedonian arms in the tomb of Lyson and Callicles at Lefkadia, dated to the time of Perseus (179–168 B.C.). This shows a rimless shield decorated with the starburst emblem, two helmets, two swords and a pair of greaves. The helmet on the left is of late

 101

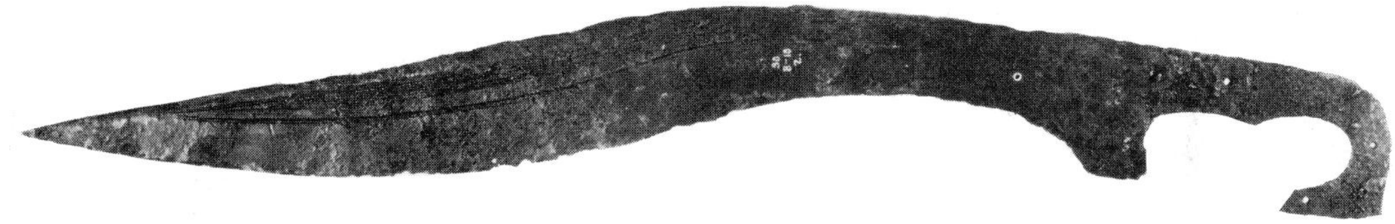 102

Thracian type. The one on the right is the high-crowned type. The sword on the left is a *kopis* with a typical bird's head handle, while that on the right is the typical hoplite two-edged type.

(Diameter of lunette approx. 3 m.)
Ch. I. Makaronas, *Makedonika* 2 (1941–52) 634–6, pls. XVIII–XIX; *id.* and S. G. Miller, *Archaeology* 27 (1974) 248–59; cf. P. J. Callaghan, *AAA* 11 (1978) 56.

101(a, b). Iron *sarissa* head and butt from Vergina. The head (**a**), which is 51 cm long, weighs 1.235 kg. The butt (**b**) is 44.5 cm long and weighs 1.070 kg. It has been estimated that a 12 cubit *sarissa* with a shaft of cornel wood would weigh 6.5 kg and a 14 cubit example about 8 kg.

(Thessaloniki, Archaeological Museum 7.192 and 193.)
M. Andronikos, *BCH* 94 (1970) 91–107. Cf. A. M. Snodgrass, *Arms and Armour of the Greeks* (1967) 118f.; M. M. Markle, *AJA* 81 (1977) 323–39.

102. Spanish *falcata*. This single-edged cut and thrust sword is almost identical to the Greek *kopis*, the most common sword of the period, and may have been derived from it. The blade length of these weapons is about 45 cm. The handle is usually in the form of a bird's head.

(London, British Museum 1890.8-10.2, presented by A. W. Franks. From Spain. Length 60 cm.)
H. Sandars, *Archaeologia* 64 (1912–13) 213–58, pl. XIII.

103. Marble trophy from Rhodes showing the panoply of a Hellenistic general. First century B.C. The decorated muscled cuirass worn over a soft leather tunic with *pteryges* protecting the shoulders and thighs was the standard dress uniform of generals.

(Rhodes, Archaeological Museum 1224 (displayed in Castello). From necropolis in Makry Steno (found 1917). White marble. Height 1.90 m.)
A. Maiuri, *ASAtene* 4–5 (1921–22) 245f., fig. 8; G. Jacopi, *Clara Rhodos* 1 (1928) 22, fig. 4; A. Maiuri, *Clara Rhodos* 2 (1932) 57–61, figs. 28–30.

104. Thracian bronze helmet with the top in the form of a Phrygian cap and the cheek-pieces decorated in imitation of facial hair. This helmet, which is typical of the fourth century, was found at Kovachevitsa in Bulgaria.

103

104

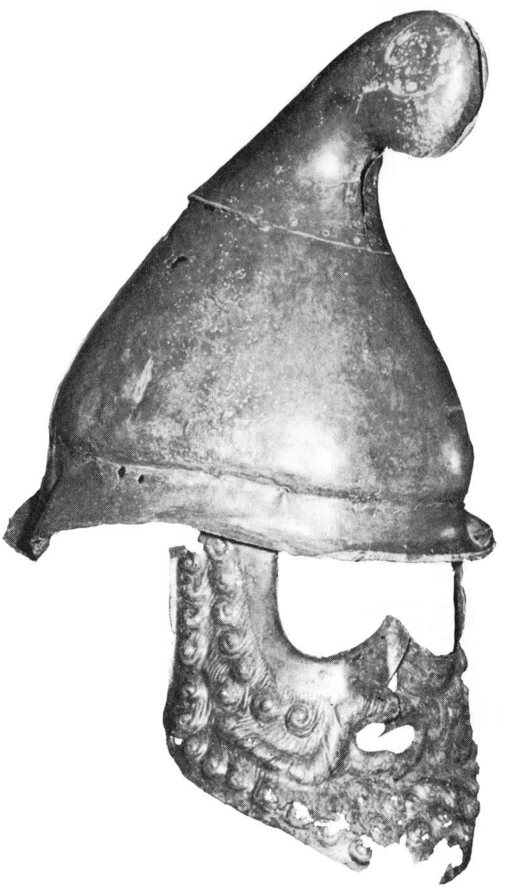

105

(Sofia, Archaeological Museum 2676. Made of three pieces riveted together. Height including cheek-piece 39 cm; helmet alone 23.7 cm; width 25 cm.)

V. Mikov, *Godishnik na narodnata biblioteka i muzei v Plovdiv* (1925) 181–6; cf. T. Ivanov, *Razhopki i prouchvaniya* 1 (1948) 99–108; R. F. Hoddinott, *The Thracians* (1981) 106, fig. 101.

105. Later bronze Thracian helmet. This is typical of the late third and early second century B.C. It is made in six pieces and carries various moulded ornaments: a head of Athena on the front, a head of Apollo(?) on the hinge of the visor, and an ear on the side of the neckpiece. There are traces of gilding. A very similar helmet made in iron was recently discovered at Prodromiou in Greece.

(Paris, Louvre Museum 1365. From Melos. Height 20 cm; width 20 cm; depth (side view) 24 cm.)

06

107

108

B. Schröder, *JdI* 27 (1912) 328, Beil. 13.2; A. de Ridder, *Les bronzes antiques du Louvre* II (1915) 2 no. 1106, pl. 65.1106.

106. Bronze helmet of later Thracian type but showing strong barbarian influences. This helmet, which comes from Bryastovets (Karaagach) in Bulgaria, is probably of the third century B.C.

(Sofia, Archaeological Museum 3454. Height 14 cm.)
Schröder, *art. cit.* 328, Beil. 13.1.

107. Bronze Boeotian helmet found in the Tigris. This possibly belonged to one of Alexander's cavalry. An identical helmet is shown on the Alexander sarcophagus in Istanbul (late fourth century B.C.). This type of helmet was recommended by Xenophon for cavalry use.

(Oxford, Ashmolean Museum 1977.256, formerly Rugby School. Height 24 cm; depth 34 cm.)
P. M. Fraser and T. Rönne, *Boeotian and West Greek Tombstones* (1957) 66–8, pl. 18.1–2; A. M. Snodgrass, *Arms and Armour of the Greeks* (1967) 94, 125, pl. 58; M. Vickers, *Arch. Anz.* (1981) 559f. no. 21, fig. 22.

108. Bronze Boeotian helmet of late type (*c.* 200 B.C.). Helmets of this type can be seen on many monuments of the later Hellenistic period. Its Boeotian derivation is shown by the 'pleating' on either side of the brim. The decoration of the cap is typical of the third century.

(Oxford, Ashmolean Museum 1971.904, formerly Bomford collection. Height 21.5 cm.)
H. W. Catling, *Archaeological Reports for 1974–5* (1975) 35 no. 56, fig. 13.

109. The reverse of a silver double shekel of the late third century B.C. from New Carthage showing a North African forest elephant and mahout. These elephants, now extinct in North

109

110

Africa, measured about 2.35 m at the shoulder compared to about 3 m for the Indian and 3.5 m for the African bush elephant.

(London, British Museum 1911.7-2.1, from Mogente hoard. Approx. double size.)

PCG 65 no. v.c. 1, pl. 37.1; H. H. Scullard, *NC* 6.8 (1948) 160–2; E. S. G. Robinson, in R. A. G. Carson and C. H. V. Sutherland, eds., *Essays in Roman Coinage* (1956) 39f., 50 no. 6a, fig. 3 c, pl. II.6a; H. H. Scullard, *The Elephant in the Greek and Roman World* (1974) 156, pl. XXI.

110. A terracotta statuette from Myrina in Turkey showing an Indian war elephant crushing a Celt. The elephant carries a tower that would have been held on by chains (cf. **32**). This statuette probably commemorates Antiochus I's victory over the Galatians (*c.* 272 B.C.) in which elephants played a significant part.

(Paris, Louvre Museum 131. From Myrina. Height 12 cm.)

E. Pottier and S. Reinach, *La nécropole de Myrina* (1888) 318–23, 559 no. 284, pl. X.1; F. Winter, *Die Typen der figürlichen Terrakotten* (1903) II, 385 no. 3; P. Bienkowski, *Les Celtes dans les arts mineurs gréco-romains* (1928) 141f., figs. 212–13; Scullard, *op. cit.* 123, pl. VIIb. Cf. B. Bar-Kochva, *The Seleucid Army* (1976) 75–83.

111. The catapult from Ampurias in Spain.

(**a**) The 'spring' holders of the catapult complete with the tightening 'washers' at either end. The frame is of iron and the washers bronze.

(**b**) A suggested reconstruction as a small bolt-shooting catapult.

(**c**) An exploded drawing of the reconstructed springs showing the power source of twisted sinew. These skeins of sinew or horsehair were tightened by twisting the washers.

(Barcelona, Archaeological Museum.)

E. Schramm, *Die antiken Geschütze der Saalburg* (1918) 40–6, 75–9, figs. 14–17, 36–7, pl. 11; P. Connolly, *The Roman Army* (1975) 67. Generally on Hellenistic artillery E. W. Marsden, *Greek and Roman Artillery* (1969–71).

112. Bronze triple-finned bolt-head bearing the name of Philip of Macedon. It may be compared with examples found at Olynthus, which Philip besieged in 348 B.C., and may perhaps have been found there.

(London, British Museum 1912.4-19.3. Provenance unknown. Length 6.8 cm.)

Cf. *Excavations at Olynthus* X: D. M. Robinson, *Metal and Minor Miscellaneous Finds* (1941) 382f. no. 1908, pl. CXX.

113. A reconstruction of Demetrius Poliorcetes' *helepolis*, based on the description by Diodorus Siculus (xx.91). This huge siege-tower, which was constructed for the siege of Rhodes, was 22 m square at the base and tapered to 9 m square at the top. It was over 40 m high and moved on eight wheels which swivelled so that it could be moved in any direction. It was stocked with catapults, the largest stone-throwers at the bottom and light 'sharp-

111

a

b

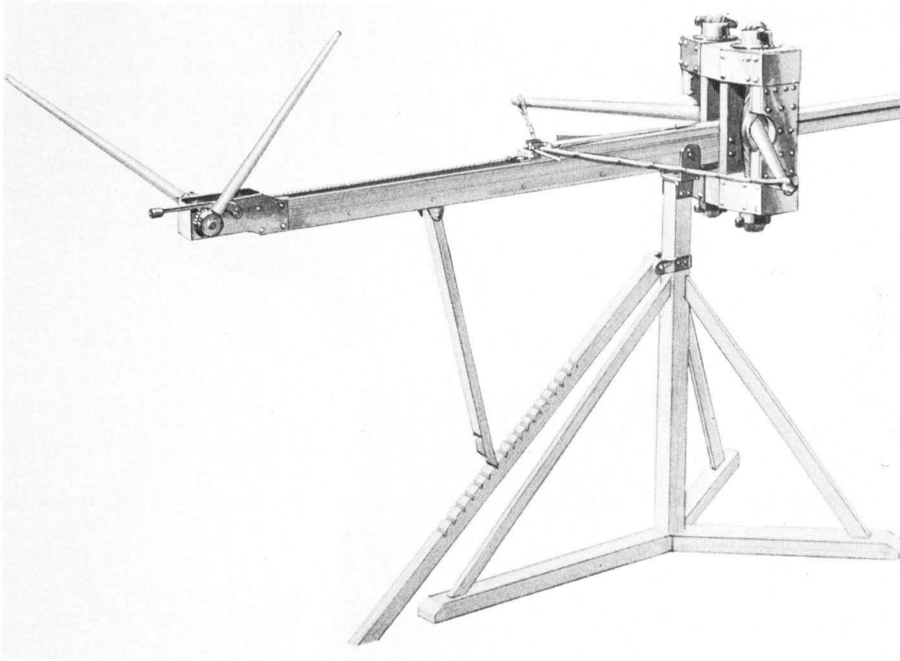

c

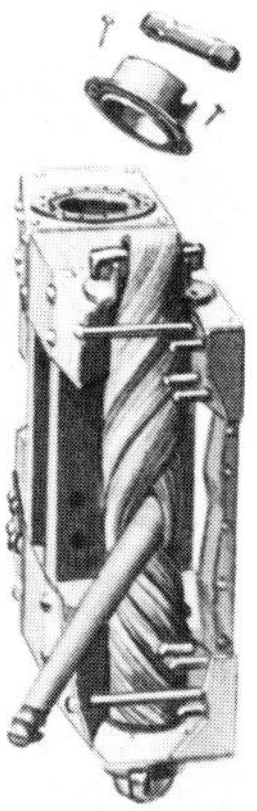

shooters' on the upper floors. The front and sides were plated with iron.

P. Connolly, *Greece and Rome at War* (1981) 282–3.

114. a tower at Perge showing the three large artillery ports in the top storey. From this elevated position the town's artillery would be able to outrange that of the enemy. Two loopholes for light artillery or archers can be seen at second-storey level. Towers were no longer crenellated but roofed over.

Walls at Perge: K. Lanckoronski, G. Niemann and E. Petersen, *Städte Pamphyliens und Pisidiens* I (1890)

112

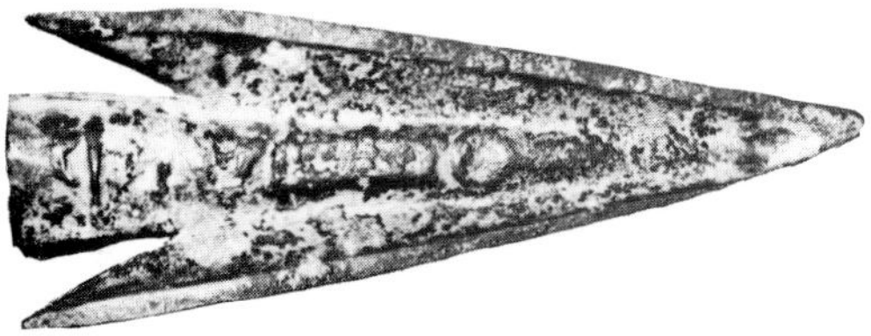

113

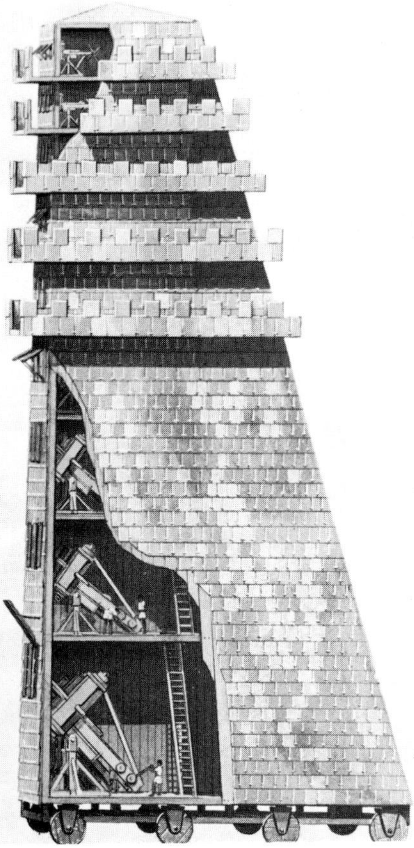

114

58–63, figs. 44–9; A. W. Lawrence, *Greek Architecture* (1957) pls. 128, 129A; E. W. Marsden, *Greek and Roman Artillery, Historical Development* (1969) 151f., 163, diagram 14. Generally on Hellenistic towers and apertures for missiles: F. E. Winter, *Greek Fortifications* (1971) 194–203, 327–9; A. W. Lawrence, *Greek Aims in Fortification* (1979) 376–418.

115. The vaulted compartments in the walls at Perge. These had platforms and loopholes for artillery. Above this would have been a sentry walk with a screening wall with loopholes for more artillery or archers.

For bibliography see **114**. See esp. Marsden, *op. cit.* 122, 155, diagram 2; Winter, *op. cit.* 142, figs. 96, 118; Lawrence, *op. cit.* pls. 76, 78–9.

116. The corbelled gateway at Assos (fourth century B.C.?). The function of corbelling was to support the immense weight of the masonry above it. Walls were usually faced with cut stone and filled with rubble.

Winter, *op. cit.* 253, fig. 282. Cf. J. T. Clarke, F. H. Bacon and R. Koldewey, *Investigations at Assos* (1902–21) 191–219; J. M. Cook, *The Troad* (1973) 241–5, pls. 32–4; Winter, *op. cit.* 253, fig. 282.

117. The base of the Victory of Samothrace, which shows the prow of an armoured galley of the late third or early second century B.C. Staggered oar-ports can be seen in the outrigger (extreme right). For an earlier form of prow compare the coin **70b**.

(Paris, Louvre Museum 2369 (cf. **52**). Height of deck 2.04 m; max. width 2.50 m; length preserved 4.30 m.)
C. Blinkenberg, *Triemiolia* (Det Kgl. Danske Videnskabernes Selskab. Archaeologisk-kunsthis-

115

116

toriske Meddelelser II.3) (1938) 37–40, fig. 13; L. Casson, *Ships and Seamanship in the Ancient World* (1971) 102f., 118f., fig. 118.

118. A rock carving at Lindus in Rhodes showing (right) the stern of a light galley. The rear end of the outrigger and the steering oar are clearly visible, and the seat of the helmsman can be seen under the curved *aphlaston*. The carving served as a base for a commemorative statue of the admiral Hagesander, set up about 180 or 170 B.C.

(Height of deck 1.80 m; max. depth of relief 1.28 m.)
Blinkenberg, *op. cit.* 22–30, figs. 2–6; *Lindos* II: C. Blinkenberg, *Inscriptions* (1941) 431–6; *Lindos* III: E. Dyggve, *Le sanctuaire d'Athana Lindia et l'architecture lindienne* (1960) 55–7, figs. III.27–8, pls. III.A–B.

Generally on Hellenistic warships, Casson, *op. cit.* 97–135. Cf. the galley in **117**.

11*

118

8. HELLENISTIC CIVILIZATION

ROGER LING

The general cultural aspects of the Hellenistic world can be treated under a number of headings of convenience: industry and trade (including ships), houses and life (including personal ornaments and fashions), sport and education, theatre, religion, death and burial, philosophy and science. The emphasis throughout will be on the apparatus of life and society, and upon the beliefs and experiences of the people of the time; strictly literary culture (for obvious reasons) and the fine arts as such (for reasons stated in the Introduction) will not be covered. Inevitably there will be a tendency to dwell on what was new in Hellenistic times, and it should never be forgotten that Hellenistic civilization developed out of what went before. Alongside the New Comedy of Menander, the traditional drama of Sophocles and Euripides remained a favourite of theatre-audiences; alongside the 'new' religions which gained ground with the mixing of the races, the old Olympian gods remained a potent force in the life of the Greek cities.

1. Industry and trade

The staple economic activity within the vastly expanded Hellenistic world was, as it had been in the world of the city-states, agriculture. There were no substantial improvements in production methods, but we know that the Ptolemies, among others, introduced new crops and fruits from the east, and that attention was given to ambitious reclamation and irrigation schemes (**119**). Some limited assistance in irrigation may have been offered by the Archimedean screw (cf. **260**), a device which is still used in parts of the Nile valley for pumping water from the river. One of the main concerns of the Ptolemies was to ensure good grain-production, and with this in mind they experimented with types of wheat which cropped more frequently; that there was a ready market for exported corn is shown by the regular appointment of grain-commissioners in several Greek cities during this period (**120**).

The vast quantities of bullion released by Alexander's conquest of Persia and the new mines which became accessible to the Greeks, for example the gold-mines of Nubia, enabled the kings at first to issue abundant money, and a money economy spread throughout the Hellenistic world (cf. **4**, **11**, **14**, **22**, **28**, **35–6**). Bronze coins with a purely nominal value came into regular use as small change (**121**). Later, when for various reasons metal supplies diminished, there was a tendency for money to grow scarcer and for prices to rise, factors which are reflected in such local phenomena as the rise of the weight standard in Athens (**122**).

New commodities and industries now came under Greek control: for example, the production of purple fabrics at Tyre, of glassware in Phoenicia and Egypt (**123**, **151–4**), of linen and papyrus in Egypt. At the same time the old Greek territories developed new specialities. Pottery with decoration in relief imitating embossed metalware became a popular line manufactured in all parts of the Greek world (**168–70**). Cos produced silks (cf. **173**), and in the later Hellenistic period, with the arrival of the Romans on the scene, Athens and various Aegean centres cashed in on the art-market by producing replicas or pastiches from classical sculpture (**124**; cf. **147**). Further east, to lessen their dependence on Egyptian papyrus, the kings

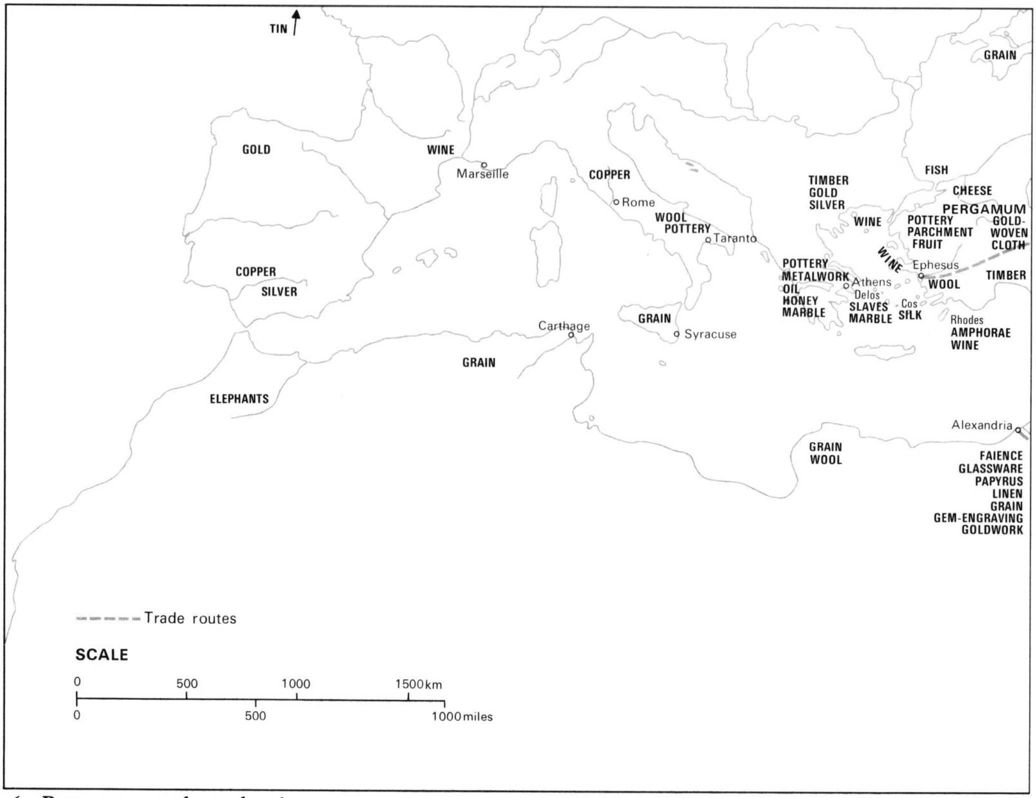

6. Resources and production

of Pergamum and the Seleucids developed the manufacture of parchment, one of the few industries where the use of large numbers of slaves may have enabled anything approximating to mass-production.

The conquest of the east opened up new trade-routes, and a feature of the Hellenistic age is the importation of oriental luxuries: dyes and spices from India, precious stones and perfumes from Arabia, ivory and elephants from both India and Africa, perhaps ultimately silks from China. These came overland via the caravan-routes controlled by the Seleucids, or by sea to the Red Sea and subsequently to Alexandria, which became the greatest emporium of the eastern Mediterranean. An aspect of the desert caravan-trade was the use of camels as pack-animals both within the Seleucid Kingdom and in Egypt (**126**).

The shift of wealth and industry eastwards meant the decline of old commercial centres such as Athens and Corinth. The major trading-state of the third and early second centuries, strategically situated at the meeting-place of sea-routes from north, south, east and west, was Rhodes, which achieved great prosperity from the tax of 2% levied on merchandise passing through its port. Rhodes was also a leading centre for the production of cheap wine and of the jars (amphorae) used in its transport (and in the transport of other fluids). The study of amphorae and their control-marks has shed a great deal of light on the trading-links of Rhodes and of its competitors (**127–8**). In late Hellenistic times, thanks to the intervention of the Romans, the bulk of the Aegean transit trade passed to Delos, where the remains of warehouses and commercial buildings provide vivid testimony to the activity of Italian and other merchants (**130–1**).

The bulk of the Mediterranean trade was naturally sea-borne, and much has been learnt about it in recent years from the archaeological examination of shipwrecks (**132–3**; cf. **125**, **144**, **149**, **261**). The ships excavated range in length from 16 m to 40 m, but we hear from literary sources of the building of much larger vessels, notably the *Syracusia* designed by Archimedes, the first 'super-tanker' in history, which turned out to be too large for most of the ports that it

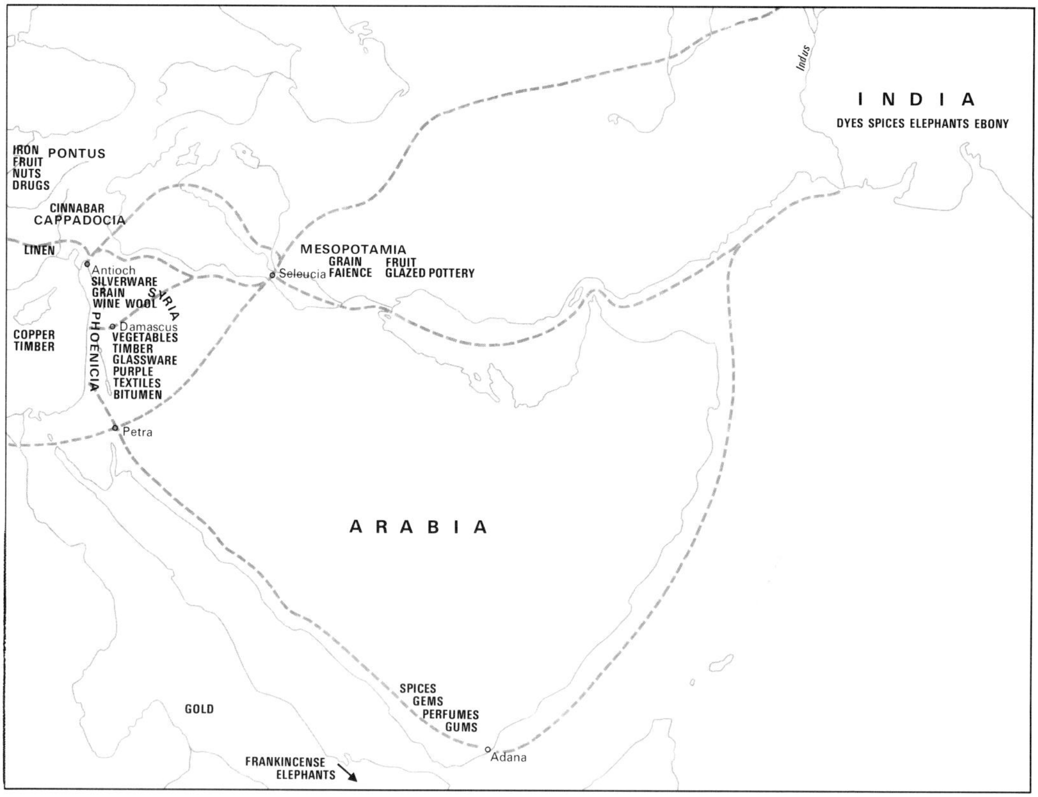

was intended to visit (**134**). On the rigging of Hellenistic ships we have very little information, but it is possible that the fore-and-aft rig, much more efficient than the traditional square sail for tacking into the wind, was developed in this period. One version, the spritsail, appears on a Thasian relief (**135**), and the Kyrenia ship too (**132**), to judge from the placing of its mast, may have had some form of fore-and-aft rig.

119. An estimate for the repair and extension of a system of irrigation in the Fayûm, possibly that of the estate of Ptolemy II's minister Apollonius (cf. **1**). 259/8 B.C. The area involved, shown in the sketchplan, is 10,000 *arourai*, to be divided by three longitudinal and nine transversal canals into 40 plots of 25 *arourai*. The canals are to be 4 cubits wide and 2 cubits deep, and the contractor estimates the amount of earth to be dug out as 137,600 *naubia* (probably units of 8 cubic cubits); the cost of the work is to be 70 *naubia* per stater (tetradrachm) in winter and 50 in the heat of summer. A supplement is payable on sloping ground, but a deduction may be made where dikes and ditches are in existence and still usable. On the verso, added at a later date, is a brief report on a tour of inspection resulting in a modification of the estimate.

(Paris, University of the Sorbonne, Institute of Papyrology 1. From Ghorân, Egypt (from the wrapping of a mummy). Length 31 cm; width 16 cm.)

P. Jouguet, P. Collart, J. Lesquies, M. Xoual, *Papyrus grecs* (Institut papyrologique de l'Université de Lille) I (1907–28) 1–23 (no. 1), pls. I–II; *Papyrologica Lugduno-Batava* XX: P. W. Pestman, ed., *Greek and Demotic Texts from the Zenon Archive* (1980) 253–65, pl. XXIX.

120. Fragment of an inscription from the Athenian Agora recording a vote of thanks to the grain-buyers (*sitonai*) of 247/6 B.C. for having taken every care to secure a good supply of grain at fair prices. 244/3 B.C. The *sitonai* were an important magistracy in cities like Athens and Delos which were dependent on imported grain to avert the danger of famine. Apart from the normal fluctuations, the Ptolemies and the grain-producing regions of Thrace and South

119

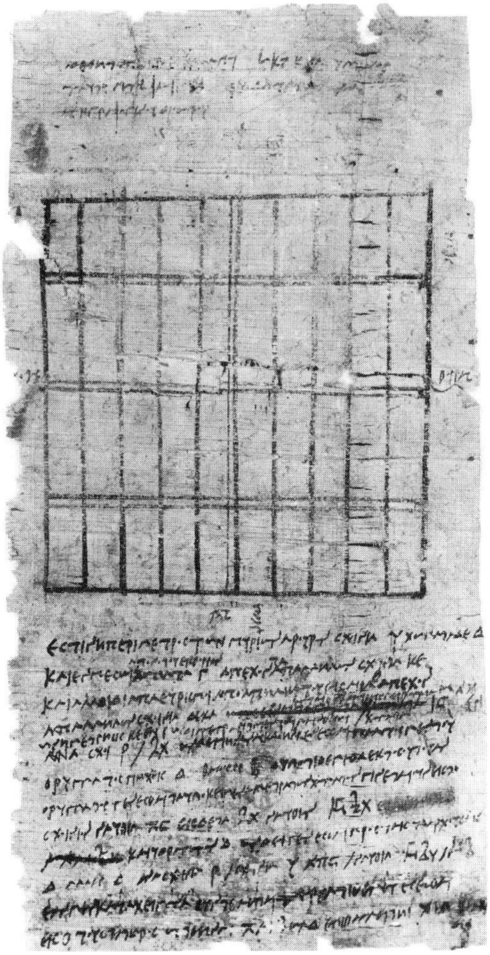

Russia were probably able to ensure a regular supply in the early Hellenistic period, but during the second and first centuries the effects of warfare, piracy and economic instability led to an increased incidence of corn-shortages.

(Athens, Agora Museum I 6064. Found built into a modern house. Hymettian marble. Height 30 cm; width 43.8 cm (inscribed part); thickness 10 cm (inscribed part).)

B. D. Merritt, *Hesperia* 17 (1948) 3f.; *id. Inscriptions from the Athenian Agora* (APB x) (1966) no. 19.

121. Athenian bronze coins. Silver coinage, now carried to all corners of the civilized world and beyond, remained the chief medium of

121

a

b

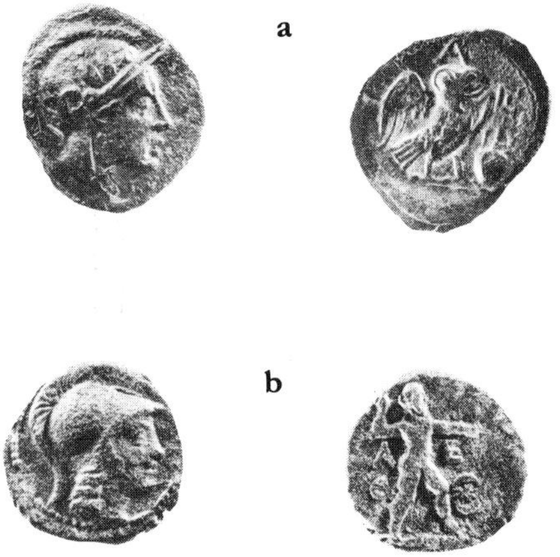

120

exchange in larger transactions; many examples are illustrated elsewhere in this volume for the historical or iconographic interest of their devices and portraits. But one of the important features of the time was the use of token bronze coins to represent the smaller denominations; this practice, which was common by the end of the fourth century in most Greek mints, facilitated small-scale transactions and was of enormous benefit to the ordinary people of the Hellenistic cities and kingdoms.

(**a**) *Obv.* head of Athena wearing late Attic close-fitting helmet with hinged visor; *rev.* owl with spread wings beside amphora. Third century B.C. At first based closely on silver types, the bronze coins soon began to ring the changes; here Athena has an up-to-date image and the traditionally sedate owl has come to life.

(Athens, Agora Museum ΠΘ – 312.)

(**b**) *Obv.* head of Athena wearing crested Corinthian helmet; *rev.* Zeus hurling the thunderbolt with the legend ΑΘΕ: (money) 'of the Athenians'. Late second or early first century B.C. Zeus 'fulminans' is one of a whole range of new types introduced on the bronze coins of the second century. The star between crescents is the symbol of the kings of Pontus, and this issue, together with the New Style silver coins which bear the same symbol, is probably to be dated to Mithridates VI's occupation of Athens from 88 to 86 B.C., despite Margaret Thompson's arguments for putting the issue back to *c.* 121 B.C.

(Athens, Agora Museum M 107. Approx. 2:1.)

M. Thompson, *The New Style Silver Coinage of Athens* (1961) 416–24, 529–31; cf. D. M. Lewis, *NC* 7.2 (1962) 275–300; M. Thompson, *ibid.* 301–33; M. J. Price, *NC* 7.4 (1964) 27–36; C. Boehringer, *Zur Chronologie mittelhellenistischer Münzserien 220–160 v. Chr.* (*Antike Münzen und geschnittene Steine* v) (1972) 22–7; F. S. Kleiner, *Greek and Roman Coins in the Athenian Agora* (APB xv) (1975).

122. Athenian lead weights. The vast majority of the lead weights found in the Athenian Agora belongs to the Hellenistic period and gives invaluable information on changing standards in the city over the last three centuries B.C. Approximately square in form, each carries a pictorial device symbolizing its value and often also a legend naming it (or alternatively an official guarantee ΔΕΜΟ or ΔΗΜΟ for δημόσιον). By combining literary and epigraphic clues with the evidence of the weights themselves, we can deduce that the standard obtaining in the fourth and third centuries was the '105 standard' (one mna, or half-stater, weight = 105 coin drachms), but that during the late third and second century the standard rose by stages to 150. This was probably due to a scarcity of silver, the main medium of exchange; as the value of silver rose, the price of other commodities in terms of silver went down, and it was thus found necessary to support the falling market by increasing weights.

122

a

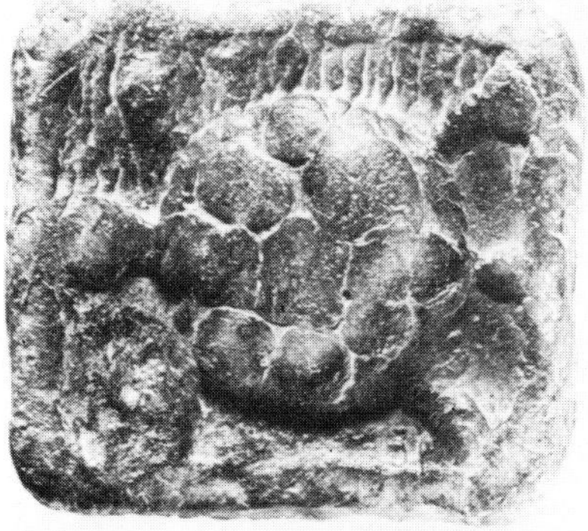

b

(**a**) One-quarter stater, with the regular symbol of a tortoise. Third or second century B.C. The weight is 222.5 g, giving a stater of 890 g (which, allowing for wear and tear and for possible chemical changes affecting the lead, conforms closely enough with the 105 standard: a stater of 915.6 g).

(Athens, Agora Museum IL 862. From deposit D 16. Length 5.2 cm; width 4.5 cm; thickness 10 mm.)

(**b**) One-third stater, symbolized by an amphora. Second century B.C. The letters τριτη(μόριον) specify the weight (here 322 g,

123

giving a stater of 966 g). This example suggests a rise in standard to 112 (a stater of 976.6 g), the first step to the 150 standard of the late second century. By the time that the 150 standard was reached, the amphora symbol had been transferred to the half-mna (quarter stater), replacing the tortoise; i.e. it remained close to a specific weight, though its denomination changed. At the same time there was a general revision of weights, the mna replacing the stater (which was now too heavy for convenience) as the basic unit of the system.

(Athens, Agora Museum IL 1041. From deposit B 17. Height 4.7 cm; width 4.5 cm; thickness 16 mm.)

The Athenian Agora X: M. Lang and M. Crosby, *Weights, Measures and Tokens* (1964) 2–33 (*passim*).

123. Colourless glass bowl with elaborate foliate patterns in gold leaf, one of the masterpieces of the glassware industry of Hellenistic times. Late third or early second century B.C. The main centres of glass manufacture were in the eastern Mediterranean, and especially at Alexandria, where new forms of decoration, such as mosaic glass and *millefiori* (**152**), became current during the third century. This type of decoration, in which the gold work is sandwiched between inner and outer shells of colourless glass, was invented there at the same time and continued till the latter part of the second century B.C. That gilded glassware was widely prized, no doubt as a luxury item, is shown by the discovery of this and other pieces in Italy, and of further examples in Asia Minor, Palestine and South Russia.

(London, British Museum 1871.5-18.2. From a tomb at Canosa, Italy (along with at least seven other glass vessels: cf. **152**). Height 11.4 cm; diameter 19.3 cm (across rim).

Rostovtzeff 372, pl. XLIII.2, 3; A. von Saldern, *JGS* I (1959) 46f. and frontispiece; D. B. Harden, *JGS* 20 (1968) 24f., 38–41, figs. 5–9; *id.* and others, *Masterpieces of Glass* (1968) 33 no. 38; *id. Arch. J.* 125 (1969) 63, 72, fig. 4, pl. X (C).

124. Portrait of an unknown Italian from Delos. Early first century B.C. One of the chief industries by which the flagging Athenian economy was revived in the late Hellenistic period was the manufacture of classicizing

24

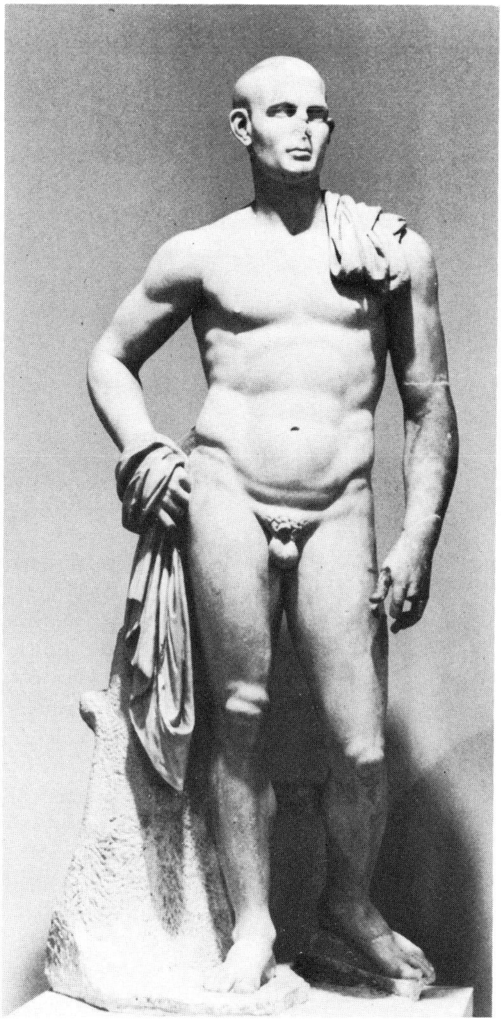

125

sculptures for the art-collectors of Roman Italy. Aided probably by the development of much more accurate techniques of mechanical reproduction, Athenian craftsmen specialized in carving replicas of famous statues, for example Polyclitan nude athletes, to which contemporary portrait-heads might be attached. The results, as here, were often incongruous, but the prevalence of the practice implies that the vanity of well-to-do Italian businessmen and officials provided a ready-made market. Known ironically as the Pseudo-Athlete, this statue combines a moderately realistic head of a man in early middle age (not bald: the hair was painted) with a Polyclitan body on a heroic scale.

(Athens, National Museum 1828. From Delos, House of the Diadumenus. White marble. Height 2.25 m (head 30 cm).)

EAD XIII: K. Michalowski, *Les portraits hellénistiques et romains* (1932) 17–22, figs. 11–12, pls. XIV–XIX; G. Hafner, *Späthellenistische Bildnisplastik* (1954) 72f. (A 24), pl. 31.

125. Marble *thymiaterium* (incense-burner). Second half of second century B.C. A typical example of the Neo-Attic marble ornaments, made at least initially in Athens, and destined

126

primarily for export to Roman Italy. A tripod base of lions' paws and griffins' foreparts supports a prismatic pedestal, from which rises an elaborate shaft of acanthus calyces; on top of all rests a shallow bowl. This item formed part of a consignment of *objets d'art* including bronze statuary and furnishings (cf. **144, 149**) which was on its way from Athens presumably to Italy when it was wrecked off the Tunisian coast at Mahdia soon after 100 B.C.

(Tunis, Bardo Museum. From the Mahdia shipwreck (one of five almost identical pieces). Pentelic marble; rear part (hidden) eroded. Height 1.85 m.)

Catalogue du Musée Alaoui, suppl. II (1922) 47f. nos. 1207–11, pl. VII. A. Merlin and L. Poinssot, *Cratères et candélabres de marbre trouvés en mer près de Mahdia* (1930) 112–30, pls. XXXVI–XL; Rostovtzeff 746, pl. LXXXIII.2; W. Fuchs, *Der Schiffsfund von Mahdia* (Bilderhefte des Deutschen Archäologischen Instituts Rom II) (1963) 27f. no. 29, pl. 37 (right).

126. Terracotta figurine of a crouching pack-camel. On the near side are two amphorae in wicker panniers; beyond (hidden) a cock in a large basket. Such representations of camels, the carriers of the desert caravan-trade, were popular types among the small terracottas and bronzes of the Hellenistic and Roman east.

(London, British Museum 1886.9–15.2. Formerly in collection of G. J. Chester. From Syria. Terracotta. Height 11 cm; length 12.5 cm.)

H. B. Walters, *Catalogue of the Terracottas in the Department of Greek and Roman Antiquities, British Museum* (1903) 247 (C 544); M. I. Rostovtzeff, *Social and Economic History of the Roman Empire*, 2nd ed. (1957) pl. 48.3.

127. Amphorae. In recent years the study of amphorae, the containers of the Mediterranean wine-trade (and of the trade in other commodities such as oil), has revolutionized our understanding of trade-relations in the Hellenistic world. Amphorae manufactured at different centres can be distinguished by their shape and fabric and, in many cases, by the control-marks stamped on their handles; while examples found in datable contexts, for example in the destruction layers of Corinth (146 B.C.) and Athens (86 B.C.), or in sealed deposits dated by associated coins and pottery (especially since the 1950s in shipwrecks), enable us to date the stamps and subtle changes of shape, and thus ultimately to chart the shifting patterns of trade over the centuries. The centre which has been most thoroughly studied, thanks primarily to Virginia Grace's work in the Agora, is Athens.

(**a**) Amphorae from a packing round a well constructed in the late second century. From left to right the sources are Roman Italy, Cnidus, Corinth (?), and an unknown Carthaginian colony (?). The Roman vessel (with one handle missing) is one of the earliest examples in Athens of the tall Dressel type I shape familiar from Italian sites and from the wrecks along the coast of south France. The Cnidian bears a stamp of the annual commissioners who administered the city of Cnidus in the early Roman period (late second and early first centuries).

(Athens, Agora Museum P 8106, SS 6599, P 6796, SS 6598. From deposit C9:7. Height 1.05 m, 92.5 cm, 78.7 cm, 77.5 cm.)

(**b**) Three Coan amphorae illustrating the development of shape from the first half of the second century to the first century B.C. During the Hellenistic period Coans, made in a clay with a pale greenish surface, tended (like Cnidians) to become taller and slimmer. Coan wine, along with Rhodian and Cnidian, was a *vin ordinaire*, in contrast with the choice products of Thasos and Chios.

(Athens, Agora Museum SS 8214, P 3981, P 11880. From well G5:3, deposit G11:1, deposit N19:1. Height 78.5 cm, 82.5 cm, 88 cm.)

(**c**) A selection of amphorae from the debris of the destruction of Athens by the Romans in 86 B.C. From the left, Rhodian, Cnidian, Chian, and Roman. Rhodian jars, which have angular handles, a peg-like toe, and a creamy surface, predominated in Athens in the third century and

a

b

127c

early second; while Cnidian, with their red clay and ringed toe, took over the Athenian market in the late second and early first centuries (they are little found outside Athens and her dependency Delos). Chian amphorae, with their distinctive tapering bodies and pointed tips, are always rarer because of the fine quality of their contents.

(Athens, Agora Museum SS 8602, SS 7918, P 19120, SS 7319. From well F19:3 (SS 8602), deposit N20:4 (SS 7918, P 19120), deposit M18:1 (SS 7319). Height 80 cm, 90 cm, 87 cm, 86.5 cm.)

128. Amphora stamps. Systematic stamping of amphorae became normal in the early Hellenistic period. Generally the stamp gives a date by means of the eponymous official ('in the term of...'), names the manufacturer, and adds an ethnic label (e.g. 'Thasion' or 'Knidion') or a state-emblem, such as the rose of Rhodes. The purpose of stamping is uncertain. It was not simply to date the vintage, because many brands were hardly special enough to justify such a policy. Another possibility is that the stamp acted as a type of official endorsement guaranteeing capacity and licensing the manufacturer to sell his goods in return for a tax-payment; a new die would be authorized each year only upon renewal of the licence.

(**a**) Thasian stamp, labelled Θασίων and bearing the name of the manufacturer or merchant Satyrus. Third century B.C. The grape-cluster is one of a large number of emblems used on Thasian jars. These jars were widely exported, being common in the Black Sea region, and occurring fairly frequently in Athens, the Aegean islands, western Asia Minor, and Egypt; but they are rarely found in Italy, despite the testimony of Roman writers as to the popularity of Thasian wine.

(Alexandria, Graeco-Roman Museum, formerly Benaki collection TABC 90. Approx. actual size.)

128a

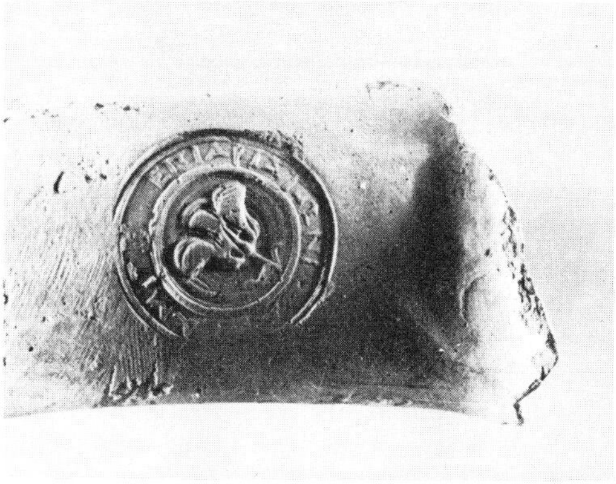

b

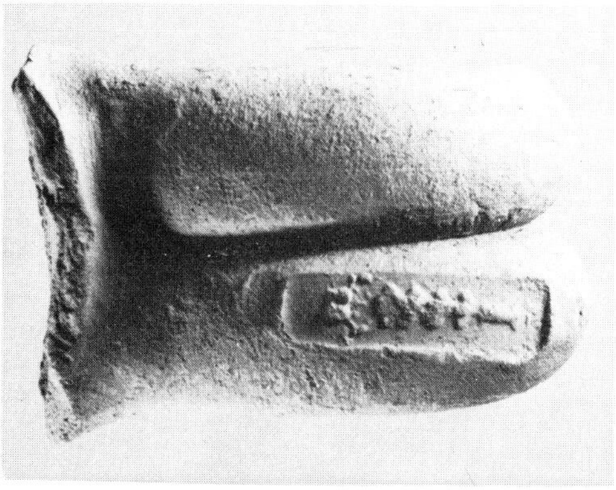

c

d, e

(**b**) Rhodian. Third century B.C. Rose stamps of the manufacturer Hellanicus, dated in the term of Aristonidas, in the month Artamitios. Rhodian stamps are unusual in that they employ an emblem taken from the city's coin-types (either a rose or the head of Helios: cf. **42**) in lieu of an ethnic 'Rhodion', and in that the stamps on the two handles provide complementary information, one naming the maker, the other giving the date. Elsewhere normally either one handle alone is stamped or the two handles bear identical impressions. The naming of the month is unique to Rhodes and supports the theory of a system of governmental controls, since such precision would seem unnecessary for any form of maker's guarantee.

(Athens, Agora Museum SS 7583. Approx. actual size.)

(**c**) Coan. Third or early second century B.C. The amphorae of Cos were made with distinctive double-barrelled handles. Here one stamp names the maker Dorimachus, the other uses coin-symbols of Cos, a crab and club.

(Athens, Agora Museum SS 12618 and SS 12048. Approx. actual size.)

(**d**) Cnidian. Late second century B.C. From a handle of the late second century naming officials of the early Roman period (Cydosthenes and Demetrius). Amphorae of this group are like those of Rhodes in having a different stamp on the second handle, here naming eponymous official, manufacturer, and place of manufacture ('Knidion').

(Athens, National Museum KT 1555 EM 2. Approx. actual size.)

(**e**) Cnidian. *c.* 90 B.C. One of the rare examples where the jar-name 'Knidion' is replaced by a Cnidian coin-device, the head of a bull. Factory of Dioscuridas, in the term of Hermon.

(Athens, National Museum KT 486 EM 1. Approx. actual size.)

Generally on amphorae and their stamps V. R. Grace, *Hesperia* suppl. VIII (1949) 175–89, pls. 19–20; *Études thasiennes* IV: A.-M. Bon and A. Bon, *Les timbres amphoriques de Thasos* (1957); V. R. Grace, *Amphoras and the Ancient Wine Trade* (APB VI) (1961); *ead. American Philosophical Society Year Book* (1955) 321–6; (1959) 472–7; (1964) 518–19; *Archaeology* 19 (1966) 286–8.

129. A public wine-measure dedicated to Hermes and the people of Thasos by the *agoranomos* Zosimus. First century B.C. The *agoranomoi* (market-commissioners) of Thasos evidently carried out duties beyond the mere control of the markets, here taking responsibility in a sphere which at Athens was entrusted to the *metronomoi*: namely the control of weights and measures. The availability of standard measuring-tables (*sekomata*) in the Hellenistic cities testifies to the general concern for fair trading; and this particular example, the companion to a dry-measure dedicated by the same man, gives valuable information on the standards of Thasos. The left-hand cavity, labelled 'stamnos', holds about 7.68 litres; the right-hand one ('half-amphora') about 15.36 litres. This establishes the capacity of a Thasian amphora in the first century B.C. as about 30.72 litres.

(Thasos, Archaeological Museum 1238. From the agora. Marble. Length 1.65 m; width 56.5 cm; depth 25 cm.)

Études thasiennes V: *Recherches sur l'histoire et les cultes de Thasos ii*: C. Dunant and J. Pouilloux, *De 196 avant J.-C. jusqu'à la fin de l'antiquité* (1957) 101f. no. 194, pl. XV.

130. General view of the foundations of the so-called Hypostyle Hall on Delos, looking west. Situated in the heart of the commercial quarter and opening southwards (left in the photograph) to the Agora of Theophrastus, this vast hall is thought to have served as a meeting-place in which various financial and commercial transactions could have been carried out: a kind of ancient stock-exchange. The building, officially known as the Stoa of Posidon, was completed in all essentials by 208 B.C. and is of architectural interest inasmuch as in function and form it is a forerunner of the basilicas of Roman times. The interior was divided up by five rows of nine columns, with a single file of Doric surrounding three ranks of Ionic; the central point was left free and the roof above it raised to form a lantern. The square foundation overlying the left-hand row of columns belongs to one of a number of Roman houses built over the ruins of the hall in Imperial times.

EAD II: G. Leroux, *La salle hypostyle* (1909); R. Vallois and G. Poulsen, *Nouvelles recherches sur la salle hypostyle* (1914); Bruneau and Ducat 105–7 (no. 50).

129

130

131

131. View of the north-west corner of the Agora of the Italians, the 'club-house' and commercial headquarters of the important Italian community which developed on Delos after Rome made the island a free port in 166 B.C. The building, which in accordance with the dominant role of Italian merchants and bankers in Delos was the largest architectural complex erected there, consists of a vast court (66.75 m × 53.47 m × 68.72 m × 48.08 m) surrounded by a two-storeyed portico behind which opened various exedrae and niches, as well as a thermal suite. The niches contained honorific statues of prominent members of the Italian community and decorative statuary (the wounded warrior now in the National Museum in Athens).

132a

132b

132c

On two sides (east and south) rows of shops faced outwards to the surrounding streets. In the foreground is the monumental entrance-porch (propylon). Begun about 110 B.C., the Agora of the Italians was probably abandoned after the sackings of Delos in 88 and 69.

EAD XIX: E. Lapalus, *L'Agora des Italiens* (1939): Bruneau and Ducat 109f. no. 52, fig. 18.

132. An early-third-century shipwreck off Kyrenia in Cyprus.

(**a**) General view of the wreck in course of excavation. Lying in the hull is part of the cargo of amphorae and stone grinders of hopper design. The amphorae belong to ten different types, but the greater part (343) was of Rhodian manufacture, and another large group, concentrated mainly in the bow and stern areas, was Samian; the grinding-stones, which were perhaps designed for use with ores rather than grain, were of a grey volcanic rock which could have come from Cos or one of the islands of the southern Cyclades. It has been suggested that the boat was 'island-hopping', picking up and depositing consignments at different ports; but it is equally possible that the whole cargo had been collected at an entrepôt such as Rhodes. The grid of plastic pipes constructed over the wreck is to assist the archaeologists in their work of photogrammetric recording.

(**b**) Some of the black-'glazed' pottery used by the crew of the Kyrenia ship. The recurrent number four (e.g. there are four of the drinking-cups at the bottom right) indicates a crew of that number, and the shapes conform with a date in the early third century. The ink-pot at the centre would presumably be used in connexion with records of cargo transactions, if not simply for the writing of the ship's log-book.

(**c**) A handful of almonds from the Kyrenia wreck. Over 10,000 were recovered in the excavation, chiefly in the bow area, where they were presumably stored in sacks. They had perhaps been loaded at Kyrenia itself, since Cyprus was renowned for its almonds. A radiocarbon determination produced a date of 288 ± 62 B.C., which agrees with the evidence of the pottery and of the coins, two of which could be ascribed to Antigonus Monophthalmus

33

(316–301 B.C.) and Demetrius Poliorcetes (306–294 B.C.). The timber of the boat had actually been cut half a century or so earlier, since a radiocarbon date obtained from the planking of the hull was 389 ± 44 B.C.

(Finds now in Kyrenia, Crusader Castle.)

H. Wylde Swiny and M. L. Katzev in D. J. Blackman, ed., *Marine Archaeology* (1973) 339–55; M. L. Katzev in G. F. Bass, ed., *A History of Seafaring* (1972) 50–3, 62–4.

133. Statue of a youth, perhaps one of a pair of wrestlers, from a shipwreck at Anticythera, between southern Greece and Crete. Second or early first century B.C. The right half of the figure was buried in the mud of the sea-bottom and is thus well preserved, but the left side was exposed so that the arm and the leg have been corroded by sea-water. The Anticythera ship contained a cargo of bronze and marble sculptures which was almost certainly on its way to the Italian art-market, perhaps from Delos, when it sank in the second quarter of the first century B.C. Here we are dealing not with works of art specially manufactured for connoisseurs but with works which had been removed from their bases. If they came from Delos, their removal could have

134

been a result of the destruction wrought by the pirate-attack in 69. Among the other items in the cargo were the bronze 'computer' (**261**), parts of couches, and a load of Coan and Rhodian amphorae.

(Athens, National Museum 2774. Parian marble: left side of body corroded. Height 1.11 m (including plinth); head 21 cm.)

P. C. Bol, *Die Skulpturen des Schiffsfundes von Antikythera* (1972) 69–72 (no. 25), pls. 38–40. Generally on the wreck *Arch. Eph.* (1902) 147–72, pls. 7–16, Α–Θ; V. Stais, *Ta ex Antikytheron euremata* (1908); Svoronos, *Ath. Mus.*, 1–86, pls. I–XX; G. D. Weinberg and others, *The Antikythera Shipwreck Reconsidered* (*Transactions of the American Philosophical Society* n.s. 55.3 (1965)); Bol, *op. cit.*

134. Engraved gem with representation of a merchant-ship. With its deep hull and its grandiose fittings, including eight towers, this may be a representation of the gigantic *Syracusia*, built under the supervision of Archimedes for Hieron II of Syracuse and subsequently donated to Ptolemy III. It has been estimated that the ship carried a cargo in the region of 1,700 or 1,900 tons on its maiden voyage. A description by Moschion, preserved by Athenaeus (v.206d–209e), not only records the eight towers – two aft, two forward, and the rest amidships – which could be used to bombard enemy ships, but also gives details of interior accommodation and amenities reminiscent of a modern liner.

(London, British Museum, formerly Hertz collection. Glass-paste imitating banded agate. 10 cm by 14 cm.)

135

H. B. Walters, *Catalogue of the Engraved Gems and Cameos, Greek, Etruscan and Roman, in the British Museum* (1926) 313 no. 3307, pl. XXXII.3307. See generally A. W. Persson, *Opus. Arch.* I (1935) 132–49, pl. II.7–15; L. Casson, *Ships and Seamanship in the Ancient World* (1971) 184–6, 191–9.

135. Fragment of a relief of a sailing-boat (second century B.C.), apart from the *Syracusia* gems (**134**) one of the very rare representations of non-naval vessels in the Hellenistic period (for a Nile boat cf. **8**). This one has the earliest attested example of a spritsail (i.e. a sail with a spar running diagonally from the foot of the mast), a type especially favoured in the north Aegean and used presumably for fishing, ferrying or the like.

(Thasos, Archaeological Museum. Marble. Height 38 cm; width 30 cm; thickness 5.5 cm.)

L. Casson, *Mariner's Mirror* 46 (1960) 241; *id. Ships and Seamanship in the Ancient World* (1971) fig. 176.

2. Houses and life

We are much better informed about private houses and their furnishings in Hellenistic times than in most earlier Greek periods, thanks primarily to the well preserved remains of residential quarters discovered at Priene (mainly second half of fourth century B.C.), Pella (late fourth and early third century), Delos (second and early first century), and, in the west, Acragas (Agrigento: late second century). Generally we are dealing with well-built, middle-class homes, rectangular in plan where fitted into a Hippodamian street-grid, as at Pella and Priene (**47**, **66**, **136**); cf. Camirus and Heraclea in Lucania (**41**, **89**), but more irregular where the street-system itself is irregular (Delos). Some of the houses at Pella are unusually grand and spacious (cf. **66**). The more normal dwelling consists simply of a small central court with rooms on three or four sides. The court was approached directly by a short entrance passage from the street, but otherwise there were few openings in the external walls, at least at ground-floor level: the house was largely inward-looking, getting its light and air from the court. In the wealthier examples the court was provided with a colonnade on one side, if not on all four (**136–7**).

Walls were normally constructed of rubble bonded with clay, or sometimes simply, as in earlier periods, of sun-dried bricks; only the grander houses had ashlar façades (**136**). The wall-surfaces were plastered, and during the third and second centuries the plaster was increasingly given a decorative treatment (**138**). At the same time floors, mainly of clay at Priene, received mosaic pavements in the more important rooms: at first composed of pebbles (**139**), these gradually evolved the 'tessera' technique familiar in Roman times (**138**, **140**; cf. **186**).

Water-supply was a matter of concern to the civic authorities, and new aqueducts were built, for example at Pergamum, where an ambitious (and probably not entirely successful) system carried water under high pressure up to the citadel. But water was rarely laid on to private houses. Householders, where not dependent on public fountains, derived their supplies from wells or from the collection of rainwater in underground cisterns. Good examples of the latter survive at Athens and Delos (cf. **141**). Street drainage systems, both open and covered, were of course a standard feature of Hellenistic

136

planned cities, and the surplus rainwater from houses was run off into the main drains, sometimes flushing a lavatory on the way (cf. **142**).

One gets the impression of an improvement in living standards, at least among the middle and upper middle strata of society (the conditions obtaining among the lower classes are difficult to assess archaeologically). This is borne out by the furnishings and bric-à-brac found in Hellenistic houses, including bronze bed-fittings (**145–6**), marble tables (cf. **137**), elaborately ornamented terracotta stoves (**143**), terracotta figurines (cf. **171–2**), and marble statuary (**147**, **173**; cf. **124**). Our illustrations also cover selected examples of bronze vessels (**149**), silver plate (**150**; cf. **32**), lamps (**162**), luxury glassware (**151–4**), and some of the finer ceramics, among which relief-moulded wares are the most important (**165–70**). Among personal ornaments and accessories illustrated are mirrors (**163–4**) and jewellery (**155–61**; cf. **235**, **237**). Jewellery in particular seems to have been produced in greater quantity than before, thanks to the greater availability of gold in the wake of Alexander's conquests (from the Persian royal treasures and from mines such as those of Nubia). It maintained the mastery achieved in Classical times, with consummate use of filigree and repoussé, as well as of new techniques, notably inset gems. Many of the gems employed, for example garnets, are new imports of the Hellenistic period.

Fashions in Hellenistic dress can be followed in contemporary sculpture and in terracotta figurines, notably the 'Tanagra' figurines (so-named after one of the most prolific find-spots) produced in many parts of the Greek world between *c.* 330 and *c.* 200 B.C. (**171–2**). Women's dress, as might be expected, shows the greater variety and interest, with high waistlines (cf. **30**, **212**, **216**) and diaphanous shawls (**173**) becoming *à la mode*. Hairstyles varied, but one favourite was the so-called 'melon' coiffure, in which the hair was swept back in a series of segmental waves to a chignon at the nape of the neck (cf. **161**). For men the chief innovation, inspired by Alexander's example, was the shaving of the beard (cf. **4**, **11**, **13**, **19**, **22–4**, **28–9**, **35–6**, **56**, **65**, **70**, **124**).

136. Remains of house XXXIII on the north side of Theatre Street, Priene, photographed shortly after it was excavated. Originally built in the late fourth century, altered in the second century B.C. The court of the original nucleus (left) is clearly distinguishable; the main reception-room (*oecus*) lay, as normal, to the north, protected at the front by a two-column porch (*prostas*), which provided shade in the summer but at the same time admitted the low sunshine of winter. Later, but still in Hellenistic

137a

times, a colonnade was carried right round the court to create a true 'peristyle', and the area of the house was doubled by the addition of the neighbouring premises (to the right).

T. Wiegand and H. Schrader, *Priene* (1904) 285ff.; M. Schede, *Die Ruinen von Priene*, 2nd ed. (1964) 96–103.

137. The House of the Hermes, Delos.

(**a**) General view. This particularly well preserved second-century house is remarkable for being terraced into a hillside; parts of three storeys have survived, each set back from the one below, and there is sufficient evidence to confirm the former existence of a fourth. The central court is provided with an upstairs gallery at first-floor level, where the ground-floor peristyle is repeated.

(**b**) Reconstruction drawing of the interior of the court facing south (towards the hillside). Stairs rising to the second storey can be seen in the doorway behind the rear gallery. The visible furnishings are a marble table in the west wing of the peristyle, a herm now set against the north-west angle-column, and a well-head which provided access to an underground cistern, the house's source of water. Among the mass of finds from the house perhaps the most interesting are three measuring-tables (cf. **129**) which together with three stone weights imply that the proprietor was a merchant. Such objects are frequently found in the houses of Delos.

J. Delorme, *BCH* 77 (1953) 444–96, pls. XLV–LVI; J. Marcadé, *ibid.* 497–615, pls. LVII–LVIII.

138. Interior of *oecus* in the House of the Trident, Delos. This detail gives a good idea of the structure and amenities of a Delian private house in the second half of the second century, the period of Delos' heyday. The walls are constructed of local stone, notably of gneiss, which splits easily into slabs of varying thickness; no mortar is employed, but the surfaces are covered with a thick layer of plaster.

b

In the more important rooms, as here, this plaster is treated in the so-called Masonry Style, in which the surface is raised to give the effect of monumental ashlar masonry, richly picked out in colour. Some such decorations include painted figure-friezes (cf. **200**). The floor is paved with polychrome mosaic. At the right a section of the wall-plaster has collapsed, revealing the underlying layer scored with herring-bone trowel-cuts to provide a key.

Generally on structures and decorations in Delian private architecture, *EAD* VIII.2: J. Chamonard, *Le quartier du théâtre* III (1924). On decorations alone, M. Bulard, *Peintures murales et mosaïques de Délos* (*Mon. Piot* 14, 1908); *EAD* XXIX: P. Bruneau, *Les mosaïques* (1972).

139–40. *Mosaic pavements*

One of the clearest marks of the increasing luxury of private houses in Hellenistic times is the provision of patterned and figured pavements. The technique of rendering clay or mortar floors both more durable and more attractive by embedding fine pebbles in the surface had begun some centuries earlier in Phrygia and became more common from the late fifth century onwards. These pebble mosaics reached their acme about 300 B.C. in the examples at Pella (cf. **66**), to be gradually superseded during the third century by the more sophisticated 'tessera' technique, in which specially cut cubes of stone or glass (*tesserae*) were employed to produce what were often astonishingly subtle pictorial effects (cf. **5**, **201**). The normal decorative arrangement

138

consisted of a central panel or panels with a pictorial treatment surrounded by concentric rectangular borders of ornamentation (wave-pattern, maeander, vegetal scrolls, etc.: cf. **138**).

139. Detail of a pebble-mosaic from Pella showing a balancing pair of centaur and centauress, from the threshold of a large *oecus*. *c.* 300 B.C. The male centaur holds a plate. The light-on-dark effect and the use of leaden strips (elsewhere also of terracotta) to render linear detail are very reminiscent of the colour-balance and the draughting technique in red-figure vase-painting. The room in front of which the threshold lay was paved with the famous lion-hunt mosaic.

(Pella, Museum. From house 1, threshold of room C. Background black, figure white and pink, details in grey, yellow and red. Panel (as framed): height 82.5 cm; length 2.63 m. Pebbles from 5 mm to 1 cm diameter.)

Deltion 16 (1960) part A, pl. 47a; P. Petsas, *Pella, Alexander the Great's Capital* (1978) 97, fig. 10 (= *La mosaïque gréco-romaine* (1965) 48, fig. 5). Generally on pebble mosaics C. M. Robertson, *JHS* 85 (1965) 72–89; *id. JHS* 87 (1967) 133–6.

139

140. Detail of a tessera mosaic on Delos showing Dionysus riding a leopard. Second half of the second century B.C. The god, who wears richly embroidered robes and an ivy-wreath, holds a tambourine in his left hand and a *thyrsus* in his right. The panel, along with two lozenge-shaped compartments containing centaurs, was enclosed in the normal manner with bands of ornament, notably saw-tooth and wave-pattern, the whole set within a broad area of marble chippings.

(Delos, House of the Masks, room E. Background black; figurework various colours (predominantly shades of blue, white, yellow and brown). Panel: height 1.01 m; width 1.02 m; tesserae mostly 2 or 3 mm square.)

EAD XIV: J. Chamonard, *Les mosaïques de la Maison des Masques* (1933) 11ff., figs. 3, 4, pl. III; *EAD* XXIX: P. Bruneau, *Les mosaïques* (1972) 240–5, figs. 177, 182–3.

141. Interior of the cistern which collected rainwater from the theatre on Delos. Third century B.C. Since Delos has no springs and only one seasonal watercourse, the inhabitants of the island were dependent on wells and on cisterns for their water-supply. On the whole the latter were preferred, as being less vulnerable to contamination; and most Delian houses of the Hellenistic period have a cistern beneath the courtyard, fed by rain from the roofs and gutters (cf. **137**). Either excavated in the rock, or (more commonly) constructed of masonry, these cisterns were lined with impervious hydraulic cement which allowed them to retain winter rainwater through the summer. This fine example, measuring about 22.50 m by 6.50 m, was punctuated by a series of eight granite arches which formerly supported the paving of the piazza above.

J. Chamonard, *BCH* 20 (1896) 312f.; R. Vallois, *L'architecture hellénique et hellénistique à Délos* I: *Les monuments* (1944) 265–8. Generally on water-supply, *EAD* VIII.1: J. Chamonard, *Le quartier du théâtre* III (1924) 323–56.

140

141

142

142. Drains on Delos. Most Hellenistic cities were provided with well organized and maintained drainage-systems to carry off surplus rainwater and effluent. The drains here served a private house; a tributary drain from a lavatory merges with the main rainwater conduit at the left. The paving-slabs which covered them have been removed in the photograph to show the carefully-constructed stone channels.

(House of Fourni, north-east corner.)
Cf. Chamonard, *loc. cit.*

143. Terracotta stove found on Delos. Second or early first century B.C. Such portable stoves were the main means of cooking and heating in Hellenistic houses, and this particular form with a high cylindrical pedestal is found throughout the eastern Mediterranean, though commonest in Egypt, Asia Minor and the Cyclades. The fire was lit in the upper part, which contained a bowl-shaped cavity pierced by three holes; and the opening in the side of the pedestal served both to create a draught and to enable the clearing of the ashes. Cooking utensils were supported on the three projections above the rim. This particular example is a *de luxe* version, elaborately decorated with reliefs, including heads of Medusa on the three supports, a representation of the mythical battle of Greeks and Amazons on the upper part of the body,

143

144

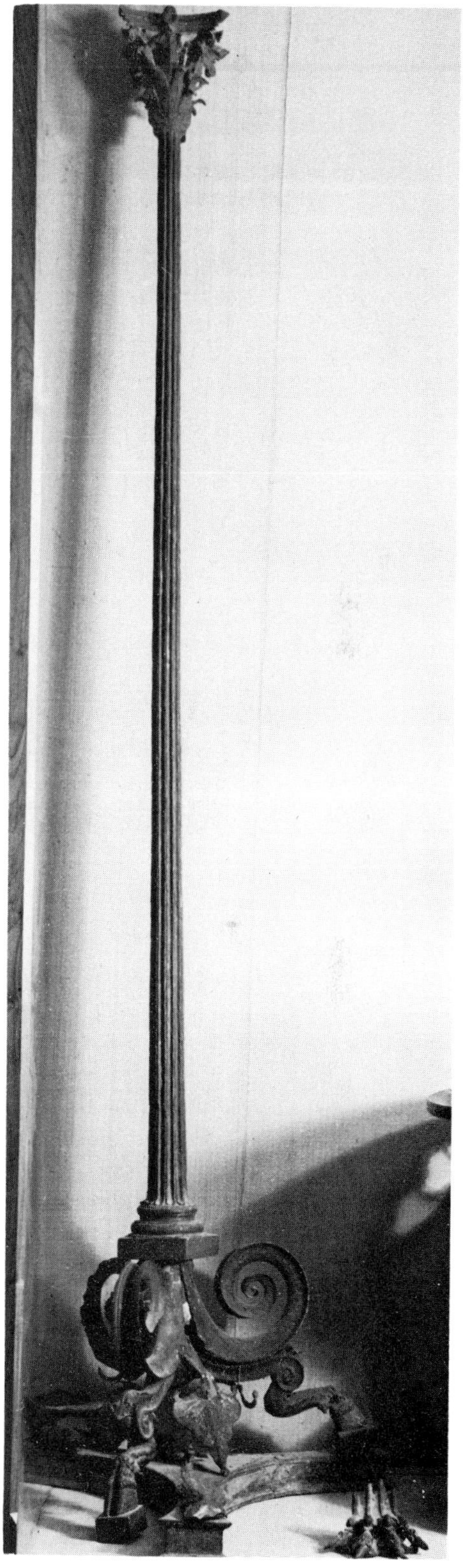

figures of Atlantes supporting garlands, and heads of Silenus below. The handles are aesthetic rather than functional, since an example as heavy as this must have been is only notionally portable.

(Delos, Museum 58.A.1. From house no. 18 in Upper Theatre Street (1958 excavations). Reconstructed from fragments; lower part restored in plaster. Height 88 cm (as restored); diameter 36 cm at base, 44 cm at rim.)

BCH 83 (1959) 785, fig. 3; C. Le Roy, *BCH* 85 (1961) 479–91, figs. 6–18, pls. xv–xvi; Bruneau and Ducat, pl. 18.2.

144. Bronze candelabrum. Second half of second century B.C. A base formed by three goats' feet and volute ornaments, with ivy-leaves between them, supports a fluted shaft. The latter is surmounted by an imitation Corinthian capital and the intended effect is unmistakably that of a very slender, elongated column. The column would have supported a plate on which lamps could be set. Similar candelabra have been preserved in the ruins of Pompeii and Herculaneum.

(Tunis, Bardo Museum F 113, 299–302. From the Mahdia shipwreck. Reconstructed from separate pieces. Height about 1.82 m.)

145

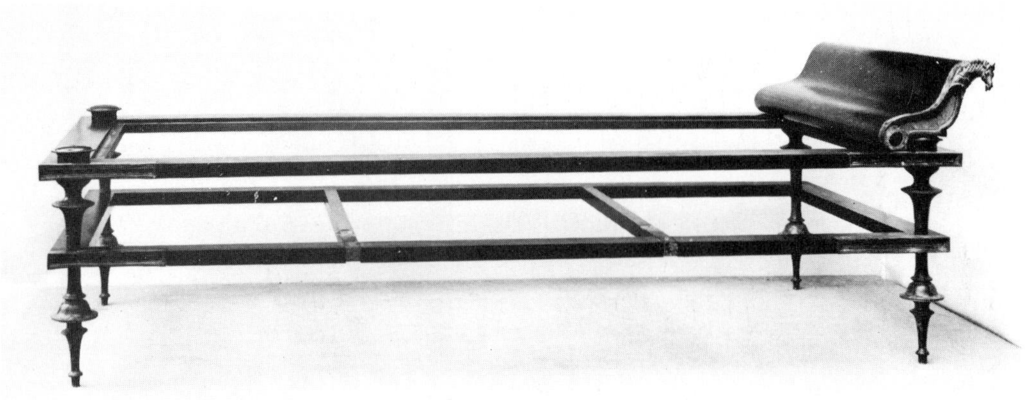

146

Catalogue du Musée Alaoui, suppl. I (1910) 130 no. 113; suppl. II (1922) 136 nos. 299–302; W. Fuchs, *Der Schiffsfund von Mahdia* (Bilderhefte des Deutschen Archäologischen Instituts Rom II) (1963) 27f. no. 29, pl. 37 (right).

145. Restoration of a couch from Priene. Late third or second century B.C. Most ancient couches had frames of wood, which have perished, leaving only the bronze fittings. Here a single couch has been reconstructed from the fittings (angle-pieces, legs, headboard ornaments) of two originals. The result gives a good idea of a typical Hellenistic couch, with a low S-curved headboard (*fulcrum*) and elaborate lathe-turned legs including a projecting bell-like member and a tapering foot. The headboard fittings terminate, as often, in a horse's head;

7

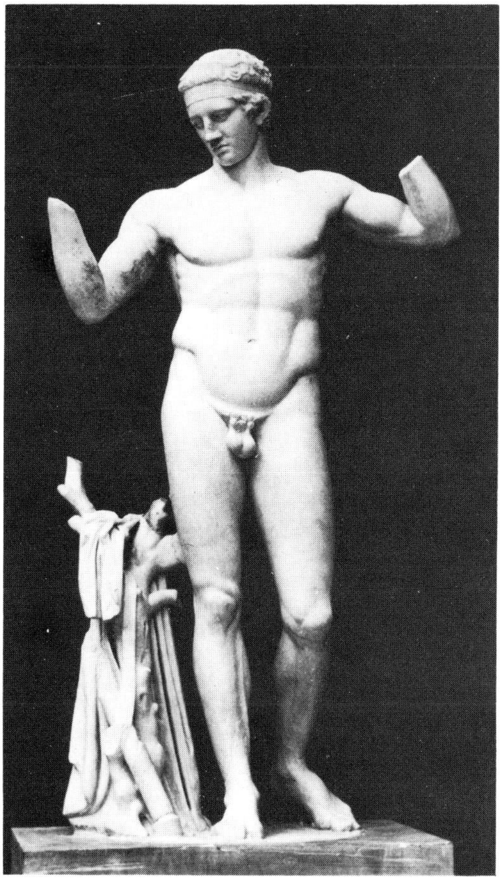

148

another ornament, now lost, would have been inserted in the hole in the lower terminal. Such couches may have been the 'Delian type' referred to by Pliny, who writes that 'bronze first acquired renown there [at Delos] in the manufacture of the feet and headboards of dining-couches' (*NH* XXXIV.9; cf. XXXIII.144). Straps would have been extended across the frame to support a mattress.

(Berlin, Pergamon Museum BR. 10053, 10054. From Priene, house XIV. Wood modern; bronze fittings ancient, apart from corner-bosses. Height 49.5 cm; length and breadth uncertain (restored as 2.10 m and 1.0 m respectively).)

T. Wiegand and H. Schrader, *Priene* (1904) 378–82, figs. 480–1; G. M. A. Richter, *The Furniture of the Greeks, Etruscans and Romans* (1966) 57, fig. 308. On 'Delian' couches K. A. Neugebauer and A. Greifenhagen, *Ath. Mitt.* 57 (1932) 29–45.

146. Hollow-cast bronze headboard ornament, decorated with busts of Hera (?) and Athena and a reclining figure of Dionysus. Third century B.C. The holes are for nails by which the plate was attached to a wooden headboard. The elongation and elegance of the form distinguishes this Hellenistic example from the more robust and upright *fulcra* of Roman times; and the use of a relief figure to decorate the middle is an early Hellenistic feature. Later examples, as at Priene, tended to have the middle part open or plain, except occasionally for inlaid ornament.

(London, British Museum 1908.4–18.2. Provenance unknown. Height 33.3 cm.)

F. H. Marshall, *JHS* 29 (1909) 162, fig. 15; Richter, *op. cit.* 57, fig. 306.

147. Copy of the Diadumenus by Polyclitus (athlete binding a fillet of victory about his head). Late second century B.C. This is the oldest known exact replica of a classical statue, and it was found, along with the 'Pseudo-athlete' (**124**) and other sculptures, in what is beyond question a private house, thus testifying to the beginnings of art-collection by wealthy private individuals in late Hellenistic times. The owner of the house, no doubt an Italian businessman or official (cf. **131**), anticipated the common practice in late-Republican Italy of decking his house with statuary.

(Athens, National Museum 1826. From the House of the Diadumenus, Delos (1894 excavations). Marble copy of bronze original (tree-trunk support added by copyist). Hands and ends of fillet missing. Height 1.95 m.)

L. Couve, *BCH* 19 (1895) 484f., pl. VIII; *id. Mon. Piot* 3 (1896) 137–53, pls. XIV, XV. On the house *EAD* VIII: J. Chamonard, *Le quartier du théatre* II (1924) 426–31.

148. Marble statue-group of Pan and Aphrodite from Delos, an interesting comment on late Hellenistic taste. *c.* 100 B.C. A mythological subject is treated in a playful, almost rococo, manner: Aphrodite, whose pose is loosely based on the famous statue carved by Praxiteles for the city of Cnidus in the fourth century, seems rather half-hearted in her rejection of Pan's advances, and it has been suggested that the slipper which she ostensibly raises to fend him off may allude to a practice which courtesans had of wearing shoes which left the message 'Follow' imprinted in their foot-tracks. Cupid's role, too, is ambivalent, since he seems both to be pushing Pan away and to be luring him on. The statue was set up by one Dionysius in the Establishment of the Posidoniasts of Beirut (for such institutions at Delos see **229**) as a dedication to the gods of his homeland.

(Athens, National Museum 3335. Parian marble; traces of colour on the hair (reddish brown), sandals (red), tree-trunk (black), and strut (blue). Minor restorations. Height 1.32 m (excluding base).)

M. Bulard, *BCH* 30 (1906) 610–31; Bruneau and Ducat 49f., pl. 10.2; Marcadé 393–6, pl. L; Lullies 141, pl. 290.

149. Bronze cauldron from the Mahdia shipwreck. Second half of the second century B.C. The projecting rim was decorated with a maeander pattern inlaid in silver, and on either side of the body was an appliqué volute and palmette ornament. The handle, now missing, was probably attached to a lug in the middle of this ornament. The cauldron has no base and was doubtless designed to rest in a stand.

14

(Tunis, Bardo Museum F282. Height 25 cm; upper diameter 45 cm.)

Catalogue du Musée Alaoui, suppl. II (1922) 135 no. 282; W. Fuchs, *Der Schiffsfund von Mahdia* (1963) 26 no. 26, pl. 35.

150. Late Hellenistic service of silver plate found at Arcisate in northern Italy, buried *c.* 75 B.C. From left to right, a hemispherical bowl, a ladle with a duck's head at the end of the handle, a small round-mouthed jug, a hemispherical strainer with holes arranged in geometric and vegetal patterns, and in the foreground a spatula (part of the blade is missing). Duck's head handles are popular in Hellenistic silverware. The main development in comparison with early Hellenistic vessels is the deepening of the bowls of the ladle and strainer.

(London, British Museum 1900.7–30.3–7. Bowl: height 5.3 cm; diameter 13.4 cm. Ladle: length 18 cm. Jug: height 13 cm. Strainer: height 6.25 cm; diameter 8.4 cm. Spatula: length 18 cm.)

H. B. Walters, *Catalogue of the Silver Plate (Greek, Etruscan and Roman) in the British Museum* (1921) 32f. nos. 126–30; D. E. Strong, *Greek and Roman Gold and Silver Plate* (1966) 115–17, pl. 34.

151–4. *Hellenistic glassware*

As is demonstrated for the Roman period by the discoveries at Pompeii, glass vessels (like bronze vessels) were probably in more general everyday use than the archaeological evidence tends to suggest: the intrinsic value of the material and the fact that it is fusible mean that broken or unwanted vessels were re-cycled, whereas pottery was merely replaced. On the other hand glass was still produced in Hellenistic

150

times by the costly and laborious moulding techniques and must have remained, relatively speaking, a luxury item, manufactured mainly in Alexandria and the eastern Mediterranean. Only with the discovery of glass-blowing in the late first century B.C. did mass-production begin.

151. Greenish glass goblet, probably made in Alexandria. Third or second century B.C. The base is decorated with eight pointed petals between which are almond-shaped bosses round the belly.

(London, British Museum 1895.10–17.1. From Aegina. Height 9.1 cm; diameter 9.8 cm (rim).)
A. von Saldern, *JGS* 1 (1959) 42f., fig. 30; D. B. Harden, *Arch. J.* 125 (1969) 62, 71, pl. VIII (B).

152. Glass dish in *millefiori* technique. Late third or early second century B.C. Though practised in Mesopotamia much earlier, this technique achieved world-wide renown only in the Hellenistic period, with the emergence of the great glass-factories of Alexandria. The effect was achieved by cutting sections from polychrome glass rods, arranging them in a kind of 'mosaic' and then fusing them into the required shape in a two-piece mould. In this example the 'flowers' consist of spirals of white enclosing a yellow centre, the whole set in a dark blue

151

matrix; and interspersed among them are irregular 'tesserae' of gold leaf, white or yellow.

(London, British Museum 1871.5–18.3. From a tomb at Canosa, Italy (cf. **123**). Height 5 cm; diameter 30.8 cm.)
D. B. Harden, *JGS* 10 (1968) 25, 41–3, figs. 10–12; Harden and others, *Masterpieces of Glass* (1968) 25 no. 21; A. Oliver, *JGS* 20 (1968) 50, 53, no. C1; D. B. Harden, *Arch. J.* 125 (1969) 62f., 72, pl. IX (B, C).

152

153

153. Glass *amphoriscus* with decoration of festoons and spiral trails. Second century or first half of the first century B.C. This type of tiny unguent vessel, formed round a sand-core, and decorated with trailed threads which were worked into the body by rolling the vessel while still soft, had appeared as early as the sixth century, but the elegant pointed form is characteristic of Hellenistic times. Here the trails are white and yellow, and the body brownish-green. The festoons were created by combing the trails after application. The main centre of manufacture of the class was the Syrian coast, though production may also have taken place in Cyprus, Rhodes and the Black Sea region.

(London, British Museum 1894.11–1.137. From tomb at Amathus, Cyprus (British Museum excavations 1893–94). Height 16.5 cm.)

D. B. Harden and others, *Masterpieces of Glass* (1968) 24 no. 19; *id. Arch. J.* 125 (1969) 55, pl. IV (B) (*g*).

154. Mould-fused glass bowl, decorated with wheel-cut grooves inside the rim: Syrian work. About second century B.C. The glass is pinkish with areas of iridescence.

(London, British Museum 1856.8–26.324, given by Lord Stratford de Redcliffe. From Calymnos. Lower part restored. Diameter, at rim, 18 cm.)

Unpublished.

155. One of a series of gold disc-medallions carrying heads mainly of goddesses (Artemis, Aphrodite, or, as here, Athena) in high relief, manufactured probably in Thessaly, where all of them seem to have been found. Probably third or early second century B.C. The richly decorated borders include inlaid garnets; blue enamel is used in the eyes and in the centres of rosettes. Of some interest is the network of chains attached to the exterior and clearly designed to hang or spread over a cylindrical or spherical surface. Suggested functions for the discs include pyxis-lids, breast-covers and hair-ornaments (perhaps applied over chignons).

(Athens, Benaki Museum 1556. Found with other similar pieces in a hoard of jewellery somewhere in Thessaly (perhaps near Karpenision) in 1929. Diameter 11.1 cm.)

B. Segal, *Museum Benaki Athen, Katalog der Goldschmiede-Arbeiten* (1938) 42–4 no. 36, pls. XIII–XIV. Cf., for parallel material, P. Amandry, *Collection Hélène Stathatos. Les bijoux antiques* (1953) 97–105; *ibid.* III: *Objets antiques et byzantines* (1963) 251 and n. 2; H. Hoffmann and P. F. Davidson, *Greek Gold. Jewelry from the Age of Alexander* (1965) 8, 222–7 nos. 90–2; T. Hackens, *Catalogue of the Classical Collection: Classical Jewelry* (Museum of Art, Rhode Island School of Design, Providence, 1976) 66–71.

154

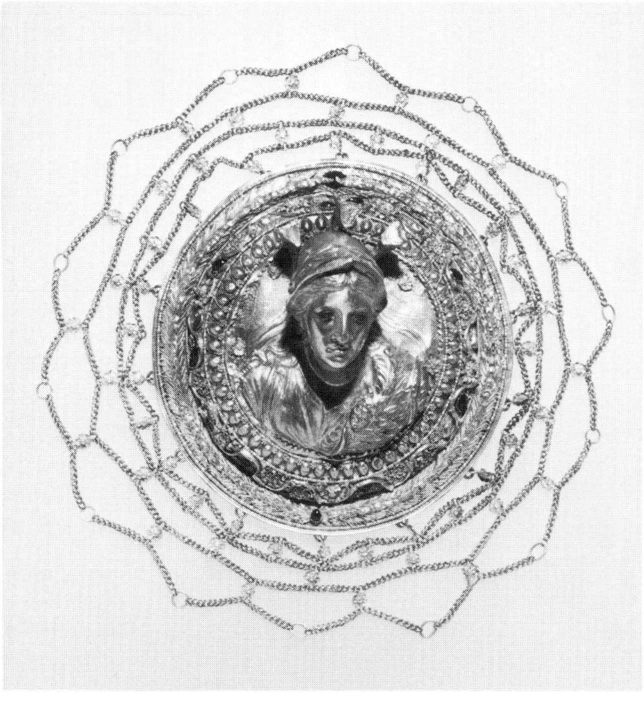

155

156. Head of gold pin with attached chains, used to fasten either the hair or a part of the dress. Probably late third, or second century B.C. Pin-finials tend to be very elaborate in Hellenistic times and often incorporate sculptural types. Here a crouching Aphrodite of the Anadyomene type, normally said to be based on a statue by Doedalsas of the third century B.C., is surrounded by four seated putti clutching toilet objects, the whole resting on a Corinthian capital. The garnet again testifies to the Hellenistic love of inset stones.

(Athens, Benaki Museum 2062. Provenance unknown, perhaps Thessaly. Total length of pin 16 cm; height of finial about 3.8 cm.)

BCH 62 (1938) 448, fig. 4; *Arch. Anz.* (1939) 226, fig. 7 (both with lower part of finial inverted). Cf. P. Jacobsthal, *Greek Pins* (1956) 83f.; Hoffmann and Davidson, *op. cit.* 192f.

156

157. Gold diadem, consisting of a tube carrying elaborate floral ornaments. Third or second century B.C. Such diadems were probably intended to be worn by women on festive occasions, though many would subsequently find their way into tombs, as this one doubtless did. The tube is decorated with a bead and reel enrichment, and the floral ornaments are composed of a vast number of minute flowers, some of which are filled with blue enamel, attached by wires to a series of openwork plates. Surmounting them is a series of small palmettes, and at the centre stands a figure of Eros holding an *oenochoe* (wine-jug) and a *phiale* (libation-dish).

157

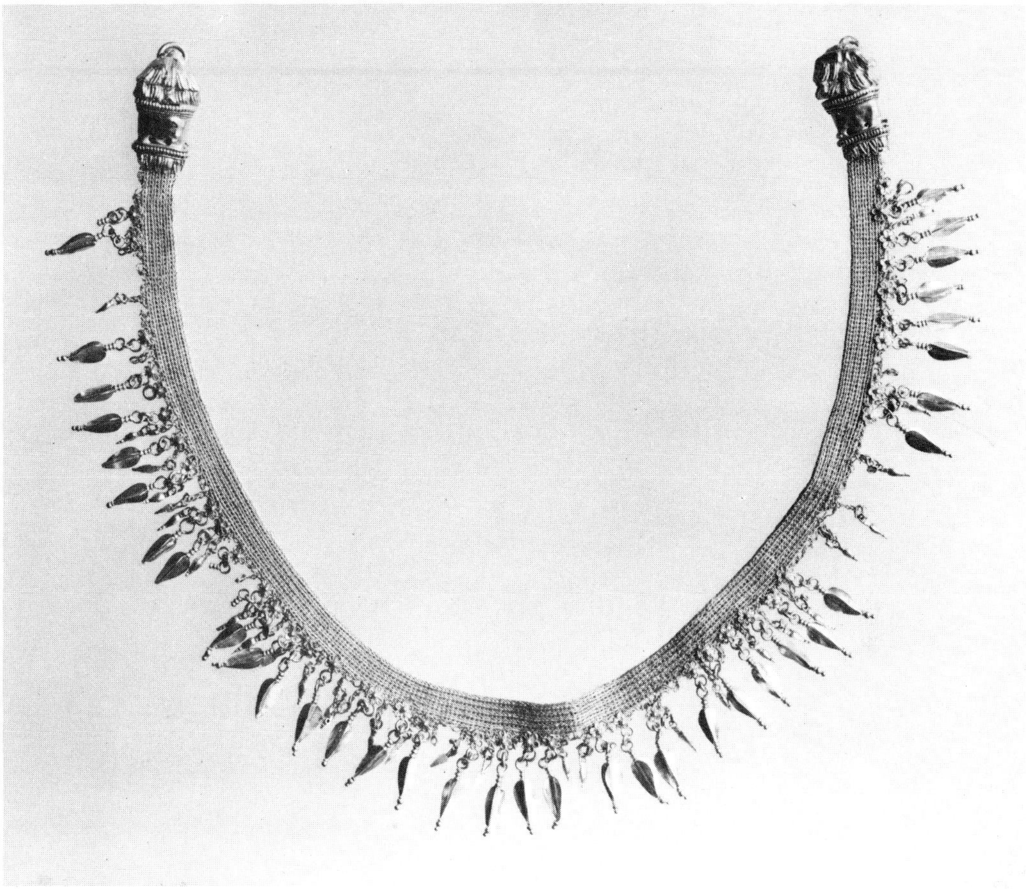

158

(London, British Museum 1898.7–16.1, formerly Tyszkiewicz collection. From South Italy. One end, along with two of the openwork plates and the attached flowers, is restored. Diameter about 18.2 cm; length about 52 cm.)

W. Fröhner, *La collection Tyszkiewicz, choix de monuments antiques avec texte explicatif* (1892) pl. 1 (4); F. H. Marshall, *Catalogue of the Jewellery, Greek, Etruscan, and Roman, in the Departments of Antiquities, British Museum* (1911) 175 no. 1631, pl. XXIX.

158. Gold strap necklace of typical Hellenistic form. Late fourth or third century B.C. This type, in which a strap of intermeshed wires is hung with pendants in the form of small amphorae and/or spearheads, became popular about the time of Alexander and continued till the late second century. It is mentioned in an inscribed inventory of treasure belonging to the temple of Artemis on Delos (279 B.C.), where the pendants are specifically termed 'amphorai' and 'longchia' (C. Michel, *Recueil d'inscriptions grecques* (1900) 682 (1.24), 683 (1.40)). Here the points of attachment between spear-heads and strap are masked by small rosettes, while the little amphorae hang on chains decorated with blue enamelled discs. The terminals are in the form of lions' heads. Such necklaces would probably not have been worn right round the neck but from shoulder to shoulder, suspended from a pair of *fibulae*, so that the pendants would hang more effectively.

(London, British Museum 1867.5–8.538, formerly Blacas collection. Length 30.5 cm.)

Marshall, *op. cit.* 212 no. 1943, pl. XXXIV.

159

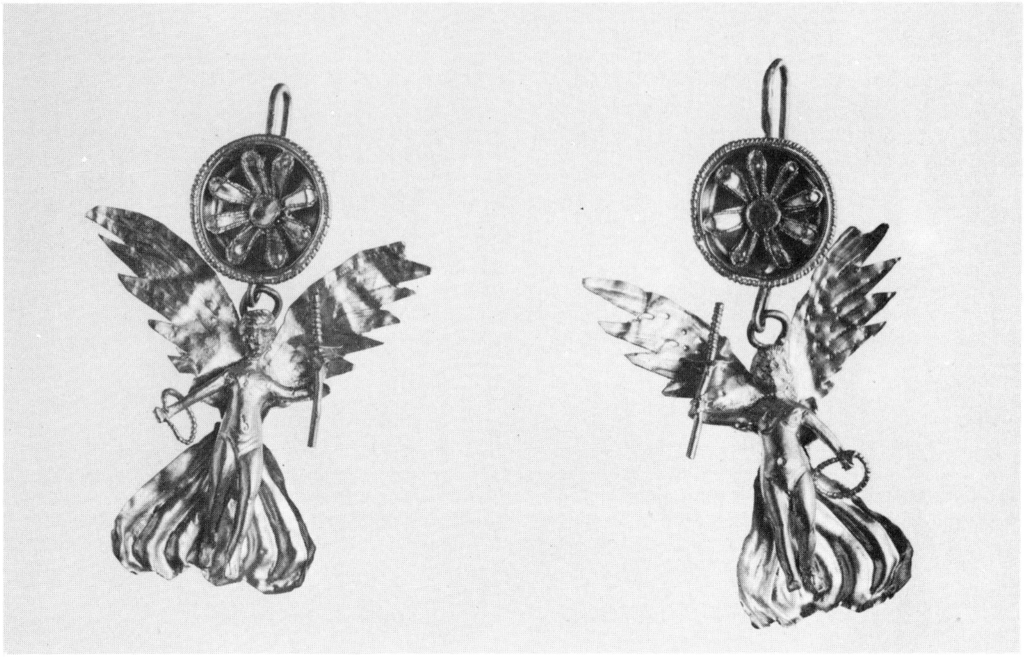

159. Gold earrings with pendants in the form of winged Victories. Late fourth or third century B.C. (if genuine). The type with a figure, usually Eros or Victory, suspended from a disc is a favourite in Hellenistic times. Here the Victories are nude apart from a cloak flying behind, and they carry each a torch and wreath of beaded wire; the discs are decorated with eight-petalled rosettes.

(London, British Museum 1872.6–4.562, formerly Castellani collection. The connexion with Castellani, an expert forger, raises doubts about the genuineness of the earrings, but they represent the type well enough. Height 4.6 cm.)

Marshall, *op. cit.* 200 nos. 1849–50, pl. XXXII.

160. Three finger-rings of Hellenistic times. The use of inset stones, whether plain or engraved, is a characteristic of the period. From left to right:

(**a**) Convex oval garnet in gold hoop, from Crete. Third century B.C.

(Length of bezel 3.0 cm.)

(**b**) Gold ring consisting of separate hoop and bezel hinged together. First century B.C. The hoop has three small inset garnets, one circular and two pear-shaped; the bezel contains an oval amethyst. Provenance unknown.

(Height 3.5 cm.)

(**c**) Convex oval glass bezel imitating amethyst, set in gold hoop. First century B.C. Provenance unknown.

(Diameter of hoop 2.3 cm.)

(London, British Museum 1917.5–1.714; 1917.5–1.843; 1866.5–4.51: (*a, b*) formerly Franks collection, (*c*) formerly Woodhouse collection.)

F. H. Marshall, *Catalogue of the Finger Rings, Greek, Etruscan, and Roman, in the Departments of Antiquities, British Museum* (1907) 119 no. 714, 138 no. 843, 121 no. 725, pls. XVIII, XIX, XXI; R. A. Higgins, *Greek and Roman Jewellery* (1961) 173–5, pl. 53 (D–F). Cf. E. Lévy, *BCH* 89 (1965) 554f., fig. 18, pl. 22A; S. G. Miller, *Two Groups of Thessalian Gold* (1979) 40f., pl. 26.

160

161

162a

162b

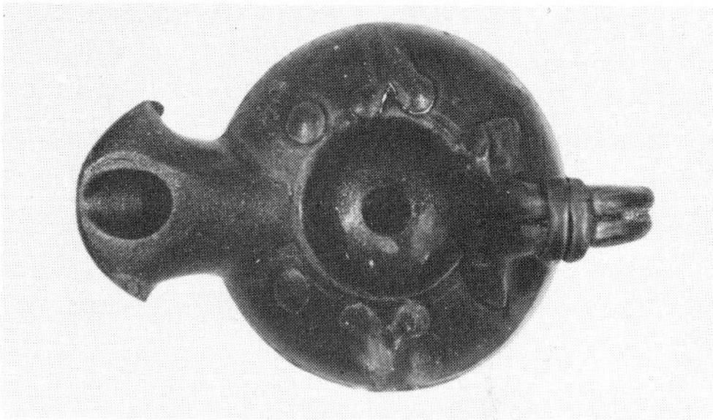

162c

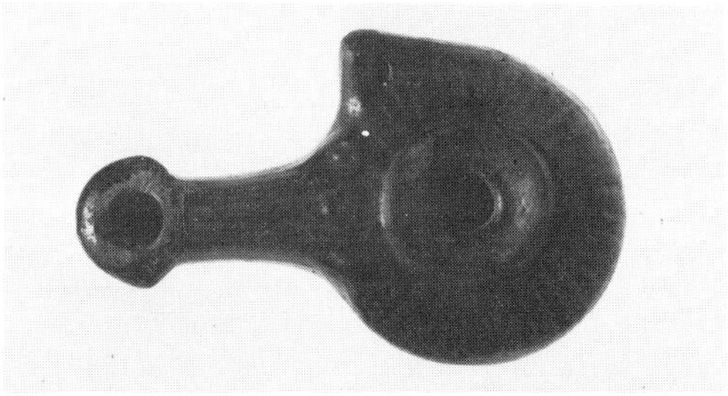

162d

161. Bone bezel with portrait of a Ptolemaic queen. First half of the third century B.C. The glorification of monarchs, symbolized by the development of the ruler-cult and the use of the ruler's image on coinage, was reflected also in the practice among court-ladies of wearing gems and metal rings with the queen's portrait. This cheap version shows one of the early Ptolemaic queens, perhaps Berenice I (half-sister and consort of Ptolemy I) or the more notorious Arsinoe II (died 271/0 B.C.).

(Athens, Agora Museum BI 815. From area of the Heliaea (backfill). Diameter 3.2 cm; thickness 3 mm.)
D. B. Thompson, *An Ancient Shopping Center: the Athenian Agora* (APB XII) (1971).

162. *Hellenistic lamps*
The pottery lamps which were the main sources of light for the less well-to-do householders underwent certain technical and stylistic changes about the beginning of the Hellenistic period. The old shallow, open type gave way to a somewhat deeper form, closed save for a central

filling-aperture; and at the same time the nozzle tended to lengthen. In addition, about the beginning of the third century mould-made lamps appeared alongside the wheel-made ones and rapidly became more popular, doubtless because of the greater decorative possibilities which they offered. Richer people could afford the more elaborate bronze lamps, which naturally survive in smaller numbers, but which evidently now sometimes assumed quite bizarre and inventive forms.

(**a**) Rhodian lamp. First half of the third century B.C., or a little later. A wheel-made variety without a handle but provided with a lug on the shoulder for hanging (a feature added mainly in the fourth and third centuries); coated with a reddish brown slip. This example was probably found on Cyprus, and would therefore be a testimony to trade between Rhodes and that island.

(London, British Museum 1967.10–27.4. No provenance, probably from 1889–90 excavations of Cyprus Exploration Fund. Length 9.7 cm; width 7.0 cm.)

D. M. Bailey, *A Catalogue of the Lamps in the British Museum* I: *Greek, Hellenistic, and Early Roman Pottery Lamps* (1975) 175 (Q 390), pls. 78, 79.

(**b**) Cnidian (?) lamp. Second century or first quarter of the first century B.C. A wheel-made variety with appliqué relief ornament on the shoulder (a double-leaf and disc on each side); coated with black slip. The reliefs and other features, such as the short nozzle with rounded end and the two-ribbed handle with similar binding, appear on numerous lamps from Cnidus.

(London, British Museum 1926.2–16.28. From Cnidus, probably from the sanctuary of Demeter. Length 10.9 cm; width 7.0 cm.)

H. B. Walters, *Catalogue of the Greek and Roman Lamps in the British Museum* (1914) 51 no. 360; Bailey, *op. cit.* 154 (Q 337) pl. 64.

(**c**) Egyptian lamp with a long nozzle; coated with black slip. Probably first century B.C. or early first century A.D. This example is mould-made and thus permits rilled ornament round the shoulder and birds' heads in relief (not discernible on the photograph) at the roots of the nozzle. Again, in the absence of a handle, a pierced lug is provided on the shoulder.

(London, British Museum 1963.7–15.11, formerly F. W. Robins collection (545). No provenance. Length 12.5 cm; width 7.1 cm.)

Journal of Egyptian Archaeology 25 (1939) 50, pl. XI.3; Bailey, *op. cit.* 258 (Q 556), pl. 109.

(**d**) Bronze lamp in the form of an elephant's head with mounted *mahout* on the lid. Hellenistic period. Representations of war-elephants in the minor arts recall the role of these creatures in the Seleucid and Ptolemaic armies (cf. **32**, **109–10**).

(London, British Museum 1922.7–12.11; formerly Fouquet collection. From Memphis. Height 8.5 cm; length 15 cm.)

P. Perdrizet, *Bronzes grecs d'Egypte de la Collection Fouquet* (1911) 86f. no. 151, pl. XXXV; P. R. Bienkowski, *Les Celtes dans les arts mineurs gréco-romains* (1928) 145f. no 10, fig. 221.

163. Gilded silver lid-mirror, perhaps Chalcidian work. First half of the third century B.C. Hinged lid-mirrors with reliefs on the exterior of the lid began in the late fifth century and continued at least till the end of the third, though becoming less common after the middle of the fourth century. This is an exceptional piece, since most Greek mirrors were of bronze; silver mirrors became commoner only in Roman times. The reliefs, representing Selene and Endymion, were cast in a separate sheet of metal, which was then attached to the lid. The reflecting surface and handle are shown below.

(Athens, National Museum 16111. Found in a grave at Demetrias in 1917. Diameter (lid) 17 cm.)

A. S. Arvanitopoulos, *Polemon* I (1929) 7–27; W. Zuchner, *Griechische Klappspiegel* (*JdI* Ergänzungsheft XIV) (1942) 63 (KS 88).

164. Base of bronze lid-mirror with turned decoration. Hellenistic period. Mirrors, whether of the lid or disc type, were normally decorated only with simple concentric mouldings and incised rings in Hellenistic times. The additional clusters of small rings on this piece are an unusual variant.

(Copenhagen, National Museum, Antiksamlingen 1080. Bought in Paris, provenanced 'Cyprus'. Diameter (base) 14.7 cm.)

Unpublished.

165–70. *Hellenistic pottery*

It would be impossible in the space available adequately to illustrate the wide range of ceramic

163

164

165

wares used in the Hellenistic world. Storage amphorae are dealt with in the chapter on trade (**127–8**), and one or two of the finer wares are illustrated in various sections (**83**, **132b**, **235**); so it will suffice here to show a small sample of the better-quality decorated wares not already mentioned. Apart from the tail-end of red-figure painting in southern Italy during the early Hellenistic period, and from one or two categories of polychrome wares, notably the so-called Centuripae ware made in western Sicily, the decoration of Hellenistic pottery is relatively subdued, consisting mainly of well-spaced painted vegetal or floral ornaments,

166

168

167

169

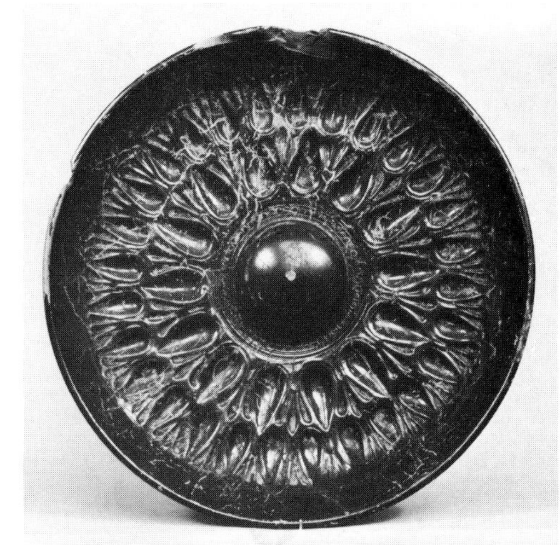

either dark on a light ground (Hadra ware, *lagynoi*) or light on dark (West Slope ware, Gnathian), or of figures and ornaments in relief ('Megarian' bowls, Calene *phialai*).

165. Ribbed *oenochoe* (wine-jug) in Gnathian style. *c.* 300–275 B.C. Gnathian ware, produced in various centres in Apulia from the mid fourth to the advanced third century, was the Italian equivalent of the West Slope ware produced in Athens, Corinth, Crete and various cities of the east. Coated with black varnish, and decorated principally with vegetal motifs (palmettes, ivy-scrolls, etc.) in yellow and white paint, it is one of the more distinctive classes of Hellenistic ceramic. Vertical ribbing was introduced in the last quarter of the fourth century. Cf. **204b**.

(Manchester, Museum MWI 6949. Provenance unknown.)

166. *Lagynos.* Late third to first century B.C. This wine-decanter is one of the most characteristic Hellenistic shapes, with its squat body, carinated shoulder, tall narrow neck and angular handle. The body was coated with a white slip, and the decoration, mainly confined to the shoulder, executed in brown paint. *Lagynoi* are widely found in Greece and the eastern parts of the Hellenistic world, but it is not clear where the principal factories were.

(Pylos, Museum 547. From Hellenistic cemetery at Yialova, tomb no. 1 (cf. **236**). Height 18 cm.)
Deltion 21 (1966), Chronika, pl. 164c.

167. Amphora in West Slope ware. First half of second century B.C. This piece is fairly typical of the series with its squat proportions, twisted handles, and simple decoration (necklace with pendants, chequers, 'Chinese boxes') carried out in white and brown on a black gloss surface.

(Athens, Agora Museum P 599. From a storage pit at the base of the Areopagus. Height 23.6 cm; diameter 19.8 cm.)

H. A. Thompson, *Hesperia* 3 (1934) 374 (D 25), fig. 59; cf. 438–47.

168. So-called 'Megarian' bowl decorated with a sheath of acanthus and lotus leaves. Third century B.C. 'Megarian' bowls, manufactured in several centres of European Greece and Asia Minor from the early third to the first century B.C., were the principal form of relief-decorated pottery in Hellenistic times, the forerunner of the Arretine and 'samian' wares popular in the Roman period. The decoration was achieved by throwing the bowl inside a mould into which the decorative motifs had been pressed with stamps; the surface was then coated with dark paint before firing. Bowls with vegetal ornament of the type represented here were inspired by embossed metal prototypes like a silver bowl with lotus leaves now in the Cairo Museum (G. Grimm, *Kunst der Ptolemäer- und Römerzeit im Ägyptischen Museum Kairo* (1975) pl. 98) and belong to an early stage in the history of the series; figured bowls, including many with scenes from Homer (a speciality of Boeotia) and Attic drama, began later in the third century.

(London, British Museum 1839.11–9.23, formerly Campanari collection. Provenance unknown. Height 9.3 cm; diameter 15.2 cm.)
Unpublished.

169. Example of a Calene *phiale*, one of the Italian representatives of the Hellenistic relief style. Third or early second century B.C. These shallow bowls were decorated with reliefs on the interior as opposed to the exterior, either figure-scenes or (as here) rings of buds ranged round a central 'omphalos'. It is thought that the decoration was frequently produced from moulds taken directly from metalwork, and *phialai* in gold and silver closely related to this one actually exist. An example in gold, though much more elaborate, was found in the late-fourth-century gold hoard at Panagyurishte in Bulgaria (I. Venedikov, *The Panagyurishte Gold Treasure* (1961) 17, pls. 35–8). The series was produced in Campania, probably mainly at Cales itself, in the third and second centuries.

(London, British Museum 1839.11–9.37c, formerly Campanari collection. Provenance unknown. Height 3.3 cm; diameter 19.3 cm.)
A Catalogue of the Greek and Etruscan Vases in the British Museum II (1870) 236 no. 1810; G. M. A. Richter, *AJA* 63 (1959) 246, pl. 59, fig. 45.

170. Elaborate *crater* with relief figure-decoration found in the Athenian Agora. Late second or early first century B.C. The figures of the neck were moulded on separate plaques and attached; they included satyrs, maenads and a three-figure group of Dionysus being supported by his followers. The clay is grey, and the gloss slip has fired irregularly black, brown and grey. The place of manufacture was perhaps Pergamum.

(Athens, Agora Museum E 153. From a cistern at the south-west corner of the Agora. Parts of lip and body and one handle are restored. Height 27 cm; diameter (lip) 20.5 cm, (body) 18.8 cm.)
H. A. Thompson, *Hesperia* 3 (1934) 423–6, fig. 111, pl. III.

171–3. *Hellenistic dress*
In women's dress one of the most striking changes in comparison with the previous age was the raising of the waist-line by placing the girdle immediately below the breasts, a mode which produced a broad-hipped and full-skirted effect. Another vogue, at least when ladies were posing for statues, was a cocoon-like wrapping of the cloak (*himation*) about arms and shoulders. Often, from the early second century onwards, the *himation* was made in a light stuff, perhaps Coan silk, and became a kind of shawl through which the folds of the dress were clearly visible.

171. Terracotta figurine, showing a lady in her 'Sunday best'. Late fourth or third century B.C. Over a full-skirted *chiton* she wears a *himation* in heavier material, tightly wrapped round both arms and drawn veil-like over the head. The raising of the right arm within the cloak is a favourite gesture for setting off the costume to best advantage. The left hand holds a fan, and on the head is a fashionable sun-hat rather like a Chinese coolie hat (perhaps the *tholia* of Theocritus, *Idyll* XV.39).

(London, British Museum 1875.10–12.8. From Tanagra, 1875. Plinth damaged; back not modelled. Himation painted blue, apart from parts over arms (red); fan and hat edged with pink. Height 19 cm.)
H. B. Walters, *Catalogue of the Terracottas in the Department of Greek and Roman Antiquities, British Museum* (1903) 208 (C 245); M. Bieber, *Entwicklungsgeschichte der griechischen Tracht*, 2nd ed. (1967) 35f., fig. 8.

172. Terracotta figurine of a youth. Third century B.C. He wears the Hellenistic form of *chlamys* (riding-cape), which differs from the classical form in having a curved, instead of a

171

172

straight, lower edge. This produces, when the garment is fastened over the right shoulder, a roughly horizontal lower hem: compare the famous statue of a youth from Tralles, now in Istanbul. In addition to the *chlamys*, the figure wears boots and a wreath or thick fillet.

(London, British Museum 1874.3–5.68. From Tanagra, 1874. Back nearly flat, with hole. Height 20.5 cm.)

Walters, *op. cit.* 222 (C 322); Bieber, *op. cit.* pl. 15.1. For the Tralles youth (Istanbul, Archaeological Museum 542) see M. Bieber, *Griechische Kleidung* (1928) 69, pl. XXXV.1; H. Sichtermann, *Antike Plastik* 4 (1965) 71–85, pls. 39–52; Lullies 143f., pls. 296–7 (with further bibl.).

173. Portrait-statues of Cleopatra and Dioscurides, set up in their house on Delos. Third quarter of the second century B.C. The couple were Athenian colonists, and the statues, commissioned by Cleopatra in honour of her husband's dedication of two silver tripods in the temple of Apollo, are dated after 138/7 B.C. by a reference to the Athenian archon of that year. Cleopatra is dressed in the second-century fashion with a diaphanous shawl of fine linen or silk over her heavy *chiton*; Dioscurides wears the traditional thick *himation*.

(Delos, House of Cleopatra (excavated 1906). Marble; heads of both figures, left arm of Cleopatra, feet of Dioscurides missing. Height: Cleopatra 1.52 m (excluding base); Dioscurides 1.52 m (base modern).)

F. Mayence and G. Leroux, *BCH* 31 (1907) 415f., fig. 9; *EAD* VIII.1: J. Chamonard, *Le quartier du théâtre* I (1922) 218f., fig. 95; Marcadé 134, 325–8, pls. LXV, LXVI, LXVIII; Lullies 136, pl. 279.

173

174. Cuttings for small trees and shrubs along the south flank of the so-called Theseum (Temple of Hephaestus) in Athens. The first pits, probably thirty-eight in all, were dug along the sides and rear of the temple in the early third century B.C.; further ones were added in the first century B.C. In accordance with the normal practice of ancient gardeners, attested also by discoveries at Pompeii, the young shrub was set in the ground together with the pot in which it had been transported from the nursery. Remains of the pots found in the 1936 excavations confirmed the purpose of the pits. Such ornamental gardens probably became more common in Hellenistic times, aided by improvements in water-distribution; a landscaped park of late Hellenistic date has recently been identified outside the city of Rhodes.

(Cuttings from 75 to 90 cm square; from 60 to 90 cm deep.)

D. B. Thompson, *Hesperia* 6 (1937) 396–425; *ead. Garden Lore of Ancient Athens* (APB VIII). Pompeian plant-pots: W. Jashemski, *The Gardens of Pompeii, Herculaneum and the Villas destroyed by Vesuvius* (1979) 238–41. Rhodian park: H. Lauter, *Ant. K.* 15 (1972) 53–8.

3. Sport and education

Grouping sport and education together is justified by the important role played by athletics in the education of the Hellenistic world, especially through the medium of the *ephebia* and its meeting place, the gymnasium. The *ephebia* was a basically Athenian institution and originated as a form of two-year military service to which all citizens were liable on attaining their eighteenth birthday; but, as the cities came to be overshadowed by the Hellenistic monarchies, its military importance declined and it tended to become a kind of college of physical education, reserved primarily for the well-to-do. Some time in the early third century military service in Athens ceased to be compulsory and was reduced to one year, with the result that the ephebes, from being five or six hundred in number, dropped dramatically to twenty or thirty. Although the revival of the city under Roman patronage after 166 B.C. brought renewed wealth and the revitalization of old institutions including the *ephebia*, the recruitment figures now generally stayed below 150 (**175**).

Outside Athens the *ephebia* and gymnasium became indispensable features of Greek cities, serving not only as a means of preserving Greek culture among the Greeks themselves but also as instruments of hellenization among the native nobility. Well preserved gymnasia have been excavated at several Hellenistic sites (**176–7**; cf. **54**), often complete with graffiti to remind us of the young men who studied there (**178**). Their importance is shown by the fact that the gymnasiarch (principal of the gymnasium) was often the foremost man in the city. Although the ephebic education remained primarily military and athletic, various forms of intellectual teaching also came to play a part, and *exedrae* where lectures and discussions could be held are never lacking in gymnasia (**176a**, **177**; cf. **72**).

Education in general is a relatively well-known aspect of Hellenistic culture, thanks to inscriptions recording, for example, private endowments for the foundation of schools, and thanks

174

especially to the countless Egyptian papyri and ostraca carrying school exercises. A couple of school papyri are illustrated (**179–80**). They show something of the methods employed and of the subjects studied, both in primary education (which lasted from the age of seven to that of fourteen) and in the secondary school (fourteen to eighteen). Elementary teaching, based on the three Rs, was a slow and painful business, in which, for example, pupils had to read and write syllables one by one in alphabetical order before they went on to words, and when finally they did graduate to words they were deliberately presented at an early stage with obscure and unpronounceable ones. In secondary education the papyri testify to the memorization of anthologized verse and to the overwhelming popularity of Homeric epic in all literary studies. Generally speaking literary studies came to predominate in Hellenistic schools, and traditional subjects like physical education, music and mathematics tended to lose ground, being left to the experts.

In both sport and education the Greek love of competition remained strong. Recitation competitions at civic festivals were the nearest ancient equivalent to our modern examination system, and athletic competitions were of course a major form of entertainment at all levels. One of the main features of the Hellenistic period was the proliferation of athletic festivals (cf. **184**), some of which, like the Ptolemaieia in Alexandria, were elevated to the rank of the 'big four' of 'the Circuit' (the Olympic, Pythian, Nemean and Isthmian). As the passion for athletics spread eastwards, one finds an increasing proportion of competitors from Alexandria and the new cities of Asia turning up in the lists of victors in the old Greek games, particularly the Olympics, which remained at the pinnacle of sporting achievement (cf. **182–3**). The traditional festivals normally retained token prizes, especially crowns (**184–6**), but in the new games money-prizes became more common. This increased the opportunities for professional athletes (not that competitors in crown-games were, or ever had been, amateurs in the true sense, since their own cities normally subsidized their training and rewarded their victories: cf. **184**). Boxers (**187–8**) and wrestlers in particular will have benefited from the increased popularity of combat events at the expense of running and field events: by Roman Imperial times the prize for the *pankration* (all-in wrestling) was six times, and boxing and wrestling three times, that for the pentathlon.

17

175. Part of an inscribed stele honouring the Athenian ephebes of 128/7 B.C. Set up 127/6 B.C. The original slab, which seems to have been erected in front of the terrace of the Stoa of Attalus, was rather over 2.35 m high and had a width of 65 cm immediately beneath the crowning moulding. The fragments illustrated came about two thirds of the way down, at the left-hand edge. Following a series of five decrees in honour of the ephebes, their trainers, and the *cosmetes* (the magistrate in charge of the ephebic college), there comes a list of the ephebes (bottom left) arranged by tribes (Erechtheis, Aigeis, etc.). The inscription reveals that there were 107 ephebes in this year, which represents a four-fold increase on the numbers in the second half of the third century but is a mere fraction

176a

176b

176c

of the recruitment figures when there was compulsory service for a two-year period in the late fourth century.

(Athens, Agora Museum I 989 a and d (forming part of I 286). Found re-used in 'Valerian' wall at south-east corner of Agora. Hymettian marble. Dimensions of the fragments as joined: height 53 cm; width 26 cm; thickness 17 cm. Letters 7 to 9 mm high.)

S. Dow, *Hesperia* 4 (1935) 71–81 (no. 37); B. D. Merritt, *Hesperia* 15 (1946) 201–13 (no. 41); 16 (1947) 169f., pl. XXXII.66; O. W. Reinmuth, *Hesperia* 24 (1955) 220–39, pl. 78.

176. Details of the lower gymnasium at Priene, one of the purest surviving examples of the Hellenistic form of gymnasium, lacking the all-important hot baths of Roman times. Sited on a terrace in the lower part of the city, immediately inside the walls, it is similar in lay-out to the gymnasium at Delos (**177**) but in at least one respect reflects more closely the norms laid down by Vitruvius: i.e. the doubling of the portico on the north side of the palaestra in order to protect the *ephebeum* from driving rain. The gymnasium was laid out in the second half of the second century B.C.

(**a**) The central *exedra* behind the north portico can be safely identified as the *ephebeum* or ephebes' common-room and lecture-hall. The entrance was supported by a pair of Ionic columns whose bases remain in position and round the remaining three walls, above a high marble socle, ran a series of semi-columns; two of these framed a statue of a benefactor at the back of the room. Supports for wooden benches against the foot of the walls are still visible in places: compare Vitruvius' 'exhedra amplissima cum sedibus'. But the proportions (3:2) are slightly more elongated than those recommended by the Roman writer (4:3).

(**b**) Detail of the wash-room (*loutron*) at the north-west corner of the gymnasium. Water spouted from lions' heads into a row of marble wash-basins along the north wall. In the front part of the room a pair of narrow foot-basins was set in the floor.

(**c**) Foundations of starting-gates in the stadium, which lay to the east of the gymnasium. The running-track was overlooked by a bank for spectators on the north, uphill side, with stone seating in the central third only; and above this again lay the covered practice-track (*xystus*). The visible starting-gates probably date to Roman times and replaced simpler versions of the Hellenistic period, now overgrown.

T. Wiegand and H. Schrader, *Priene* (1904) 259–75; M. Schede, *Die Ruinen von Priene*, 2nd ed. (1964) 81–9.

177. A general view of the remains of the gymnasium on Delos, looking north west. The gymnasium existed in the first half of the third century, but the surviving remains represent the final form achieved in the last quarter of the second century. The central court or palaestra, 31.80 m square, was enclosed by an Ionic peristyle of thirteen columns each side, and behind it, to north and west, open the normal rooms of a gymnasium: a changing room (*apodyterium*) behind the triple-arched doorway, a wash-room (*loutron*) reached through the marble-framed door at the corner, a large *exedra* with a bench along the walls (Vitruvius' *ephebeum*), and (at the back right) perhaps the *sphairistra* or games room. The identification of the rooms has been rendered possible by an inscribed inventory of 156/5 B.C., listing the sculptures and other offerings in the gymnasium (*ID* no. 1417. A. I, ll. 118–54).

177

J. Audiat, *BCH* 54 (1930) 95–130, pl. III; Bruneau and Ducat 127f. no. 76; *EAD* XXVIII: J. Audiat, *Le gymnase* (1970).

178

178. One of many graffiti cut in marble benches from the area of the gymnasium on Delos. This one, from a curving bench found in 1911 at the south end of the *xystus*, records the friendship of Archias and Diognetus, names which occur together on two other benches. They were probably, to judge from the names, ephebes of the period of the Athenian colony (after 166 B.C.). Other graffiti show boats, animals, gaming-boards, torches, prize-amphorae and human figures, some of the subjects being perhaps inspired by dedications set up in the gymnasium.

(*In situ.* Letters 1.6 cm high.)

See generally M.-T. Couilloud, in Audiat, *op. cit.* 101–37.

179. Part of a papyrus scroll containing school exercises. Last quarter of the third century B.C. (after 217). This section shows a list of proper names (Arktos, Nereus, Neileus, Neilos, Thoas, etc.) divided up into syllables to help pupils with their pronunciation; they progress from disyllabic to polysyllabic names (Hippomedon, Antilochos, and in the next column Anaxagoras, Arkesilaos, etc.). It is significant that the vocabulary is that of mythology, geography and history, not of everyday speech; the whole scroll displays a highly artificial approach, geared entirely to the reading of literature. It begins with methodical lists of purely notional syllables, set out in order like our modern multiplication tables, proceeds to obscure and tongue-twisting monosyllabic words, goes on to gods, rivers and the names illustrated, then jumps straight to passages from Euripides, Homer and more recent poets. The neatness of the script indicates that it is a teacher's manual rather than a schoolboy's copy-book. Normally schoolboys

179

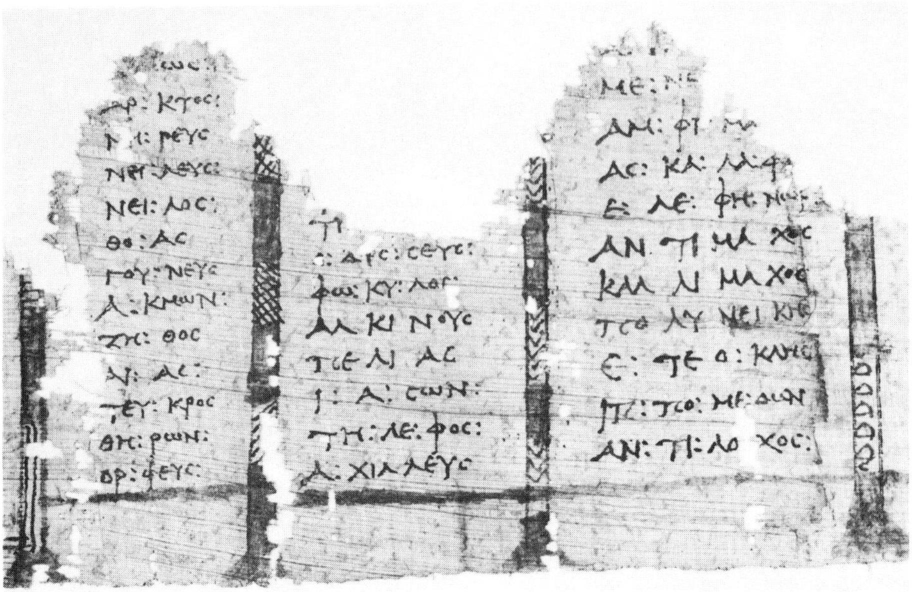

did their exercises on scrap pieces of papyrus (often the backs of old official documents) or even on potsherds.

(Cairo, Egyptian Museum 65445. Said to be from the Fayûm. Papyrus scroll in two fragments 66 cm and 176 cm long; original overall length approximately 2.85 m. This detail approx. 18 cm long (the three columns combined).

O. Guéraud and P. Jouguet, *Un livre d'écolier du IIIe siècle avant J.-C.* (Publications de la Société Royale Égyptienne de Papyrologie. Texts et documents II) (1938).

180

180. Part of a school papyrus from Egypt, carrying in columns a glossary of words used in Homer. Second or first century B.C. Compiled no doubt by a *grammaticus* (teacher of literature), this glossary contains dittographies and alphabetical inconsistencies which suggest somewhat unmethodical collating of other lexica: for example, some words occur twice at different points and with different definitions. The left-hand column, partly preserved, lists the Homeric words, all beginning ου (οὐτιδανός etc.), and the right-hand column gives the meanings; at the bottom right is a fragment of a list beginning with the letters πα. This is one of countless Egyptian papyri which testify to the importance of Homer in secondary-school studies in Hellenistic and Roman times. On the other face (recto) there are disconnected excerpts from poetry, including a

181

piece from the *Iliad*, a simile from an unknown epic, and some trimeters from New Comedy, which would have been set for learning, much as passages from Shakespeare are set in modern schools in Britain.

(Freiburg, University Library, Department of Manuscripts 12. Provenance unknown? Height 27 cm; width 11 to 12 cm.)

W. Aly, *Mitteilungen aus der Freiburger Papyrussammlung* 1 (Sitzungsberichte der Heidelberger Akademie der Wissenschaften. Philosophisch-historische Klasse (1914), Abhandlung 2) 7–22, pl. 1.1.

181. The stadium at Perge (Pamphylia), looking south. Although the existing auditorium is of Roman Imperial date (probably second century A.D.), the stadium was certainly laid out in the Hellenistic period, when athletic festivals were first instituted at Perge and other Asian cities. The arena measures 34 m by 234 m. The northern end of the seating (foreground) is curved rather than straight, a typically Roman feature designed to accommodate additional spectators near the finishing-line.

K. Lanckoronski, *Städte Pamphyliens und Pisidiens* 1: G. Niemann and E. Petersen, *Pamphylien* (1890) 46f., 55f.; G. E. Bean, *Turkey's Southern Shore* (1968) 51, pl. 10; Akurgal 278, pls. 14b, 96b.

182. The Palaestra and Gymnasium at Olympia.

(**a**) Model by A. Mallwitz showing, in the foreground, part of the Gymnasium and, behind it, the Palaestra. In the great panhellenic sanctuary these complexes lacked their normal civic function as the focus of ephebic activities but were, rather, practice grounds for athletes taking part in the Olympic games. The Palaestra (cf. **72**), built in the third century B.C., served primarily for boxers, wrestlers and pancratiasts, while the Gymnasium, which is dated to the second century, accommodated also those practising for the running, jumping and throwing events. Even here, however, the social and educational functions of such complexes were not forgotten, as is shown by the *exedrae* in the Palaestra. When the Gymnasium was built, a doorway was opened into it through the Palaestra's north *exedra*; and further access was provided by a door further to the west when the Gymnasium was enlarged. Both complexes were directly accessible from the athletes' 'village' to the west (off the picture to the right). In the far

182a

182b

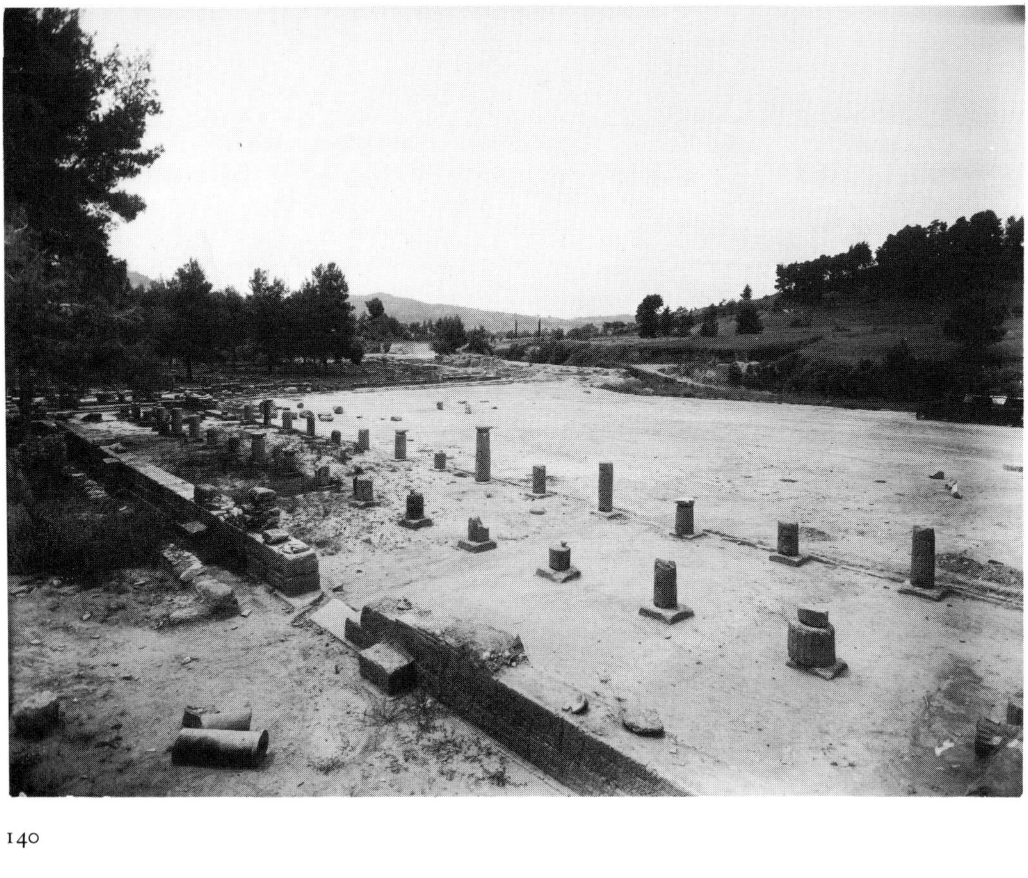

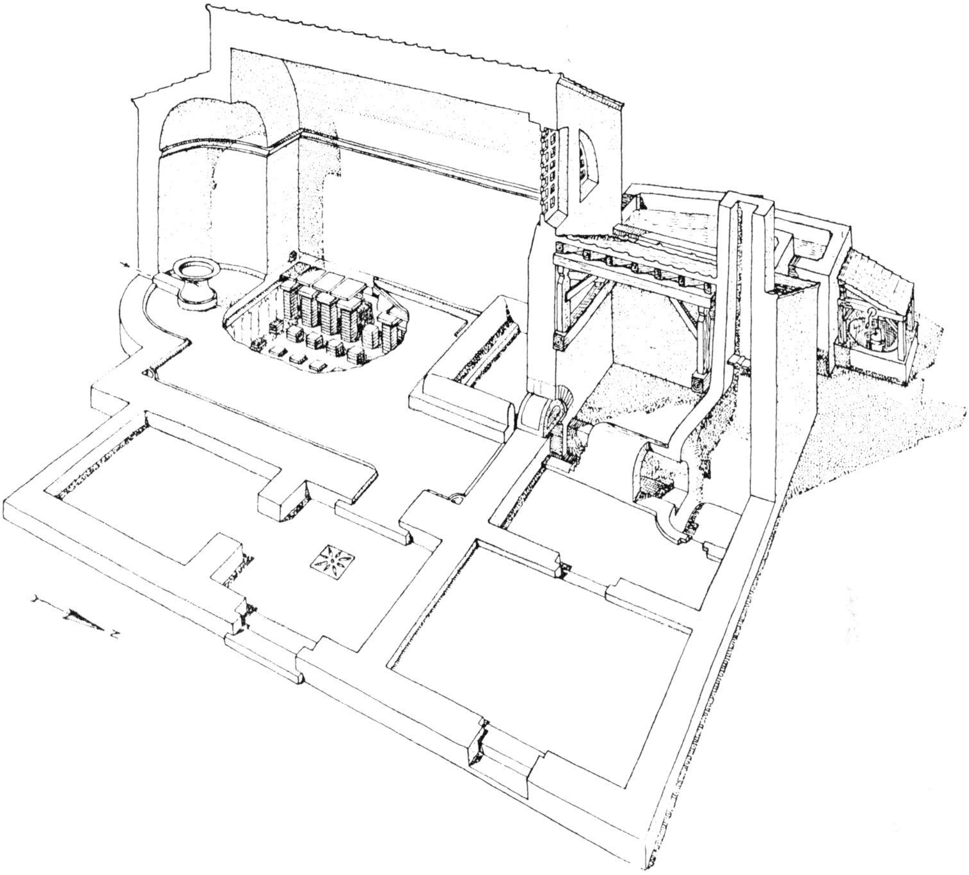

background is the Leonidaeum, a hotel complex built in the second half of the fourth century B.C. to house wealthy visitors to the festival and games.

(**b**) The Gymnasium in the course of excavation, looking south-west. In the foreground is the two-aisled east portico which served as a covered practice-track: its length (approximately 220 m) slightly exceeded that of the actual Olympic stadium. To the west the Gymnasium was at first roughly co-terminous with the Palaestra, but later it was enlarged to produce a vast exercise-ground unequalled in Greek times. The new western portico, along with the athletes' 'village', has been destroyed by river-erosion, and almost nothing is known of the north portico: only the south-eastern sector of the complex is exposed. At the actual south-east corner a grand Corinthian *propylon* was added at the end of the second century B.C.

F. Adler and others, *Die Baudenkmäler von Olympia* (*Olympia, die Ergebnisse der von dem Deutschen Reich veranstalteten Ausgrabung* II) (1892) 113–28, pls. LXXIII–LXXVIII; H. Schleif, in W. Dörpfeld, *Alt-Olympia* (1935) 269–73; E. Kunze and H. Schleif, *Ol. Bericht* III (1938–39) 67–75; H. Schleif and R. Eilmann, *Ol. Bericht* IV (1940–41) 8–31; A. Mallwitz, *Olympia und seine Bauten* (1972) 278–89.

183. Partial perspectival reconstruction of the Greek hypocaust bath at Olympia. Bathing facilities are a necessary concomitant of athletic sports, and in the Greek baths at Olympia, thanks to the skill of the German excavators, we can follow the development of one complex from a simple wash-room with a well, through the typical classical installation with hip-baths, to something approaching the Roman *thermae*. Here, dated about 100 B.C., is the culmination of the process. The main bath-chamber, a barrel-vaulted room about 6 m wide and 8 m long with an apse at the south end, had an underfloor heating system; the floor was raised on ninety brick pillars 85 cm high and the resulting cavity was heated via a flue from a furnace (incidentally

184

sunk into two of the fifth-century hip-baths) in the adjacent room to the north. The same flue heated water in a rectangular basin in the corner of the bath-room, while a pedestal set in the apse probably supported a heated bowl (*labrum*). If dated correctly, this would be the earliest fully evolved underfloor heating-system known; that underfloor heating was invented by the Greeks is suggested by the Romans' use of the Greek name '*hypocausis*' and by the presence of more primitive hypocaust systems in two other sets of baths earlier in the Hellenistic period, at Gortys in Arcadia and Gela in Sicily.

H. Schleif and R. Eilmann, *Ol. Bericht* IV (1940–41) 51–6, 79f., pls. 8–10, 18–20; Mallwitz, *Olympia* 272f., fig. 226.

184. Marble plaque from the pedestal of a statue set up on Delos in honour of the Athenian wrestler and pancratiast Menodorus. Four rows of nine crowns, carved with some attempt to represent the actual plants used at the different festivals, record his victories and (the last four in the bottom line) honours voted to him by Athens, Rhodes, Thebes and King Ariarathes of Cappadocia. Inscriptions above the crowns name the festivals and within the crowns the events. The dedication, inscribed on the actual statue-base which rested on the pedestal, describes him as 'victorious in the Circuit and the other sacred games', but one of the festivals of the traditional Circuit, the Isthmian, is not mentioned, and so the victories of Menodorus may have belonged to a period when the Isthmian games were suspended following the destruction of Corinth by the Romans in 146 B.C. Ariarathes is probably therefore Ariarathes V (163–130 B.C.). The fact that Menodorus won so many victories in 'crown' games does not mean that he was a true amateur, since his own city would have rewarded him handsomely for his exploits. His name is not found in the better-quality Athenian families and his father was evidently a Roman, so he may have been something of a *parvenu* in athletic circles.

(Delos, Museum 174. Found to the south of the Agora of Theophrastus. White marble; right end worked to fit another slab (at right angles?). Length 1.83 m; height 91 cm; thickness 30 cm.)

L. Bizard and P. Roussel, *BCH* 31 (1907) 432–5 (no. 26), fig. 3; S. Dow, *Hesperia* 4 (1935) 81–90 (no. 38); *ID* no. 1957; *EAD* XVIII: W. Deonna, *Le mobilier délien* (1938) pl. XCI.808.

185

186

185. Fragment of a slab in honour of a victorious athlete, set up by a man from Rhamnus in Attica, perhaps in honour of his father (Ale)xandros. Both ends are broken off, but reliefs representing four of the athlete's prizes are preserved: the Panathenaic amphora of oil from Athens, the Isthmian pine-crown, the shield from Argos, and the Nemean celery-crown. The shape of the amphora and the style of lettering suggest a date in the late third or second century B.C.

(New York, Metropolitan Museum of Art 59.11.19 (Rogers Fund), formerly collection of Lord Hatherton. Provenance unknown. Marble. Height 32.5 cm; length 67.0 cm.)

D. von Bothmer, *Metropolitan Museum of Art Bulletin* n.s. 19 (1960–61) 182f., fig. 1.

186. This mosaic panel (late second or early first century B.C.), from the floor of a room in the House of the Trident on Delos, bears witness to the popularity of agonistic sports in the Hellenistic period. It shows a Panathenaic prize-amphora, evidently awarded for a victory in the chariot-race (see the device on the belly), a palm of victory, and an olive-crown. The apparent reference to the Panathenaic games would be highly appropriate in the period of the Athenian colony, but there is no need to think that the mosaic was laid in honour of a particular victory, whether won by the householder or by anyone else; the motif is a purely decorative one, what we would call today a still life. At least three other Delian mosaics showed athletic prizes.

In situ. Colours predominantly browns, reds and greens; figures on amphora black. Height (disregarding borders) 75 cm; width 55 cm.)

M. Bulard, *Peintures murales et mosaïques de Délos* (*Mon. Piot* 14) (1908) 194–6, pl. XA; *EAD* XXIX: P. Bruneau, *Les mosaïques* (1972) 73–5, 264, figs. 216–18, pl. B, 3 (no. 234).

187 

 188

187. Bronze head, the only remnant of the 187 statues of victorious athletes which Pausanias singled out for mention in his description of Olympia. Last quarter of the fourth century B.C.? Recognizable as a boxer from its flattened nose and swollen ears, it is clearly a close likeness of a particular individual, unlike the more generalized boxer in the Terme Museum (**188**). It has been linked with the portrait of Satyrus by Silanion (Pausanias VI.4.3), but statistical probability is against this or any other specific identification. The groove in the hair marks the position of the victor's olive-crown, now lost.

(Athens, National Museum 6439. From Olympia (found north of the Prytaneum). Height 28 cm.)

A. Furtwängler, *Die Bronzen und die übrigen kleineren Funde von Olympia* (*Olympia, die Ergebnisse der von dem Deutschen Reich veranstalteten Ausgrabung* IV) (1980) 10f. no. 2.2a, pl. II; Robertson 517, pl. 160a; P. C. Bol, *Grossplastik aus Bronze in Olympia* (Olympische Forschungen IX) (1978) 40–3, 114f. (no. 159), pls. 30–2; Lullies 117, pls. 228–9.

188. Bronze statue of a seated boxer. First century B.C.? Though sometimes interpreted as a mythological character, this figure is almost certainly a genre creation. The flattened nose, gashed cheeks and cauliflower ears testify to the brutality of the sport and perhaps to its increased professionalization in Hellenistic times.

(Rome, Terme Museum 1055. From the Horti Sallustiani in Rome. Rock seat restored. Height 1.28 m.)

W. Helbig, *Ant. Denk.* I.1 (1886) 2, pl. 4; Robertson 520, 716 n. 40; Lullies 142f., pls. 294–5.

189. Bronze race-horse and boy-jockey found in the sea off Cape Artemisium. The foreparts of the horse and the rider were recovered in 1928, the rear of the horse in 1937; the whole group has been recently restored, with the middle of the horse completed in synthetic resin. Doubts which have been expressed over the unity of the two elements are groundless: the urgent vitality of both horse and rider points to the late third or second century B.C., and the disparity of scale reflects the reality of the horse-race, in which jockeys must evidently be as light as their modern counterparts. The boy's semi-negroid features raise interesting questions about his racial origin. The original source and function of the group (a dedication in a sanctuary by a victorious owner?) are uncertain; presumably it was being transported as plunder or merchandise

for Roman patrons when the boat carrying it and the famous early-Classical striding 'Posidon' was sunk.

(Athens, National Museum 15177. Length, as restored, 2.50 m (minus tail); height 2.05 m.)

N. Bertos, *Deltion* 10 (1929), suppl. 89–95, figs. 3–6; H. von Roques de Maumont, *Antike Reiterstandbilder* (1958) 34–6; V. G. Kallipolitis, *AAA* 5 (1972) 419–26.

4. Theatre

In the Hellenistic period the main form of public entertainment alongside the athletics and other sports dealt with above was the theatre. Theatres were as indispensible a part of the new foundations of the Seleucids and other monarchs as were stadia and gymnasia.

In theatre-architecture and staging-technique the chief development was the introduction of a forebuilding or proscenium (*proskenion*) up to 3 m high in front of the actual stage-building (*skene*) (**193–8**). This development, which took place as early as the late fourth century at Epidaurus and perhaps Eretria (**194**), signalled (or was the consequence of) a clear divorce between acted drama, which now took place on the roof of the proscenium in front of the *skene*'s upper storey (*episkenion*), and choral performances, which presumably continued to be staged in the orchestra. The reduction in size and importance of the chorus marked a further stage in the separation of drama from its religious origins; and it is significant that the theatre in Athens (**196–7**), where the traditions of choral drama might be expected to have survived longest, was probably not provided with a proscenium till the third or early second centuries.

Proscenium-acting was especially well suited to the production of comedy, and particularly of the New Comedy associated with the early-Hellenistic Athenian playwright Menander (**199**), in which the chorus merely performed entr'actes. This type of comedy, involving stock characters (the angry old man, the dissolute son, the impertinent slave) and stock situations (the discovery of long-lost children, a young man's passion for a *hetaera*), is in some sense the ancestor of our modern comedy of manners. Its popularity is attested by representations of scenes from the plays in wall-painting, mosaic and sculpture (**200–2**), by terracotta figurines of actors (**203**), and by decorative versions of comic masks (**204–5**; cf. **192**, **207**). The dress of the actors, except at first for slaves, abandoned the grotesqueness (padding, prominent phalli, etc.) of Old and Middle Comedy, approximating instead to the everyday dress of contemporary Athenians; but masks were retained. These tended to conform with certain standard types which could not be taken, as in Old Comedy, for caricatures of particular living people. A list of these types compiled in the Roman period by the lexicographer Pollux can be used, with due caution, to identify the types portrayed in Hellenistic art.

The outlandish costumes of Attic Old and Middle Comedy continued in a form of south-Italian farce, the so-called 'phlyakes', whose subjects included burlesques of mythology and slapstick comedies of daily life (**207**; cf. **208**). At the same time tragedy remained popular. The success of new playwrights, however, seems never to have rivalled that of the classical masters, and especially of Euripides, whose works were constantly revived. Our illustrations (**190–1**) belong to the threshold of the Hellenistic age, since the end of red-figure vase-painting soon afterwards removes the principal source of visual information; but other forms of evidence attest the frequency of revivals in later times: e.g. a late-third-century inscription from Tegea which records the achievements of an actor and names five plays of Euripides in a catalogue of seven titles (*IG* v.2, no. 118 = *SIG*, no. 1080). These revivals must have been staged in traditional fashion in the orchestra, unless they were adapted in some way to the new raised stage, for example by the reduction in numbers of the chorus.

A final important aspect of the history of Hellenistic theatre was the organization of theatrical performers into guilds of 'Dionysiac artists' (*technitai*). These guilds, which included not only actors, singers and musicians but also poets and producers, first appeared in the 280s and 270s as a response to the spread of theatres and dramatic festivals and to the need to protect the interests of the profession as well as to serve the interests of the festival-organizers. Their members often acquired considerable privileges, such as exemption from taxation and military service (cf. **209**), and the guilds themselves enjoyed almost the status of independent states, with accredited ambassadors in various cities and representatives at the great festivals.

19

190. Sicilian vase-painting of a scene from Sophocles' *Oedipus Tyrannus*, the only representation of an identifiable tragedy which shows the actual stage. Third quarter of the fourth century B.C. The floor of the stage was supported by posts, and the backdrop was formed by a series of four Doric columns. It thus appears that a raised stage was known in Sicily at a time well before it was introduced in Athens (in the third or early second century). The scene portrayed is probably lines 924ff. in which a messenger reports the death of Polybus and reveals the circumstances of Oedipus' adoption. The messenger is at the left, white-haired and bearded, wearing a yellow tunic and chlamys, and high boots; Oedipus stands listening at the centre, fingering his beard; and Jocasta watches at the right, drawing her veil to her face in a gesture of horror. Their two daughters, though not referred to in Sophocles' text, are shown in the spaces between the adults. As in the following plate, the illustration is not entirely literal, since the characters do not wear theatrical masks.

191

(Syracuse, National Archaeological Museum 66557. Red-figure calyx-crater (fragmentary) by the Capodarso Painter.)

A. D. Trendall, *The Red Figured Vases of Lucania, Campania and Sicily*, suppl. I (*BICS* suppl. XXVI) (1970) 105 no. 98a; *IGD* 66, 68–9 (III.2.8).

191. Apulian vase-painting showing a scene from Euripides' *Alcestis*. Third quarter of the fourth century B.C. Alcestis, who has agreed to take Admetus' place in the Underworld, is taking leave of her family. She is seated on a couch with her arms round her two children, while Admetus and his mother stand one on either side, hands raised to head and chin respectively in characteristic gestures of mourning. An aged servant watches at the right, and the first of a pair of Alcestis' handmaids is visible at the left. In staging the play the appearance of Alcestis on a couch was perhaps achieved by means of the *ekkyklema*, a platform on wheels which was pushed forward or revolved into the central doorway of the *skene*.

(Basel, Antikenmuseum Loan S.21. Red-figure *loutrophoros* by a forerunner of the Ganymede Painter.)

IGD 75 (III.3.5).

192. This stele was set up in the theatre of the Attic deme Aixone, south-east of Athens, in honour of the *choregoi* Auteas and Philoxenides. The date, given by the name of the archon Theophrastus, is probably 313/12 B.C. (an alternative date of 340/39 is less likely). Incised in the stone beneath the inscription are symbols of the gold crowns awarded to the *choregoi*; above is a relief of a satyr bringing a jug to fill Dionysus' wine-cup. Most interesting are the comic masks carved on the fascia below the pediment: probably, from left to right, an old man, an old woman, a young woman with long hair, a young man, and a young woman with short hair. They cling to the more traditional types of Middle Comedy which were soon to be modified by New Comedy.

(Athens, Epigraphical Museum 13262. Found at

192

Glyphada in 1941. Total height 95 cm; width of shaft 36 cm at top, 40 cm at bottom.)

N. Kyparissis and W. Peek, *Ath. Mitt.* 66 (1941) 218f., pl. 73; Pickard-Cambridge, *Festivals* 49, 215f., fig. 25; *IGD* 122 (IV.8a); T. B. L. Webster, *Monuments Illustrating Old and Middle Comedy*, 3rd ed. (1978) 118 (AS 2).

193 (a, b). View and reconstruction of the interior of the theatre at Priene (begun in the second half of the fourth century B.C.). This small (only about fifty rows of seats arranged in five wedges) but well-preserved theatre is crucial for the study of dramatic production in Hellenistic times and has been a focus for much of the controversy which has raged on the subject. Von Gerkan argued that the proscenium existed from the first stone phase of the theatre (dated by him *c.* 300), but that the action did not take place on its roof till the second half of the second century, when the upper part of the *skene* was opened up by the creation of three large *thyromata* (see **195**). Most writers believe that the action was transferred to the roof of the proscenium as soon as it was constructed, whether this was in the first phase of the theatre or later. The upper storey of the *skene* is now missing, but the surviving elements of the proscenium have been re-erected. A series of eleven piers with attached half-columns supported the front ends of stone beams (four can be seen still in position) over which were laid the wooden planks of the stage (*logeion*). In the spaces between the piers were three two-leaved doors alternating with painted wooden panels.

A. von Gerkan, *Das Theater von Priene* (1921); Bieber, *Denkmäler* 29–37 no. 8, figs. 27–38, pl. 13; Bulle, *Untersuchungen* 250–3; Pickard-Cambridge, *Theatre* 202–4, figs. 68–9; Dinsmoor 301 n. 3; Bieber, *History* 108–10, figs. 416–25; M. Schede, *Die Ruinen von Priene*, 2nd ed. (1964) 70–9, figs. 84–92; D. De Bernardi Ferrero, *Teatri classici in Asia Minore* III (1970) 10–20, figs. 1–13, pls. I, II.

194. Remains of the theatre at Eretria, which acquired its basic lay-out in the Hellenistic period, probably in the late fourth or third centuries B.C. Since, unlike most Greek theatres, this one was situated on flat ground rather than being cut into a hillside, the auditorium was hollowed out to a depth of 3.20 m below the natural surface, and ramps led down to the orchestra; the roof of the proscenium remained at ground-level. A vaulted tunnel (centre) passed under the stage-building to a stairway which gave more direct access to the *skene*. An interesting feature is an underground passage leading from the proscenium to a staircase which opened in the centre of the orchestra, perhaps an entrance for arrivals from Hades (Pollux's 'Charonian steps') or other 'miraculous' manifestations.

Dörpfeld and Reisch 112–17, figs. 44–5; Fiechter, *Entwicklung* 4–9, figs. 6–9; Bieber, *Denkmäler* 20f. no. 3, figs. 14–15, pl. 8; Bulle, *Untersuchungen* 87–91; Fiechter, *Das Theater in Eretria* (1937); Pickard-Cambridge, *Theatre* 198f., figs. 64–5; Dinsmoor 300 n. 1, fig. 110; Bieber, *History* 77–8, 118, figs. 284–8, 452–4; P. Auberson and K. Schefold, *Führer durch Eretria* (1972) 46–52.

193a

193b

195. The theatre in the sanctuary of Amphiaraus at Oropus.

(**a**) View of the remains of the stage-building. The piers with half-columns on the front formed part of a proscenium which was unusually low (only about 2.50 m) and was approached by ramps at the sides; these seem to have existed from the initial phase, which is dated to the third century B.C. An inscription from the architrave (*IG* VII, p. 745) records the dedication of 'the *proskenion* and the *pinakes*' (the latter evidently painted panels set in the intercolumniations), while a second inscription (*IG* VII, no. 423), ascribed to the upper storey of the *skene*, refers to the dedication of 'the *skene* and the *thyromata*' (evidently wide openings in this upper storey employed either as doorways to the interior or as settings for the display of painted scenery).

(**b**) Fiechter's reconstruction, which makes convincing use of the available evidence.

Dörpfeld and Reisch 100–9, figs. 35–42, pl. VI.1; Fiechter, *Entwicklung* 1–4, figs. 1–5, 64a–b; Bieber, *Denkmäler* 21–4, figs. 16–18; E. R. Fiechter, *Das Theater in Oropos* (1930); V. C. Petrakos, *Ho Oropos kai to hieron tou Amphiaraou* (1968) 84–93, figs. 11–16, pls. 10–13.

196. Interior of the theatre of Dionysus at Athens, the birthplace of Greek drama. The stone auditorium was constructed in all probability in the period of the statesman Lycurgus (338–326 B.C.) and remained largely unchanged throughout antiquity. Its lower part, slightly greater than a semi-circle, was divided by stairways into thirteen wedges of seats; and above a broad cross-passage (*diazoma*) further radiating wedges ran up the lower slope of the Acropolis. There were seventy-eight rows of seats in all according to Dörpfeld's calculation, and the theatre could perhaps have accommodated about 14,000 spectators. Either in the time of Lycurgus or about a generation later the first true stage-building was constructed, consisting of a *skene* with projecting wings (*paraskenia*) at either end; in this phase the action took place at ground-level or on a low stage between these wings and in the *orchestra* in front. Only in the third or early second centuries (for a different

195a

195b

196

view see *CAH* VII².I, ch. 8) was the proscenium, which had appeared as early as the late fourth century at Epidaurus and elsewhere, introduced in Athens. The actors probably now moved up on to the roof of the proscenium, and the *paraskenia*, no longer required to frame the action at ground-level, were accordingly shortened. The present paving in the orchestra and the sculptured podium behind it date to the Roman Imperial period.

Dörpfeld and Reisch 36–82; E. R. Fiechter, *Das Dionysos-Theater in Athen* I (1935); III (1936); Pickard-Cambridge, *Theatre*, chapters IV, V; J. Travlos, *Pictorial Dictionary of Ancient Athens* (1971) 537–52.

19

197. Closer view of the front seats in the Athens theatre. The thrones in the front row were for priests and city-officials who enjoyed the right of *prohedria*, and many of them, including the central throne for the priest of Dionysus (with lion's-paw feet), probably go back to the reconstruction of Lycurgus, or at least are close replicas of thrones installed at that time. The remains of a marble parapet in the foreground date to the Roman period.

98

199

Dörpfeld and Reisch 45–9, figs. 14, 15; Bieber, *Denkmäler* 17, pls. 4, 5; S. Risom, *Mélanges Holleaux* (1913) 257–63, pls. VIII–XIII; Fiechter, *Dionysos-Theater* I, 64–72, figs. 54–9; Pickard-Cambridge, *Theatre* 141–4, figs. 39–43; T. Kraus, *JdI* 69 (1954) 32–48; Bieber, *History* 70f., figs. 267–9; M. Maass, *Die Prohedrie des Dionysostheaters in Athen* (Vestigia XV) (1972).

198. Post-sockets for the rear of the stage-building of the theatre at Pergamum (cf. **64**). Although apparently built in the reign of Eumenes II (197–159 B.C.), the Pergamum theatre lagged behind almost every other Greek theatre in having a wooden stage-building at a period when the normal material was stone. The reason was that a permanent building would have blocked the terrace leading to the temple of Dionysus, whereas a wooden structure could be readily dismantled when not in service. The sockets, all about 40 cm square, were made of hard trachytic lava, and the surrounding pavement (missing at this point) of soft, darker-coloured tuff; the rebates inside the edges of the sockets were designed to carry lids. There were three rows of sockets in all, of which the back two were 1 m deep and the front one only 70 cm, a difference which led Dörpfeld to his convincing restoration of a two-storey *skene* fronted by a one-storey *proskenion*. The spacing of the posts indicates the presence of three doorways in both *skene* and *proskenion*. Oblique settings of sockets at either end of the building may possibly have served in some way for the installation of rotating side-sets (*periaktoi*).

Altertümer von Pergamon IV: R. Bohn, *Die Theater-Terrasse* (1896) 12f., 15f., pls. IV, V X; W. Dörpfeld, *Ath. Mitt.* 32 (1907) 220–31, figs. 12–14; Bieber, *Denkmäler* 37f., fig. 39, pls. 14–18; Bulle, *Untersuchungen* 256f.; Bieber, *History* 62f., figs. 245–7; D. De Bernardi Ferrero, *Teatri classici in Asia Minore* III (1970) 28f., figs. 23, 24, pls. III, IV.

199. Sculptured portrait of Menander (*c.* 342–292 B.C.), the greatest exponent of New Comedy. First century B.C.? This Roman herm-bust is thought to have been copied from a statue set up in the theatre in Athens, of which the base, carrying the signature of Praxiteles' sons Cephisodotus and Timarchus, was found in 1862. The identification of portraits of Menander, long a matter of controversy, has now been

200

201a

firmly established as a result of the discovery of an inscribed bronze bust (Malibu, J. Paul Getty Museum).

(Boston, Museum of Fine Arts 97.288 (Catherine Page Perkins fund). From neighbourhood of Torre Annunziata. Italian (?) marble. Height 51.5 cm (face 19.6 cm).)

Bieber, *Denkmäler* 83f., pl. 47; Bieber, *History* 90, fig. 318; Richter, *Portraits* 233 no. 38, figs. 1621–3 (with further bibl.); Robertson 518f., 716 nn. 37–8.

200. Part of a painted frieze from the main dining- and reception-room of the House of the Comedians in Delos, showing scenes from New Comedy. Last quarter of the second century B.C. From left to right a three-figure scene on a brownish red ground, another three-figure scene on a black ground, and a two-figure scene on a brownish red ground. Some of the figures are badly effaced, but it is possible clearly to see a white-haired slave with the typical trumpet-mouth (Pollux's no. 21: the *pappos*) at the right of the first two scenes, in each case speaking in

201b

agitation with arm outstretched (cf. **203d–e**). The central figure of the second scene (no. 10: the admirable youth) raises his finger to his mouth in a gesture of perplexity and the left-hand figure (no. 35?: the second false maiden) clasps her hands together in consternation; the general action is similar to that of a Pompeian painting where an old slave speaks excitedly while a young couple draw back in alarm. Webster compares an episode in the *Mostellaria* of Plautus, where the slave Tranio warns Philolaches of the return of his father from a voyage abroad.

(Delos, Museum S.62.8. Plaster, reconstructed from fragments. Colours predominantly purple, yellow, white and tones of red, against a brownish-red or black ground. Height 25 cm; length 1.46 m.)

Webster, *MNC* 295f. (DP 1–2); *EAD* XXVII: P. Bruneau and others, *L'Îlot de la Maison des Comédiens* (1970) 169f., 176–9, pls. 21 (3, 4), 22 (7, 8), 23, 24 (3).

201. Mosaic copies of third-century paintings representing scenes from New Comedy. Late second or early first century B.C. The mosaics, which reproduce the brush-strokes and rich colouring of the originals by means of tiny stones often less than 1 mm across, were inset panels (*emblemata*) in the centre of a pavement in the so-called Villa of Cicero at Pompeii; they were contained in shallow trays of marble and were perhaps imported ready-made from the Greek east, a supposition strengthened by the Samian origin of the artist Dioscurides whose signature appears on each piece. The scenes portrayed have now been linked with plays of Menander by comparison with labelled scenes in a mosaic pavement at Mytilene.

(**a**) Musicians, perhaps derived from the *Theophoroumene*. The castanet-player and the child reappear in the relevant scene on the Mytilene mosaic, but the other two figures are replaced by a slave and by a young man standing still. A slightly different juncture in the play must be intended; but, since our knowledge of the play is very sketchy, we can only make conjectures as to the relationship of the two scenes. The two male musicians reappear among the Myrina terracottas (cf. **203a**), though with masks exchanged.

(**b**) The opening scene of the 'Breakfasting Women' (*Synaristosai*). An old hag, Philaenis (Pollux no. 29), and her daughter, Pythias (no. 39: the little youthful *hetaera*), take wine with Plangon (no. 35: the second false maiden). Although the play of Menander is lost apart from a few fragments, a Latin version by Plautus is preserved in the form of the *Mostellaria* and as long ago as 1930 F. Marx recognized the source of the mosaic, a conjecture which was taken up by Webster in 1956, five years before the discovery of the Mytilene mosaic. The action is set in an interior, probably revealed by one of the wide openings (*thyromata*) in the episcenium.

(Naples, National Museum 9985 and 9987. Colours predominantly shades of blue-green, red, brown, yellow, grey and white. (a) Height 43.7 cm; width 41.7 cm. (b) Height 42 cm; width 33 cm.)

M. Bieber and G. Rodenwaldt, *JdI* 26 (1911) 1–22; Bieber, *Denkmäler* 160f., pls. 92, 93; F. Marx, *Rheinisches Museum* 79 (1930) 197–208; A. K. H. Simon, *Comicae Tabellae* (*Die Schaubuhne* xxv) (1938) 14–24 nos. 8, 10; Pickard-Cambridge, *Theatre* 223f., figs. 85–6; T. B. L. Webster, *Greek Theatre Production* (1956) 23f., C19, C20; S. Charitonidis, L. Kahil and R. Ginouvès, *Les mosaïques de la Maison du Ménandre à Mytilène* (*Antike Kunst* suppl. vi) (1970) 41–4, 46–9, pls. 5, 6; Webster, *MNC*, pp. ix, 183 (NM1, NM2), 285; *IGD* 145 (v, 1 and 3), frontispiece, col. pl. opp. 8; Robertson 581, 732 n. 216.

202. Relief showing a typical scene from New Comedy. First century A.D.? An angry father emerges from his house to chastise his son who is returning drunk from a revel, supported by one of the wily slaves who so often abet youths in their misdemeanours. The father is restrained by a milder neighbour. The four main actors wear masks which can be identified with Pollux's series: the angry father is no. 3 (leading old man), the son is no. 16 (second youth with wavy hair), the neighbour is no. 4 (old man with long beard and wavy hair) and the slave is no. 27 (wavy-haired leading slave). The curtain at the right is excluding part of the stage-building not required in the play, or alternatively is veiling unwanted props.

(Naples, National Museum 6687, formerly Farnese collection. Provenance unknown. Marble. Height 45 cm; width 53 cm.)

Robert, *Masken* 6f., 61f., figs. 11–13, 85; J. Sieveking, in Brunn-Bruckmann, text to pl. 630a (1912); Bieber, *Denkmäler* 157 no. 130, pl. 89; Bieber, *History* 92, fig. 324; Webster, *MNC* 30, 192, 195 (NS 25).

203. A selection of terracotta figurines (formerly painted) of characters from New Comedy, made at Myrina, south of Pergamum, during the second century B.C. The popularity of such pieces recalls the vogue for similar figurines of characters from Old and Middle Comedy in fourth-century Athens.

(**a**) Youth playing castanets, probably Pollux no. 10, the admirable youth. The particular interest of the type is its similarity to the middle figure in one of the Dioscurides mosaics in Naples (**201a**); the terracotta, like the mosaic, may have been inspired by a third-century painting.

(Athens, National Museum 5060, formerly Misthos collection (543). Height 19 cm.)

Bieber, *Denkmäler* 167 no. 155, pl. 100.3; *ead. History* 95, fig. 342; Webster, *MNC* 81 (MT15); *IGD* 147 (v.10).

(**b**) Youth wrapped in cloak: Pollux no. 15, the first youth with wavy hair, described as 'a soldier and a braggart'.

(Athens, National Museum 5025. Right hand missing. Height 22 cm.)

Webster, *MNC* 81 (MT 17); Pickard-Cambridge, *Festivals* 226, fig. 117.

202

03a

203b

203c

203d

(**c**) Parasite (Pollux no. 18), carrying an oil-flask and a strigil, conventional attributes of the character.

(Athens, National Museum 5027, formerly Misthos collection (544). Height 19 cm.)

Robert, *Masken* 23f., figs. 51–2; Bieber, *Denkmäler* 164 no. 144, pl. 97. 1–2; *ead. History* 100, fig. 372; Webster, *MNC* 82 (MT 19); Pickard-Cambridge, *Festivals* 226, fig. 119.

(**d**) Curly-haired slave (Pollux no. 24). He wears a wreath concealing the bald forehead which is one of the features recorded by Pollux, but traces of red paint on the face agree with Pollux's description of the character as 'red-skinned'.

(Athens, National Museum 5048, formerly Misthos collection (540). Height 20 cm.)

Robert, *Masken* 10f., figs. 22–3; Bieber, *Denkmäler* 166 no. 150, pl. 98.4; *ead. History* 103, fig. 399; Webster, *MNC* 83 (MT 28).

(**e**) Slave running: Pollux no. 25, the bald slave, normally a cook. The type was called Maison after a Sicilian actor who popularized the character.

(Athens, National Museum 5058, formerly Misthos collection (60). Hands broken away. Height 19 cm.)

Robert, *Masken* 15, fig. 27; Bieber, *Denkmäler* 166 no. 154, pl. 100.2; *ead. History* 103, fig. 397; Webster, *MNC* 83 (MT 30); Pickard-Cambridge, *Festivals* 227, fig. 125.

(**f**) *Hetaera* wearing a snood (Pollux no. 41).

(Athens, National Museum 5032, formerly Misthos collection (427). Height 18 cm.)

Webster, *MNC* 86 (MT 45).

204. Necks of Gnathian ribbed oinochoai (cf. **165**). Each shows a theatrical mask suspended on a string.

(**a**) Tragic mask, probably female: Pollux's no. 25 (second *kourimos*)? *c.* 300–275 B.C. She

203e

203f

wears the high triangular *onkos*, probably introduced in tragedy between *c.* 350 and *c.* 330 B.C.

(Paris, Louvre Museum K 596. From Gnathia.)

T. B. L. Webster, *JHS* 71 (1951) 223 no. 4, 231f.; *id. Monuments Illustrating Tragedy and Satyr Play*, 2nd ed. (*BICS* suppl. xx) (1967) 81 (GV 9).

(**b**) Comic mask: woman with melon hair, perhaps Pollux's no. 39 (little youthful *hetaera*). *c.* 300–275 B.C.

(Manchester Museum MWI 6949. Provenance unknown. Parts of paint of mask eroded.)

T. B. L. Webster, *JHS* 71 (1951) 223 no. 35; Webster, *MNC* 123 (GV 5(a)), 281.

205. Miniature mask of old man from New Comedy: with a knob of hair on top and a flowing beard, he is best equated with Pollux's no. 7, the Lycomedean, described as 'curly-bearded, long-chinned', and 'meddlesome' (the raising of one eyebrow mentioned by Pollux is not found in Hellenistic versions of the type). A good example of a character who may have been given this mask is Smicrines in Menander's *Epitrepontes*. *c.* 300–250 B.C.

(Athens, Agora Museum T 213. From a third-century well in the Agora (G 14:2). Terracotta, left half of beard missing. Height 4.9 cm.)

T. B. L. Webster, *Hesperia* 29 (1960) 276, 282, pl. 68 (C4); Webster, *MNC* 52 (AT 2); Pickard-Cambridge, *Festivals* 224, fig. 111; *IGD* 147 (v, 6).

206. Roman relief after a Hellenistic type representing Menander with three characteristic masks of New Comedy. First century B.C. or A.D. It is derived from the same prototype as a well-known relief in the Lateran Museum, which however has an extra figure at the right (the Muse of Comedy? Menander's girl-friend Glycera? a personification of Skene?). The masks are perhaps to be equated with Pollux's no. 11 (dark youth), no. 34 (first false maiden), and no. 4 (old

204a

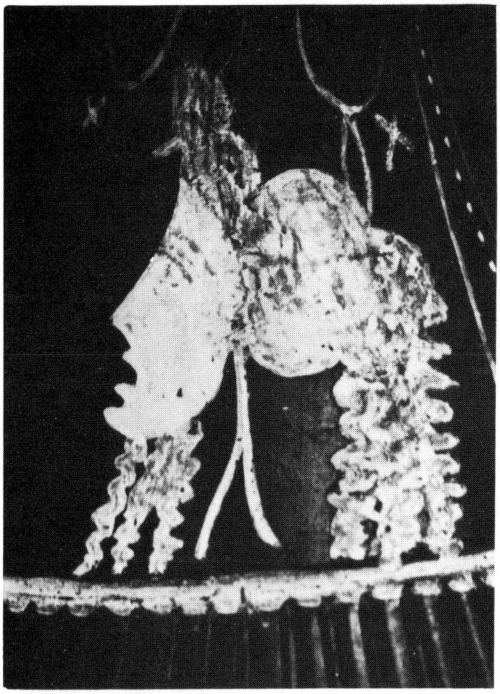

204b

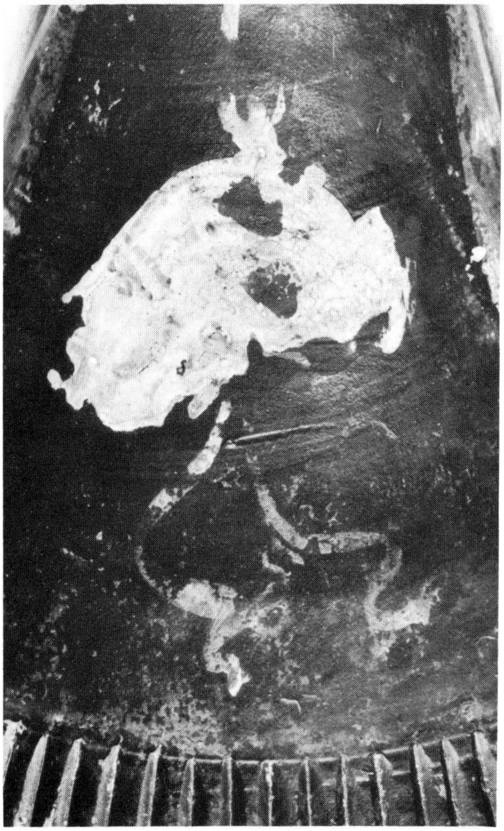

205

man with long beard and wavy hair); but Bieber's attempt to identify them with the protagonists of Menander's *Samia* is certainly too optimistic. The figure of Menander is probably based on the seated statue in the Athenian theatre (cf. **199**).

(Princeton University, Art Museum 51–1 (Caroline G. Mather fund), formerly Stroganoff collection, Rome. Provenance unknown. Pentelic (?) marble. Restored: part of Menander's right leg, the legs of his seat, the cross-struts of the table. Height 49.5 cm; width 59 cm; thickness 2 to 4 cm.)

J. Sieveking, in Brunn-Bruckmann, text to pl. 626b (1912); M. Bieber, *Festschrift Andreas Rumpf* (1952) 14–17, pl. v; Bieber, *History* 89f., fig. 316; Bieber, *Sculpture* 53; Webster, *MNC* 30, 161 (AS 6).

207. Vase-painting showing a scene from the rustic farces known as *phylakes*, popular throughout Magna Graecia and Sicily in the fourth and third centuries B.C. Third quarter of fourth century B.C. An old man carrying a walking-stick holds the arm of a younger man with a *situla* in one hand and a plate of eggs in the other; the younger man seems to reel backwards, and it has

206

207

been suggested that he is the old man's slave who has over-indulged at a feast to which he has accompanied his master. Both characters wear the short tunics (here white), tights and phalli characteristic of the genre, and the action takes place on a raised stage supported by columns, a more permanent-looking arrangement than often seems to have been used.

(London, British Museum 1873.8–20.347. From Capua. Paestan red-figure bell-krater by Python.)

Catalogue of the Greek and Etruscan Vases in the British Museum IV: H. B. Walters, *Vases of the Latest Period* (1896) 97f. (F 189); A. D. Trendall, *Phlyax Vases*, 2nd ed. (*BICS* suppl. XIX) (1967), 36 no. 39; *IGD* 132f. (IV.17).

208. Model of a stage-building from southern Italy (exact provenance uncertain). Dating to the late fourth or early third centuries, the model resembles the stage in a Paestan vase-painting by Asteas showing the madness of Heracles, and may reflect an Italian type of stage in which the action took place on a low *pulpitum* in front of

the *skene*. The façade of the latter is articulated by four Ionic columns with doors painted between them; above is a type of loggia with four Corinthianizing columns; and the whole is surmounted by a pediment with disc-*acroteria* similar to those of the roughly contemporary theatre at Segesta. The side-towers painted with arched openings may represent some form of projecting *paraskenia*. The stage carries traces which indicate the former presence of terracotta figurines of actors (cf. **203**).

(Naples, National Museum, Santangelo collection CS 362. Terracotta coated white, with painted details (arched openings in side-towers red-brown; doors between columns brown; ashlar masonry of side-towers black). Height 32 cm; width 28 cm.)

E. Petersen, *Röm. Mitt.* 12 (1897) 139–43; E. Bethe, *JdI* 15 (1900) 59–81; Bieber, *Denkmäler* 76f. no. 23, fig. 80; A. Levi, *Le terrecotte figurate del Museo Nazionale di Napoli* (1926) 173f. no. 773, fig. 134; A. D. Trendall, *Paestan Pottery* (1936) 32 n. 41, fig. 12; Bieber, *History* 130, fig. 480.

209

209. The last part of an inscription recording grants of privileges and exemptions by the Amphictyonic Council at Delphi to the Athenian guild of Dionysiac artists. Copy made in 130 B.C. The grants include perpetual *asylia* (freedom from *syle*, the exercise of reprisals), *ateleia* (exemption from public duties), and immunity from seizure of person and property; any transgressor will be liable to trial before the Amphictyons. Copies of the decree, which is almost certainly datable to 278 B.C., were set up both in Delphi and in the theatre at Athens. The Athenian ambassadors are named as Astydamas, a tragic poet, and Neoptolemus, a tragic actor.

(Delphi, engraved on the south *anta* of the façade of the Athenian Treasury. Height of letters 9 mm; space between lines 8 mm.)

G. Colin, *BCH* 24 (1900) 82–92; A. Wilhelm, *ibid.* 216–19; *Fouilles de Delphes* III.2 (1909–13) no. 68, lines 62–94, pl. VI.1 (top); Pickard-Cambridge, *Festivals* 282, 308 no. 2.

5. Religion

The Olympian religion lost ground in the Hellenistic age, but it would be wrong to exaggerate the decline. The old Greek gods were an essential bulwark of hellenization in the new cities of the east, and the well-to-do classes, who had benefited from the moral order guaranteed by those gods, continued to endow festivals and vie for priesthoods. The Hellenistic kings also took great pains to cultivate the favour of the Olympians, lavishing vast sums on building projects such as the new temple at Didyma (**51**, **210**), and the revival of work on the temple of Olympian Zeus in Athens (**87**). There was also of course prestige to be got from donating buildings to the great international sanctuaries: thus the stoas and monuments illustrated in **79–80, 84, 88**.

Of the changes and additions to the old order first and foremost is the emergence of ruler-worship. This practice began spontaneously in Asia Minor and the east in the time of Alexander and was then officially cultivated by his successors, notably the Ptolemies and the Seleucids. A first stage was the deification of dead rulers, an extension of the regular Greek practice of heroization of great men after their deaths. Alexander naturally led the way; his head, equipped with various divine attributes (the ram's horns of Zeus Ammon, the lion's scalp of Heracles, and the elephant's scalp of Dionysus), is a favourite type on the coinage of his successors (**211**). Subsequently Ptolemy I was deified by his son Ptolemy II, and Seleucus I by Antiochus I; then cults of the *living* rulers were added to those of Alexander and/or their ancestors. The fullest evidence for the worship of rulers, whether living or dead, comes from Egypt which, in addition to coins portraying kings and queens in divine guise (**4**, **11**, **14**), has yielded a series of blue faience *oenochoae* evidently used in the ruler-cult (**12**). The situation in Egypt, however, shows considerable cultural complexity; in the sculptures of the native temples, while the dead Ptolemies were portrayed in company with the Egyptian gods, the living rulers appeared chiefly in the traditional guise of pharaohs or in the role of officiating priests (cf. **13**, **15**).

Another aspect of the time is the religious role of abstract concepts. The tendency to give divine form to abstractions had grown in the fourth century (cf. **212**) but reached a climax in the following century in the worship of Tyche, or Fortune. This deity was popularly regarded more as a form of divine providence than as blind chance, and she appears both as a personal guardian spirit (often termed Agathe Tyche: cf. **12**) and as the protector of a city, in which capacity she was given monumental artistic form by Eutychides' statue for Antioch (**213**).

The Hellenistic age also saw increased popularity for healing gods such as Asclepius (**214**; cf. **49**, **215**, **265–6**), for oriental cults such as that of Cybele and Attis (**216**), and for the so-called 'mystery religions', which offered some form of salvation to their initiates. Some of the mystery cults, such as those of the Eleusinian deities, the Great Gods of Samothrace (**217–19**), and the universal Dionysus (**220**), were already well established in the Greek world; but a newcomer, perhaps not yet strictly endowed with the 'mystery' element, was the religion of the Egyptian deities Sarapis and Isis. Sarapis was a creation of Ptolemy I, a hellenized version of the Egyptian Osor-Apis, with which Ptolemy may have hoped to achieve some sort of cultural linking of the Greek and Egyptian elements in his kingdom, though his main object was probably to provide a patron deity for the Greek population (**221**). The new god, along with his consort, the old-Egyptian goddess Isis, their son Horus (Harpocrates) and the conductor of souls Anubis, achieved a considerable success in Greek circles. From Egypt their cult was carried to all corners of the Greek world, and Isis in particular came close to being a universal goddess (**222–5**), partly as a result of her ability to subsume other great deities, such as Aphrodite and Tyche (**226**).

Apart from widely popular deities like Isis, the Hellenistic world is notable for the diversity of its religions, reflecting the mixed nature of its populations. The natives of the east and Egypt generally retained their old deities, though sometimes, as in Commagene, identified with deities of the Greek pantheon; while in cosmopolitan centres such as Delos numerous cults existed side by side. A feature of the time was the growth of associations of immigrants and other groups, often focused round the worship of a particular deity (e.g. the Sarapiasts, the Samothraciasts, the Posidoniasts of Beirut). Similar in name if not in organization were the colleges of magistrates set up by the Italian community of Delos to supervise their traditional worship, including that of the Lares Compitales (**228–9**).

210. Interior of the Hellenistic temple of Apollo at Didyma (cf. **51**). One of the largest building-projects of antiquity, the temple was begun in the latter part of the fourth century B.C., with financial assistance from Seleucus I, and was still unfinished five centuries later. Like Apollo's sanctuaries at Delphi and Clarus, the Didymaeum owed its fame and success to an oracle, whose favourable response to Alexander in 331 no doubt played a major part in re-establishing its fortunes after a century and a half under the shadow of the Persian Empire. The new temple replaced a sixth-century predecessor destroyed in 494, from which it probably inherited its most unusual feature, the open-air interior. This may have been designed to incorporate a pre-existing

210

211

a

b

sacred laurel-grove. A small shrine within the court presumably housed the cult-image, brought back from Persia by Seleucus.

Didyma I: H. Knackfuss, *Die Baubeschreibung* (1941); Berve and Gruben 463–70, figs. 129–35, pls. 164–9; R. A. Tomlinson, *Greek Sanctuaries* (1976) 132–6.

211. Silver tetradrachms of (**a**) Lysimachus, (**b**) Ptolemy I; head of Alexander with the horns of Zeus Ammon and elephant-scalp of Dionysus. The worship of Alexander, symbolized by the adoption of his head with various divine attributes as an obverse type on the coins of his successors, paves the way for the deification of the Ptolemies, the Seleucids and other Hellenistic kings, at first after their deaths, but later during their lifetimes. For other coins showing rulers with divine attributes or actually named as gods see **14** (Ptolemy II and Arsinoe II as the 'theoi adelphoi'), **4** (Ptolemies wearing aegis, Cleopatra described as 'thea') and **65d** (Mithridates VI as Dionysus).

(Cambridge, Fitzwilliam Museum. Actual size.)

(a) *McClean* II, 190 no. 4488, pl. 168.4. (b) Unpublished (Hart collection). For the type Svoronos, *Nom. Ptol.* 29 no. 169, pl. VI.8; *SNG* III, no. 3390.

212. Over-lifesize statue dedicated to Themis by Megacles of Rhamnus. End of fourth or beginning of third century B.C. Themis, an ancient earth-deity who in the increasingly intellectual climate of late-Classical and Hellenistic times tended to become a personification of Time-honoured Custom, or Justice, shared a sanctuary at Rhamnus in the north of Attica with Nemesis; and this statue was found in the hall

212

of the smaller of two temples within the sanctuary. The goddess wears the typically Hellenistic high-girdled *chiton* and may have held a libation-bowl in her right hand and scales in her left. The sculptor, Chaerestratus, names his father as Chaeredemus, perhaps to be identified with a personality named on an inscription of 315–314 B.C.

(Athens, National Museum 231. Pentelic marble. Right forearm and attributes (of bronze?) missing. Height 2.02 m.)

V. Stais, *Arch. Eph.* (1891) 45–53, pl. 4; Karouzou 166 no. 231, pl. 56; Lullies 121f., pl. 244.

213

213. Roman statuette based on the statue of Tyche of Antioch. As often in Hellenistic times the goddess Tyche (Fortune) becomes the tutelary deity of a city. Characterized by the swimming youth beneath her feet, who represents the river Orontes on which Antioch stands, and by a bunch of palm-leaves (probably corn-ears in the original statue) in her right hand, Tyche wears the mural crown which was to become the standard headgear of city goddesses (compare the ship's prow worn by Alexandria, mistress of the sea: **5**). The original statue was of bronze, the work of Eutychides, and was presumably commissioned soon after the city was founded in 300 B.C.

(Rome, Vatican Museum 2672. Found in Rome, outside Porta San Giovanni (about 1780). Marble. Details restored from Syrian coins. Height 89.5 cm.)

W. Helbig, *Führer durch die öffentlichen Sammlungen klassischer Altertümer in Rom*, 4th ed., I (1963) 433–5 no. 548; cf. T. Dohrn, *Die Tyche von Antiochia* (1960).

214

214. View of the sanctuary of Asclepius at Corinth, looking north east. Initially a sanctuary of Apollo to which his son Asclepius had perhaps been admitted as a junior partner in the fifth century B.C., it was soon transformed into an Asclepieum and was totally rebuilt in the late fourth century, thus becoming one of several Hellenistic sanctuaries of the healing-god to which the sick flocked, as to present-day Lourdes, for miraculous cures (cf. **49**). Built on a terrace behind the north walls of the city, it enjoyed the amenity of a pleasant view and received healthy breezes from the Gulf of Corinth. In the court (centre) can be seen the foundations of the temple itself (the stone was robbed in later periods); and at the left, partly excavated, is the *abaton*, where cures were effected while the patients slept. A flight of steps descended to a lustral area. In the foreground, blocked by later cross-walls, is a ramp which led down to the health-centre proper, sited to the west to take advantage of an abundant source of fresh water called Lerna. To the south lay a large gymnasium where patients and others could take exercise. Huge numbers of votive terracottas representing parts of the anatomy upon which the god had successfully operated were found in the sanctuary; most date to the clearing-up operations which preceded the construction of the late-fourth-century complex.

Corinth XIV: C. Roebuck, *The Asclepieion and Lerna* (1951); M. Lang, *Cure and Cult in Ancient Corinth* (American Excavations in Old Corinth: Corinth Notes I) (1977).

215. A cylindrical altar from Delos, one of the most characteristic of all altar-forms in the late Hellenistic period. Late second or early first century B.C. The decoration with ox-heads or *bucrania* linked by garlands was particularly common in the Dorian states of the south-east Aegean (Rhodes, Cos, Cnidus and Halicarnassus), where the type may have been invented. In those cities, however, the decoration was confined to funerary altars, whereas in Delos and elsewhere it is standard for both funerary and votive ones. The form was also used, hollowed out, for well-heads. Here, as the inscription reveals, the

215

altar was dedicated as an *ex voto* to the Graces by a Roman, Sp. Stertinius, in thanks for a cure.

(Delos, Museum 483. Found in the ruins of Byzantine structures above the Hypostyle Hall (1907 excavations). Height 55 cm; diameter 42 cm.)

P. Roussel and J. Hatzfeld, *BCH* 33 (1909) 506f. no. 22; *EAD* II: G. Leroux, *La salle hypostyle* (1909) 59, fig. 82. Generally on cylindrical altars Fraser 25–33.

216. Votive relief, perhaps from Asia Minor, representing the Great Mother, Cybele, and her attendant Attis, approached by worshippers. Second century B.C. Cybele, who is shown wearing a high-girdled *chiton*, holds a sceptre in her right hand and a tympanum in her left, while her lion squats at her feet. Attis is dressed in the oriental fashion with sleeves and leggings and a Phrygian headdress. The deities, represented conventionally on a larger scale than the humans, stand within their temple, through the open door of which their worshippers, a woman and her maid (or daughter), have just entered. The cult of Attis and Cybele was one of the eastern religions which became increasingly popular in Hellenistic times.

216

(Venice, Archaeological Museum 118, formerly Grimani collection. Provenance unknown. Grey marble. Height 57 cm.)

C. Anti, *Il regio museo archeologico nel Palazzo Reale di Venezia* (1930) 104–6, no. 17; B. Forlati Tamaro, *Il museo archeologico del Palazzo Reale di Venezia* (Itinerari dei musei e monumenti d'Italia 88) (1953) 21 no. 17.

217. The sanctuary of the Great Gods on Samothrace, viewed from the south west. Samothrace was the home of the cult of the Great Gods, a group of native divinities comprising a Great Mother, a fertility god, a pair of twins (the Cabiri), and an underworld god and his consort. In this cult, which involved initiation ceremonies and a ritual drama rather like those of the Eleusinian mysteries, the Cabiri, identified by the Greeks with the Dioscuri, came to acquire special importance and popularity as protectors and guides of sailors. Votive gifts ranging from pottery and metalwork to shells and fishhooks were dedicated in gratitude for safe voyages. While important throughout the Classical period, the sanctuary enjoyed its hey-day in Hellenistic times. The Macedonian dynasty of Philip and Alexander and the Hellenistic kings donated several buildings. At the right are the remains of the Hieron, the hall in which initiation to the higher degree of the mysteries, the *epopteia*, took place; in its present form it belongs to the late fourth century B.C., except for the colonnaded porch, here re-erected, which was added in the second half of the second century. In the middle distance are the circular foundations of the Arsinoeum, the largest rotunda in Greek architecture, dedicated by Arsinoe II while she was married to Lysimachus (289–281 B.C.). It evidently housed sacrificial ceremonies and gatherings at the annual festival.

On the Hieron, *Samothrace* III: P. W. Lehmann, *The Hieron* (1969). On the sanctuary in general, K. Lehmann, *Samothrace, a Guide to the Excavations and the Museum*, 4th ed. (1975).

218. Terracotta head from Samothrace, perhaps representing the underworld god Axiokersos, identified by the Greeks with Hades. Second or first century B.C. As with Hades, his mythology involved the rape of a fertility goddess who became his consort, Axiokersa; and their union formed the subject of a sacred drama enacted in the course of the Samothracian festival.

218

(Samothrace, Museum 53.307. From a late-first-century filling at the south end of the Hieron. Relief applied to object with concave rear surface. Height 5.5 cm; width 3.4 cm; greatest thickness 1.5 cm.)

M. L. Hadzi, in P. W. Lehmann, *op. cit.* 256–8, no. 177.

219 Remains of the temple of the Samothracian gods on Delos. Though initiation into the cult could only take place at Samothrace itself, initiates formed themselves into associations of Samothraciasts and built centres for their religion in various parts of the Greek world. The Delian sanctuary goes back to the fourth century, but its final form belongs to the late second. The façade of the actual temple is marked by a line of column-stumps at the back; at the left end is a niche constructed in granite, part of the second-century reconstruction. In front of the temple, on the right, are the foundations of a monument erected by a priest of the Great Gods in honour of Mithridates VI of Pontus in 102/101 B.C.; and at the left a curved

219

220

foundation belonged to a special altar for offerings to the underworld gods. The marble door-frame lying on the ground in the middle of the picture was dedicated to the Great Gods and to Heracles.

EAD XVI: F. Chapouthier, *Le sanctuaire des dieux de Samothrace* (1935); Bruneau and Ducat 139f. no. 93.

220. One of two sculptured bases flanking a niche-shrine of Dionysus, immediately outside the main sanctuary of Apollo on Delos. End of fourth or beginning of the third century B.C. Set up by a Delian named Carystius in commemoration of his *choregia* (cf. **192**), it carries on the front face a relief of a cock whose head and neck have been converted into a phallus, and on the sides reliefs of Dionysus in company with his mythical followers, Pan and a maenad on the left, and Silenus and another maenad on the right. The base was surmounted by a phallic emblem; the stump now placed on top was found nearby and, even if not the original, gives a good idea of the monument's appearance. Inscriptions refer to a wooden phallus or 'agalma' (perhaps the bird-phallus shown on the front of the base) carried in a procession during the Dionysiac festivals on Delos.

(Base: height 1.29 m; width 53 cm; thickness 40 cm.)

On the niche and its sculptures in general L. Bizard and G. Leroux, *BCH* 31 (1907) 498–524, pls. X–XII; Bruneau, *Recherches* 296–304, pls. III, IV.4–6; on the phallus or *agalma* R. Vallois, *BCH* 46 (1922) 94–112; Bruneau, *op. cit.* 314–17.

221. Bronze statuette of Sarapis. The great god of Ptolemaic Egypt was created by Ptolemy I by grafting Greek elements on to the old Memphite god Osor-Apis, but this image, based almost certainly on the great cult-statue in the Sarapeum at Alexandria, shows him in completely hellenized form, the iconographic type being derived from Greek statues of Zeus, Pluton and Asclepius. His left hand held a sceptre at his side, while his right hand was extended above a figure of Cerberus, the three-headed watchdog of the Underworld. On his head is a corn-measure (*modius*), a symbol of fertility. The original statue was probably made in precious materials (several copies show traces of gilding on the face) and will have dated to the time of Ptolemy III (246–221 B.C.).

(London, British Museum 1824.4–78.1, formerly Payne Knight collection. From Paramythia in Epirus. Throne and arms missing, left leg restored. Height 16 cm.)

H. B. Walters, *Catalogue of the Bronzes, Greek, Roman and Etruscan, in the Department of Greek and Roman Antiquities, British Museum* (1899) 37 no. 276. On the cult-statue A. Adriani, *Repertorio d'arte dell'Egitto greco-romano* ser. A.II (1961) 40–3.

221

222

222. Restored façade of the temple of Isis within Sarapeum C on Delos. Sarapeum C is the largest of three sanctuaries of the Egyptian gods found on Delos and was certainly the official headquarters of the cult, a position which it occupied from 181 B.C. Dedications show that Sarapis retained primacy among the deities honoured there (the order in which they were invoked was Sarapis, Isis, Anubis, Harpocrates); but Isis was not far behind him. She was his consort (*IG* XI, no. 1299, lines 32f.), she was invoked alone, and she had her own temple. Within the temple (hidden) stands a damaged marble statue set up in her honour by the Athenian *demos* in 128/7. To the left are the remains of a smaller shrine, and in front of it an Egyptian-style horned altar (the horns now missing), both dedicated to the trinity of Sarapis, Isis and Anubis, the former in 135/4, the latter in 136/5. In the left foreground are the foundations of another temple, probably that of Sarapis alone.

On Sarapeum C in general P. Roussel, *Les cultes égyptiens à Délos du IIIe au Ier siècle av. J.-C.* (1916) 46–67, pl. III, figs. 8–11; Bruneau and Ducat 144f., fig. 32; Bruneau, *Recherches* 462f. On the statue of Isis Marcadé 429f., pl. LVII (top centre).

223. Bronze rattle, or *sistrum*, used in the cult of Isis (being shaken, according to Plutarch, to ward off evil). The discovery of this example in a tomb on Rhenea, where the necropolis of Delos was situated, is a further testimony to the

223

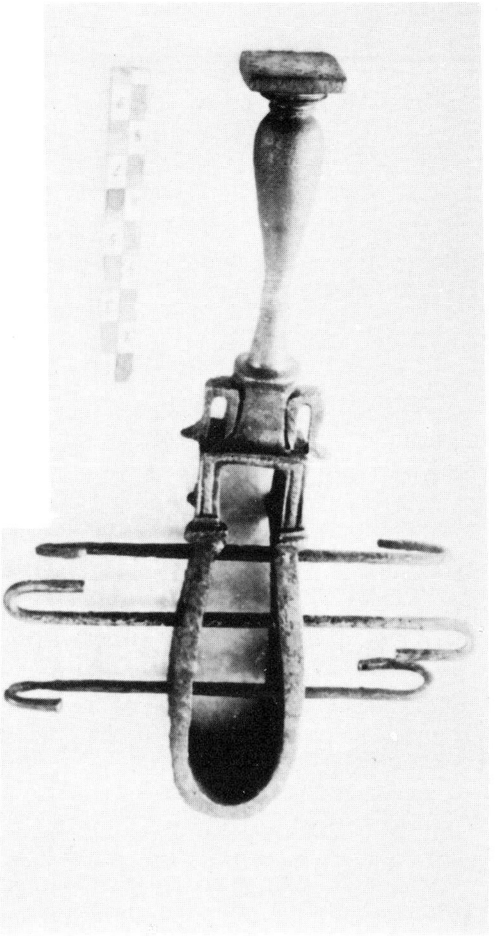

224

presence of the Egyptian religion on Delos; it had been placed in the right hand of a dead woman, perhaps to guarantee protection and well-being in an existence beyond the grave.

(Myconos, Museum 92. Height 24.5 cm.)

D. Stavropoullos, *Praktika* (1898) 103ff.; *EAD* XVIII: W. Deonna, *Le mobilier délien* (1938) 324, pl. XCII. 810.

224. Portrait of a priest of Isis from the Athenian Agora. Mid-first century B.C. The man, portrayed in the matter-of-fact style of the first century B.C., is characterized as a priest by the rolled diadem which he wears round his head, and as a priest of Isis by his shaven head. There is epigraphical evidence for a cult of Sarapis and Isis in Athens, and of an association of Sarapiasts (cf. **229**) there, by the mid third century B.C.; and a cult of Isis alone is recorded on the south slope of the Acropolis in the third quarter of the first century (*IG* II, 2nd ed., no. 4994).

(Athens, Agora Museum S 333. Pentelic marble; broken from a bust or statue. Nose and ears damaged. Height 29 cm.)

T. L. Shear, *Hesperia* 4 (1935) 402–7, figs. 30–1; *The Athenian Agora* I: E. B. Harrison, *Portrait Sculpture* (1953) 12–14, no. 3, pl. 3; *ead. Ancient Portraits from the Athenian Agora* (APB V) (1960), fig. 32.

225. Fragment of a marble tripod-base from Corinth carrying a dedication to Sarapis and Isis by Philotis, the daughter of Philonidas. Third or second century B.C.? Found in a water-system in the south-west part of the city, it is the first material evidence for the location of the sanctuaries of the Egyptian deities recorded by Pausanias at the beginning of his climb to Acrocorinth. It is also the first evidence for the existence of the cult at Corinth in Hellenistic times.

(Corinth, Museum I 2650. Height 5.7 cm; width 12.2 cm.)

G. Daux, *BCH* 90 (1966) 756, fig. 10; H. S. Robinson, *Deltion* 21 (1966), Chronika 139, pl. 129 (c–d); L. Vidman, *Sylloge inscriptionum religionis Isiacae et Sarapiacae* (1969) 20 no. 34a.

225

226

226. Marble figurine of Isis–Tyche, found near the theatre on Delos. Second century B.C. The goddess is unmistakably characterized as Isis by the sacred knot between her breasts, but at the same time she carries the cornucopia, an attribute of Tyche. This would then be a case of the assimilation of the two most successful goddesses of the Hellenistic age.

(Delos, Museum A 2255. White marble, head and right arm missing. Height 24 cm.)

BCH 77 (1953) 561, fig. 51; Marcadé 430f., pl. LVII (centre left).

227. Votive relief, probably in honour of Zeus Meilichius. Third century B.C. The bearded god is shown seated on the horned head of the river-god Achelous. Behind him, holding a *phiale* and a cornucopia, stood the goddess Meter, who was associated in his cult; next to her is Hermes; and at the right, with his club in his left hand and the lion's scalp helmet on his head, is Heracles. Meilichius, Hermes and Heracles all hold jugs, and the last-named seems to be pouring a libation. The meaning of the scene is obscure. It has been suggested that the relief, found in the Ilissus stream in Athens, indicates the presence of a shrine of Meilichius nearby.

(Athens, National Museum 1778. Upper part destroyed. Height 85 cm; width 58 cm; thickness (at base) 16 cm.)

A. N. Skias, *Arch. Eph.* (1894) 137–9, pl. 7; Svoronos, *Ath. Mus.* pl. CXXXI; A. B. Cook, *Zeus, a Study in Ancient Religion* II (1925) 1115–19, fig. 948; H. Möbius, *Ath. Mitt.* 61 (1936) 247–9; Karouzou 93f.

228. Scenes of cult-practice, painted beside the entrance-door of a house on Delos. Shortly before 69 B.C. Such religious, or 'liturgical', paintings are a familiar Delian feature, decorating altars outside street-doors or the adjacent walls during the late second and early first centuries B.C. They give a fascinating glimpse of the popular religious beliefs and practices of the Italian community on the island. Most of the scenes, as here, refer to the worship of the Lares Compitales, protecting gods of the streets and cross-roads (cf. **229**); at the top three figures dressed in the Roman toga make an offering at an altar, beneath them an attendant brings a pig to sacrifice, and at the bottom a trumpeter sounds a fanfare. It is interesting that the Roman cult is

227

228

here penetrated by Greek features: the officiants carry out the ceremonies in the Greek manner, wearing crowns rather than the priestly veil. The legend 'THEOGIPIASON' painted in Roman characters above their heads is the abbreviated form of three Greek names, Theog..., Hip..., and Iason, no doubt freedmen of Italian families. Other 'liturgical' paintings show games at the festivals of the Lares Compitales, as well as favourite protectors of the household, such as Heracles and Hermes.

(Delos, Museum. From a house-façade west of the House of the Hill. Figures, pig, altar, trumpet brown-red; details purple; framing garland green, dark red and yellow. Overall measurements of plaster fragment: height 1.30 m: width 55 cm. Figures 21 to 25 cm high.)

N. Zaphiropoulos, *Deltion* 18 (1963), Chronika 274, pl. 316; *BCH* 89 (1965) 989, fig. 1; Bruneau and Ducat 60, pl. 16.2; U. Bezerra de Meneses and H. Sarian, *Études déliennes* (*BCH* suppl. 1) (1973) 77–109. Generally on Delian religious paintings, *EAD* IX: M. Bulard, *Description des revêtements peints à sujets religieux* (1926); Bruneau, *Recherches* 589–615.

229. The Agora of the Hermaists, the commercial centre of the Italian community on Delos before the creation of the Agora of the Italians (**131**). The Italians formed colleges of magistrates (the Hermaists, Apolloniasts and Posidoniasts) who were probably charged with maintaining the cults of the different deities. The Hermaists, the best attested in the inscriptions, were responsible for a number of dedications in the Agora which has received their name, a large paved square situated strategically adjacent to the commercial port and its warehouses. The circular foundation in the foreground carried a four-columned rotunda (*tholus*) dedicated by six Roman citizens or freedmen who were presumably Hermaists; remains of its entablature and marble roof, carved with false tiles in scale-pattern, have been grouped on the second step. The rectangular structure behind it was a little Doric shrine dedicated by the Hermaists to Mercury and Maia. Later dedications were set up by the Competaliasts, the association of slaves and freedmen which supervised the cult of the Lares Compitales (**228**), and the Agora is alternatively named 'of the Competaliasts'.

J. Hatzfeld, *BCH* 36 (1912) 153ff.; F. Salviat, *BCH* 87 (1963) 252–64; Bruneau and Ducat 74f. no. 2. On the Italian religious colleges Bruneau, *Recherches* 585–9, 615–20.

230. Lead curse-tablet, folded and pierced by an iron nail. Such lead tablets, inscribed with imprecations against the hated individual, were buried as a dedication to the infernal deities, who were expected to put the curse into effect. The practice goes back to the fifth century but becomes much more common from the fourth century onwards, partly as a result of the spread of literacy, but also partly because of an increasing belief in the efficacy of magic. The use of magic was widespread in Hellenistic times, as is attested by papyri with magic formulae from Egypt.

(Oxford, Ashmolean Museum G 514.5. Provenance unknown. Length 9 cm.)

Kurtz and Boardman, pl. 45.

229

6. Death and burial

In so far as it is possible to generalize about burial and attitudes to death in the Hellenistic age, we can say that the chief novelty of the time was a greater tendency to glorify the dead individual. As kings were deified (see above), so the nobles and wealthy middle classes were heroized. This is reflected in the greater number of grand tombs and grave-monuments built during the period (**243–6**) and in the assimilation of grave-reliefs to votives, with the dead shown on a large scale like deities, and the living on a smaller scale like worshippers (**239–41**; cf. **265**). In the late Hellenistic period, especially in Rhodes, Cos and south-west Asia Minor, the increasing replacement of tombstones by funerary altars (**238**) indicates the practice of cult for the dead, now fully heroized. Along with this goes a new optimism about life after death, reflected in the concern expressed in epitaphs that the remains of the dead should be safeguarded against disturbance.

Actual burial practices varied from region to region. Cremation and inhumation existed side by side, though certain regions preferred one to the other – Athens, for instance, inhumation. Athens was exceptional in the Hellenistic world in shunning carved grave-stones and elaborate monuments in favour of an austere style of burial (**231–4**); for varied grave-deposits and artistic memorials we have to look elsewhere (**235**ff.; cf. **43–4**, **90**, **265**). A selection of tomb-stones from different areas is illustrated below (**239–42**) and one can clearly see how regional variations affected both general form and iconography: for example western Greece favoured heraldic reliefs of mourning Sirens on vertical pedimented slabs (**241**), and eastern Greece liked the 'death-feast' relief with numerous subsidiary figures in a horizontal panel (**239**), while some areas such as Demetrias in Thessaly favoured

230

painted stones with simple representations of the dead set shrine-like in architectural frames (**242**).

Monumental tombs again took different forms. The grandest of all must have been that of Alexander and the Ptolemies at Alexandria, to which we have only tantalizing literary references. Other princes in the east probably favoured mausolea modelled on the great tomb of Mausolus at Halicarnassus; the mausoleum at Belevi (**243–5**) is a case in point. More common are the so-called Macedonian tombs, which consist of a simple vaulted burial-chamber, with or without an ante-room and a fine decorated façade, approached by an entrance-passage (*dromos*), the whole covered by a tumulus (**247**; cf. **67**). This type was transmitted by the Macedonians to different regions such as Thessaly and Euboea (**248**), and even the mausoleum at Belevi contained a Macedonian-style vaulted burial-chamber. Within the chambers were frequently stone couches (*klinai*) and other furnishings, used as receptacles for the remains of the dead (**248**) or as platforms on which the dead were laid; and the walls were often decorated with representations of the dead man's possessions or of commemorative wreaths (**248**; cf. **100**). Similar decorations, as well as painted figure-scenes (cf. **92**), are found in chamber tombs in southern Italy, and further grand tumulus-tombs were built by Greeks in south Russia, partly inspired by their Scythian neighbours. In Thrace tumuli covered the *tholos* tombs of tribal chieftains, most of whom employed Greek artists and were buried with imported Greek *objets d'art* (**249**).

Apart from the unusually elaborate stone sarcophagi of the royal cemetery at Sidon and of the mausoleum at Belevi (**245**), most sarcophagi were of wood and have perished. Only in south Russia and Egypt were examples discovered more or less intact during the last century and the early years of the present one (**250–1**). They attest a development from simple chests to forms modelled upon houses with applied columns and entablatures. Most were richly decorated with gilded appliqués of terracotta or stucco.

In certain areas of the east and the Ptolemaic kingdom rock-cut tombs prevailed, no doubt as a result of geological factors and indigenous tradition. In Lycia simple chambers cut at various levels in cliff-sides received Greek architectural façades (**252**); at Cyrene similar chambers were set in rows with recessed façades whose architectural treatment was inspired by house-courtyards (**253**). At Alexandria there were complexes of underground rooms, often grouped round an open-air peristyle courtyard (**254**). One of the suburbs of Alexandria, a veritable city of the dead, has given us our word 'necropolis', and the underground complexes of the Ptolemaic city were the forerunners of the Roman catacombs.

231

231. A collection of *kioniskoi*, the small column-like grave-markers which predominated in the cemeteries of Athens after the sumptuary legislation of Demetrius of Phalerum (317/16 B.C.) had put a stop to elaborately carved tomb-stones and other prestigious monuments. The *kioniskos* was inserted into a rectangular base or directly into the ground; it carried a short inscription naming the dead; and above this a torus moulding encircled the shaft, probably to hold in place a wreath which was attached at the top (compare the bosses on the Rhodian altar, **238**).

(Athens, Kerameikos cemetery (not *in situ*). Hymettian or Pentelic marble. Height approx. 50 cm to 1.20 m; diameter 15 to 35 cm.)

Cf. *Kerameikos, Ergebnisse der Ausgrabungen* III: W. Peek, *Inschriften, Ostraka, Fluchtafeln* (1941) 44–9; K. Gebauer, *Arch. Anz.* (1942) 224, 231ff., figs. 10, 11; Kurtz and Boardman 166f.; *The Athenian Agora* XVII: D. W. Bradeen, *Inscriptions: The Funerary Monuments* (1974) *passim.*

232. Hellenistic stone-lined graves in the Kerameikos cemetery in Athens: the sort of graves which were marked by *kioniskoi*, though in this case the relevant *kioniskoi* were not found by the excavators. Each compartment contained a wooden coffin, in which the dead were laid with their heads to the east, i.e. looking west towards the mythical location of the Underworld. To judge from the associated offerings, the first and third burials were of men (iron strigils), and the second and fourth of women (bronze mirrors). Three of the tombs also contained 'tear flasks' (cf. **234**) and one contained a pair of ear-rings similar in type to those shown in **235**.

K. Gebauer, *Arch. Anz.* (1942) 239f., figs. 13, 14.

233. 'Charon's fees', little gold plaques bearing the imprint of coins and placed in the mouth of the dead as his fare across the Styx on the journey to the Underworld. The practice first appears in Athens in Hellenistic times, and men seem to have been given their fare more regularly than women. Most of the pieces shown here carry the familiar owl of Athens, but the bottom left and bottom right examples have the eagles derived probably from types of the Black Sea cities.

(Athens, Kerameikos cemetery (various graves).)

K. Gebauer, *Arch. Anz.* (1942) 236, 243, fig. 17.

232

233

234. An assemblage of 'tear-flasks', the spindle-shaped oil- or perfume-bottles which are the characteristic grave-goods of Hellenistic Athens. Second century B.C. Made of grey clay with occasional white stripes round the neck and body, they show little development in form apart from a general tendency to elongation. Some graves have only one example or lack them altogether, but others contain large quantities (the deposit here consisted of 43, the only other item in the grave being a strigil).

(Athens, Kerameikos cemetery (South Hill, 1932 excavations, grave f 4). Height 10.1 to 14.3 cm.)

Kerameikos, Ergebnisse der Ausgrabungen IX: U. Knigge, *Der Sudhügel* (1976) 187 (E 99), pl. 97. 2. Generally for 'tear-flasks' *ibid.* 59f. and *passim*; H. Thompson, *Hesperia* 3 (1934) 472–4.

4

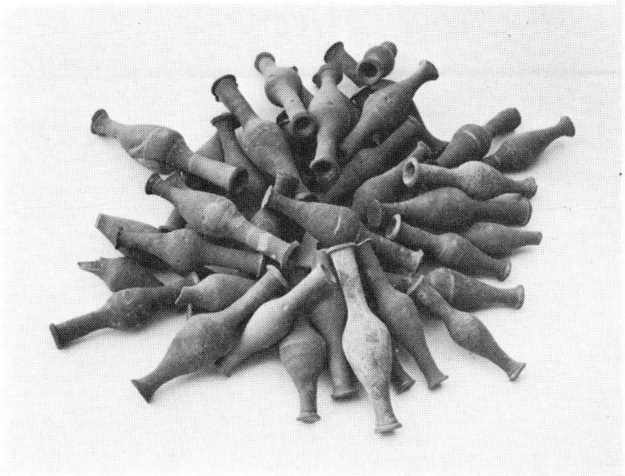

235a

235 (a–c). An early-Hellenistic grave-deposit from Corinth. *c.* 300 B.C. The variety of pots represented contrasts sharply with the restricted range of vessels in contemporary Athenian graves (cf. **234**). The six vessels are (from left to right): (**a**) (1) a small amphora; (2) a *skyphos* (deep cup) of Attic type, with the lower part of the body contracted in the early Hellenistic manner; (3) a 'tear-flask' with the bulbous form of early Hellenistic times; (**b**) (4) a lamp (cf. **162**); (5) a squat trefoil-mouthed *oinochoe* (jug); (6) a tiny *pyxis* (toilet-box). The pair of gold ear-rings (**c**) belongs to a familiar early-Hellenistic type consisting of a hoop of coiled wire tapering to a point at one end and ornamented with an animal's head at the other; the point is designed to pierce the lobe of the ear and hooks on to a ring in the animal's mouth. The grave, which was lined with limestone slabs, was that of a woman in her fifties.

(Corinth, Museum C–60–216; C–60–221; C–60–222; L 4121; C–60–223; C–60–224; MF 10138; MF 10137. From cemetery on north slope of Acrocorinth. Scale approx. (*a*) 1:5; (*b*) 1:2; (*c*) 3:2.)

H. S. Robinson, *Hesperia* 31 (1962) 119 (grave 4), pl. 45, c–e. On the ear-rings cf. R. Higgins, *Greek and Roman Jewellery* (1961) 161–2, pl. 47.

235b

235c

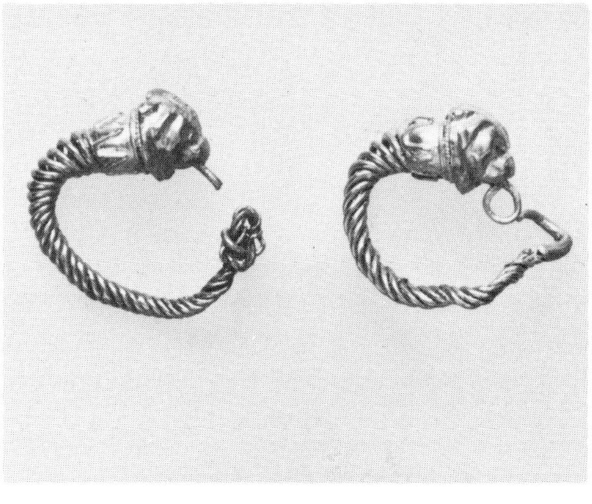

236. Grave with skeleton and grave-goods in position, in the Hellenistic cemetery at Yialova, outside ancient Pylos (Messenia). The variety of vessels present again contrasts with the situation in contemporary Athenian burials; and, as well as pottery, finds from the cemetery included coins, bronze mirrors, terracotta figurines, glassware and gold ear-rings. Associated with

236 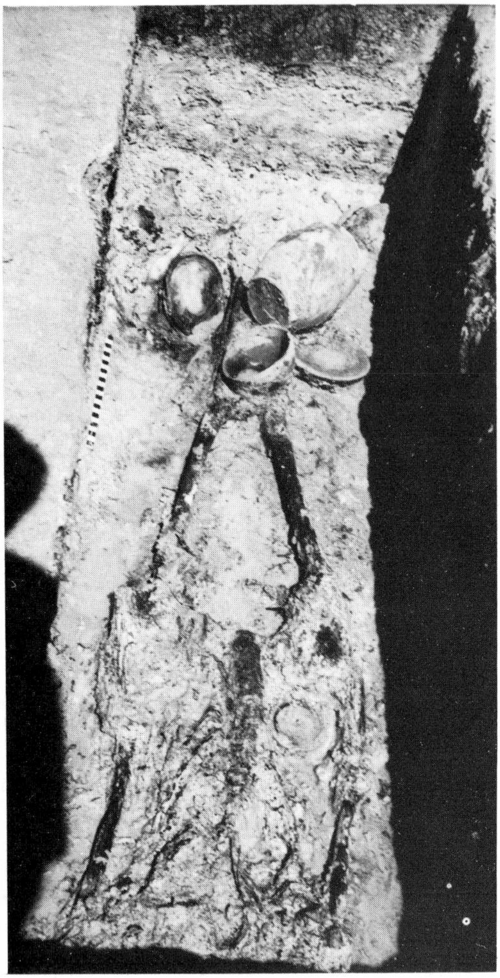

the groups of burials were remains of large pyres of offerings, including broken pots and carbonized fruits.

N. Yalouris, *Deltion* 21 (1966), Chronika 164–5, pls. 158–65.

237. Gold wreath from Armento in southern Italy, the finest and most elaborate of the gold funerary wreaths of late-Classical and Hellenistic times. Late fourth or early third century B.C. It exploits the techniques of repoussé, filigree and granulation with dazzling virtuosity to produce a farrago of oak-leaves, acorns, roses and ivy tendrils populated by bees and winged genii of both sexes. Crowning all is a winged goddess (Nike?) about to pour a libation; the jug in her right hand is missing, but a *phiale* survives in her left. Her pedestal carries the inscription 'Crithonius dedicated the wreath', and it is possible that the piece was originally a dedication to Victory which only later found its way into a tomb.

(Munich, Antikensammlungen 2335. Height 36 cm.)

J. Sieveking, *Ant. Denk.* 4 (1927–31) 80–3; G. Becatti, *Oreficerie antiche* (1955) 192 no. 354, pl. XC; D. Ohly, *Die Antikensammlungen am Königsplatz in München* (n.d.) 67, fig. 59.

238. Funerary altar from Rhodes set up in honour of Comus of Laodicea (presumably Laodicea ad Lycum, which lay just outside Rhodian territory on the mainland at its greatest extent). Second or first century B.C. The relief on the front face shows a common parting scene (the dead man taking leave of his seated wife), but the overall form of the altar is a characteristic one for Rhodes and its territory; its most striking features are the pediment crowning each of the side faces and the hollowed-out upper surface containing a pair of round bosses. The latter were perhaps intended as stands round which to place wreaths during ceremonies in honour of the dead.

(Vienna, Kunsthistorisches Museum I 432. White marble. Badly chipped at the bottom left and on the top moulding; heads of figures broken off. Height 59 cm; width 71 cm; depth 42 cm.)

O. Benndorf and G. Niemann, *Reisen in Lykien und Karien* (1884) 25f., fig. 22; Fraser 17f., fig. 46; E. Pfuhl and H. Möbius, *Die ostgriechischen Grabreliefs* I (1977) 268 no. 1081, pl. 163.

239. East Greek funerary relief representing the dead at a banquet (the 'death-feast' or *Totenmahl*). Second half of the second century B.C. Many elements, for example the banqueter's pose with raised right hand holding a *rhyton* (drinking-horn) and lowered left holding a *phiale*, the horse's head in the corner, and the sacrificial attendant leading a pig, go back to Attic reliefs of the Classical period; but the complex multi-figure treatment is characteristic of Hellenistic Asia Minor. Many of the Attic antecedents were votive offerings to heroes, and the use of the motif for tomb-reliefs is a clear indication of the Hellenistic tendency to heroize the dead. The snake which winds round the tree and reaches towards the *rhyton* may be a further

reference to heroization, since the snake is a characteristic attribute of heroes, especially chthonic heroes (cf. **43–4**, **265**). The horse, too, is closely related to the chthonic powers, though its presence here may merely serve as a symbol of the social ranking of the dead (possession of a horse was always a privilege of the better-off classes). That the banqueter is a real person rather than a legendary hero is indicated by the inscription on the upper frame, which gives the name Teiades, certainly a personal name rather than an epithet of a god. The true place of the *Totenmahl* in Hellenistic thinking about death and after-life is uncertain; it is more likely to symbolize the well-being of the deceased in another existence than to refer to a funerary

238

239

240

241

banquet at which he was conceived as being present.

(Leiden, Rijksmuseum van Oudheden Pb 158. From Smyrna (or Clazomenae?). Parian marble. Height 45.5 cm; width 83 cm; depth 19 cm.)

L. Malten, *JdI* 29 (1914) 219 n. 1, fig. 13; R. N. Thönges-Stringaris, *Ath. Mitt.* 80 (1965) 61, 94 no. 171; F. L. Bastet, *Beeld en reliëf* (1979) pl. 24a; Pfuhl and Möbius, *op. cit.* 374f. no. 1520, pl. 219.

240. Tombstone in honour of Apollonia, daughter of Cephisophon. Second half of the second century B.C. One of a series of East Greek funerary reliefs recalling the fourth-century Attic type in which the dead are portrayed in high relief within a semi-architectural niche with crowning pediment. The representation of Apollonia on a much larger scale than the two attendants (whose attributes, the torch and the perfume-flask, must refer to funerary rites) is another sign of the heroization of the dead. The wreath carved above the relief contains the words ὁ δῆμος, indicating that the state had honoured Apollonia with a civic crown.

(Oxford, Ashmolean Museum. Probably from Smyrna. Light grey marble. Base restored. Height 97 cm; width 51 cm.)

A. Michaelis, *Ancient Marbles in Great Britain* (1882) 578 no. 149; Pfuhl and Möbius, *op. cit.* 137f. no. 409, pl. 67.

242

241. Tombstone of Parmeniscus from Apollonia in Illyria (within the territory of modern Albania). Second century B.C. The stele probably formed the upper part of a pillar-like monument whose lower element was an *aedicula* (apparently designed to contain a painting of the deceased); the over-all form of the monument is of a type peculiar to Apollonia, but in style and iconography the decoration shows the influence of western Greece and southern Italy. The pair of Sirens and the oak-branches above them recall motifs on west-Greek tombstones, while the Amazonomachy frieze and the female head in the pediment are related to elements in the art of southern Italy, and especially of Apulia, whose largest city Tarentum was only a short sea-voyage away. Mourning sirens are a common motif in Greek tomb-decoration from the fourth century onwards; but their precise eschatological significance is uncertain.

(Vienna, Kunsthistorisches Museum I 1024. From Apollonia in Illyria. Limestone. Top of pediment broken away. Height 1.06 m; width 55 cm.)

C. Praschniker, *JOAI* 21–2 (1922–4), Beiblatt 128ff., fig. 47; P. C. Sestieri, *Le Arti* 5 (1942–3) 116f. no. 1, fig. 1; E. Buschor, *Die Musen des Jenseits* (1944) 77, fig. 59; P. M. Fraser and T. Rönne, *Boeotian and West Greek Tombstones* (1957) 193f., pl. 31.2.

242. Tombstone of Demetrius, son of Olympus; one of a fine series of painted stelae built into the fortifications of Demetrias in Thessaly. Since the city was founded only *c.* 293 B.C. and the hasty enlargement of its defensive towers to which the stelae fell victim can best be connected with the wars of the early part of the second century, these stones are neatly dated to the third century. The use of painted scenes in preference to reliefs for the decoration of funerary stelae is a practice little attested elsewhere in the Hellenistic world, except at Alexandria; but doubtless it was more widespread than the surviving evidence suggests (for an example from Vergina see *Balkan Studies* 5 (1964) 301f.). The dead man is shown seated on a stool, attended by a young page. It is thought that the painted stelae were originally set in *aediculae.*

(Volos, Museum L 351. Marble. Painting black, brown, purple and white on pink ground. Height 59.5 cm; width 26.3 cm; thickness 14 cm.)

A. S. Arvanitopoulos, *Graptai stelai Demetriados-Pagason* (1928) 162–4, figs. 195–6, pl. x; J. Charbonneaux, R. Martin and F. Villard, *Hellenistic Art* (1973) 129, fig. 126.

243 (a, b). The foundations and a reconstruction drawing of the mausoleum at Belevi, near Ephesus, the grandest known princely tomb of Hellenistic times, seen from the south east. Closely modelled upon the Mausoleum of Halicarnassus, it evidently consisted of a podium about 27 m square and 13 m high (containing the actual burial chamber), a cella with a Corinthian peristyle of eight columns per side, and a crowning pyramid. Heraldic pairs of griffins flanked the foot of the pyramid, with teams of horses standing at the corners. There has been much controversy surrounding the date and ownership of the tomb, but a recent reappraisal of the pottery from the construction debris has confirmed that it was built soon after 300 B.C., and this would suggest that it was intended for Lysimachus, who re-founded Ephesus about 290

243a

243b

B.C. If so, the fact that it was left incomplete would be due to his death in 281, when the Ephesians handed over their city to Seleucus and Lysimachus' body was taken for burial in the Thracian Chersonnese. Whether, as some have suggested, the mausoleum was re-used later by a Seleucid king such as Antiochus II (died 246), is still open to question.

Forschungen in Ephesos VI: C. Praschniker and M. Theuer, *Das Mausoleum von Belevi* (1979).

244

244. One of the griffins from the roof of the peristyle of the Belevi mausoleum. Early third century B.C. The unfinished state of the carving is striking; one can compare details of the sarcophagus in the burial-chamber and the steps and mouldings of the monument's *krepidoma* (stepped foundation). These lion-griffins are closely related to Persian types and, along with a palm-leaf capital from the cella and the Persian dress of a statue from the burial-chamber, provide a strong Iranian connexion which has given support to those who claim the mausoleum for a Seleucid prince. But the use of griffins in tomb-decoration has no parallels in Persia, whereas it is a well attested practice in the Graeco-Roman world (cf. **241**).

(Selçuk Museum 301. Light grey marble. Height 1.17 m; length 1.54 m.)

Praschniker and Theuer, *op. cit.* 89–91, 142–5.

245. Sarcophagus from the mausoleum at Belevi. Early third century B.C. Both the frieze on the body of the sarcophagus and the reclining figure on the lid are unfinished, and this common factor implies that the sarcophagus and its lid are

245

246

contemporary, despite anomalies which have led some to argue that the lid was a later addition. The motif of a reclining figure on a sarcophagus is unique in the eastern Mediterranean before Roman times, but the pose of the figure, and especially the presence of a *phiale* in its left hand, recalls the *Totenmahl* so popular in funerary reliefs (cf. **239**). The face of the dead man is too badly damaged to be identified as a portrait; the groove carved in the hair was designed to hold a hero's fillet in metal, or perhaps a gold wreath appropriate to the death-feast.

(Selçuk Museum 1610. Light grey marble. Sarcophagus 2.57 m long; 93 cm high; 1.25 m deep. Lid 2.67 m long; 1.09 m high; 1.43 m deep.)

Praschniker and Theuer, *op. cit.* 99–104, 148–56.

246. Funerary relief of Hieronymus, from Rhodes. Late third or early second century B.C. The surviving block probably formed the central part of the entablature from a *heroum* dedicated to the dead man. The scenes portrayed, though details of the interpretation are uncertain, seem to express conventional views of the Underworld. At the left, separated from the rest by a pillar with horizontal grooves, is a scene which may belong to the world of the living and perhaps represents a philosophical debate. At the right are (from left to right) a group of Hermes Psychopompus (the Conductor of Souls), Persephone and Pluton, a smaller-scale standing figure which may be the dead man, a pair of seated figures (spirits of the dead?), a winged figure with a staff (an underworld judge?), another seated figure, and a female figure rising out of, or sinking into, the earth (a sinner condemned to the lower depths of Tartarus?). It has been suggested that Hieronymus, named in the inscription above the relief, is the Rhodian philosopher of that name, who died about 220 B.C. The signature of the sculptor, Demetrius, is inscribed on the lower fascia.

(Now destroyed; formerly Berlin, Hiller von Gaertringen collection. From Ialysus. Marble. Length 1.00 m; height 31 cm; average thickness 9 cm.)

F. Hiller von Gaertringen and C. Robert, *Hermes* 37 (1902) 121–46; Brunn-Bruckmann, no. 579; Fraser 34–6, 129f. nn. 197–203, fig. 97.

247. Painted figure of Rhadamanthys, the judge of the dead, on the façade of the Great Tomb at Lefkadia (**67**). Early third century B.C. The figure, identified by a painted inscription above the head, leans on his stick watching while his fellow-judge Aeacus receives a soldier (presumably the owner of the tomb) who is brought into his presence by Hermes Psychopompus. The subject is unique in the visual arts but is related to a passage in Plato in which Rhadamanthys and Aeacus are linked as judges of the dead, the former having jurisdiction over Asia, the latter over Europe (*Grg.* 523E–526D). For another possible Underworld scene see **246**.

(*In situ.* Painting on plaster; face badly damaged by crack. Colouring predominantly in shades of brown and yellow. Approx. 1.10 m tall.)

Ph. M. Petsas, *Ho taphos ton Leukadion* (1966) 132–4, pls. Θ′, Ι′(3), 8; and generally on the judgement scene pp. 114–58.

248. Interior of a chamber-tomb at Eretria. The type of a vaulted burial-chamber preceded by an ante-room and/or an entrance-passage

247

(*dromos*) and enclosed within a great earthen tumulus spread into Greece from Macedonia (cf. **67**, **100**), and this example probably dates to the period of Macedonian control in Euboea (third century B.C.). The tumulus was evidently here crowned by some form of marble monument carried on a great cubic brick foundation. Inside the burial chamber, as in many Hellenistic tombs of Macedonia, southern Italy and elsewhere, there were imitation couches (*klinai*) and thrones, here carved of marble. These were hollowed out as receptacles for the cremated remains of the dead. Inscriptions reveal that the couches contained male cremations, and the thrones female. Among the rich finds from the chamber were terracotta figurines of Erotes, fragments of gold ornaments and funerary reliefs, bronze and pottery vessels, and painted clay shields, some imitating the Macedonian type; and the walls were painted with wreaths, vases and armour, shown as if hanging from iron pegs.

(Chamber 2.97 m wide; 2.85 m deep; 3.06 m high (to crown of vault).)

K. G. Vollmöller, *Ath. Mitt.* 26 (1901) 333–65, pls. XIII–XV; G. Kleiner, *Tanagrafiguren* (*JdI* Ergänzungsheft XV) (1942) 19f.

249. Painted dome of a *tholos* tomb at Kazanlak, Bulgaria. *c.* 300 B.C. The native princes of Thrace were strongly influenced by Greek art and culture, as shown by the imported *objets d'art*, especially gold and silver plate, in their tombs and by their patronage, as here, of Greek painters. The subjects portrayed in the conical cupola are chariot-races, a favourite motif in Greek art of the fourth and early third centuries B.C., and a procession of figures bringing offerings to a seated couple, presumably the owners of the tomb.

(Diameter 2.85 m; height of main frieze 58 cm.)

V. Micoff, *Le tombeau antique près de Kazanlak* (1954); A. Vassiliev, *Das antike Grabmal bei Kasanlak* (1959).

250. Drawing of a wooden coffin found in a tumulus near Anapa (south Russia). Early third century B.C. Dated by a gold coin of Lysimachus found with the skeleton, this is an example of the chest-type of coffin, which was gradually superseded in popularity (in Russia at least) by the columnar house-type from the late fourth century onwards. The inset panels contained carved and gilt wooden appliqués on a red ground: a vertical acanthus-scroll on each of the corner-posts, Nereids riding sea-monsters on the sides, and single warriors with swords and shields along the top. The lid was never recorded and is now lost. Later coffins, of which there are examples both in south Russia and in Egypt, are generally lower in proportion to their length (cf. **251**).

(Leningrad, Hermitage Museum (in fragments). Appliqués on red background. Measurements not available.)

Compte-rendu de la Commission Impériale Archéologique (St. Pétersbourg) (1882–8), pp. xxiii–xxv, 48–70, 73–5, pls. III–V, VI (5); C. Watzinger, *Griechische Holzsarkophage aus der Zeit Alexanders des Grossen* (1905) 36f., 78, 80 no. 12, fig. 64; E. H. Minns, *Scythians and Greeks* (1913) 324–8, figs. 235–8.

249

250

Coffin found near Anapa. C.R. 1882-8. VI. 5. Dark red ground of Panels. Figures &c. gilt.

251

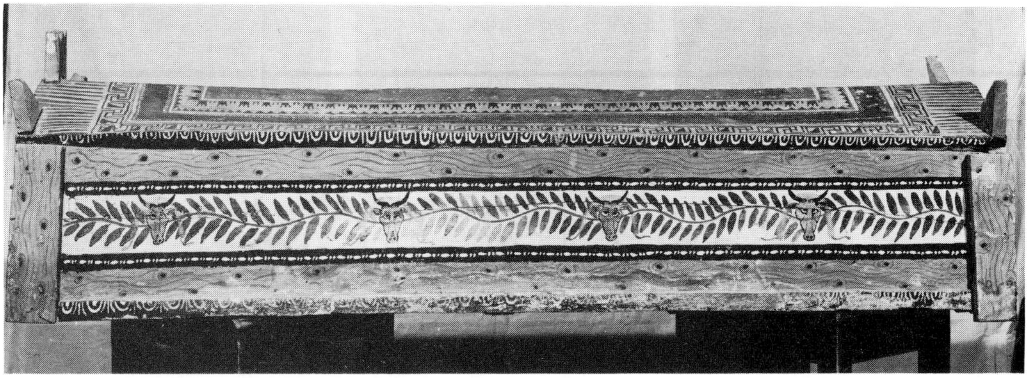

252

251. Side-view of a wooden coffin from the Fayûm. Second half of third century B.C. The decoration is of great interest since it shows a fusion of Greek and Egyptian elements. While the frieze of bulls' heads and laurel-garlands, the framing enrichments (egg-and-tongue, bead-and-reel, maeander etc.), and a rose-garland on one of the short sides are all Greek in inspiration, the panel at the foot of the coffin (not visible) shows Egyptian deities in the form of jackals and apes. In front of each jackal is a hieroglyph naming Anubis, 'the lord of the Underworld'. For other monuments in which Egyptian religious ideas are combined with Greek decorative forms (or inscriptions) see **9**, **10**.

(Cairo, Egyptian Museum 33123. From Magdola (Medinet en Nahas) in the Fayûm (1903 excavations). Wood plastered and painted (imitation wood dark yellow with red grains and black knots; bulls' heads yellow with black horns; laurel red with blue leaves; egg-and-tongue and bead-and-reel white on black ground; decoration of lid red, white, yellow and black). Length 1.85 m; height 53 cm (to top of *acroterium*); width 53 cm.)

Watzinger, *op. cit.* 33–5 no. 9, figs. 60–2; C. C. Edgar, *Graeco-Egyptian Coffins*, *Masks and Por-*

253

traits (Catalogue général des antiquités égyptiennes du musée du Caire, nos. 33101–33285) (1905) 10f. no. 33123, pl. v; G. Grimm, *Kunst der Ptolemäer und Römerzeit im Ägyptischen Museum Kairo* (1975) 2, 23 no. 39, pls. 74–5.

252. Rock-cut tombs at Telmessus (modern Fethiye). Fourth–third centuries B.C. The larger tombs represent a marriage of Lycian funerary tradition (tomb-chambers cut in hillsides) and the Greek architectural orders. The grand Ionic façades conceal small tomb-chambers with benches for sarcophagi along each wall.

O. Benndorf and G. Niemann, *Reisen in Lykien und Karien* (1884) 40f., 111–13, pls. XIV–XVII; E. Akurgal, *Die Kunst Anatoliens von Homer bis Alexander* (1961) 129f., figs. 81–3; G. E. Bean, *Lycian Turkey, an Archaeological Guide* (1978) 40, pls. 2–3.

253. Tomb façade (N 65) at Cyrene. A series of Cyrenaican tomb-façades of the Ptolemaic period probably derived, not from external façades, but from internal courtyards, and as such they may have been influenced by the open-air courtyards in the necropoleis at Alexandria. But whereas the Alexandrian equivalents are literally courtyards, with walls or doors on all four sides, here the concept is applied to a recessed façade opening off a street or terrace. The lower part

254a

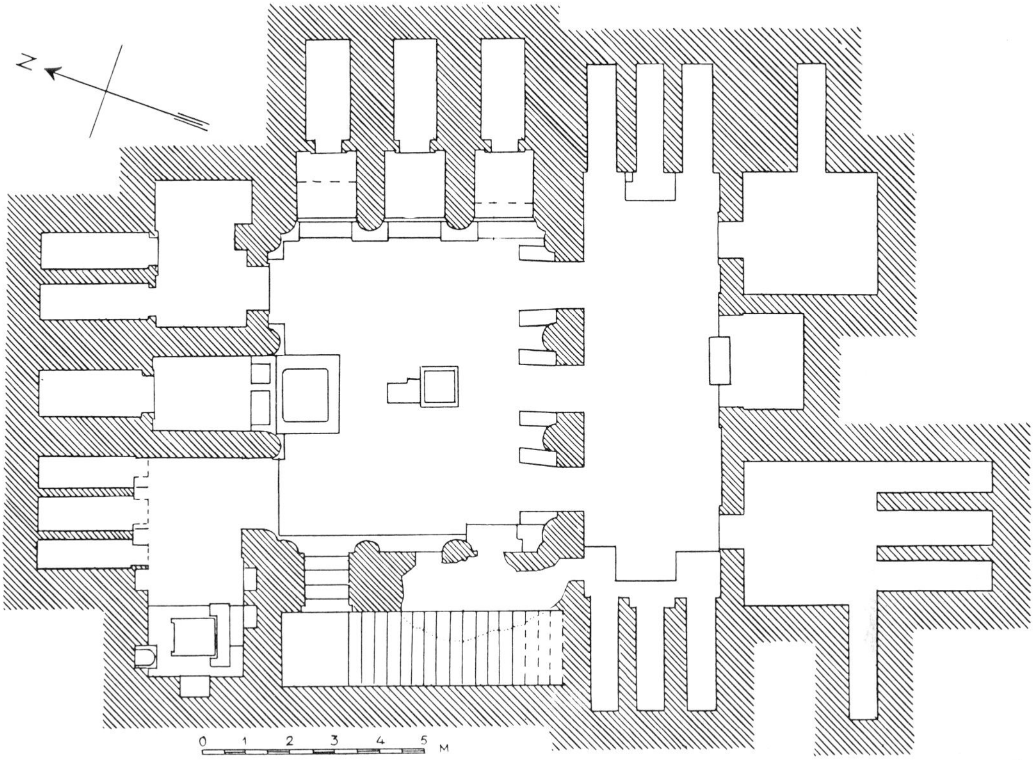

254b

of the façade is cut from the living rock, while the entablature and the upper part of the side-wall are constructed. The continuation of the entablature along the side-wall strengthens the effect of an inward-looking architecture.

S. Stucchi, *Architettura cirenaica* (Monografie di archeologia libica IX) (1975) 149ff., esp. 151f., 155, figs. 126–8, 134.

254. Underground cemetery at Alexandria (necropolis of Mustafa Pasha, hypogeum no. 1). Second half of the third century B.C.? Unlike the more normal rock-cut tombs of the Greek world and neighbouring regions, those of Alexandria do not run back from a monumental façade cut in a cliff-face or the like, but are entirely below ground-level, being reached by descending stairways. The commonest arrangement has a central court, reminiscent of the court in Greek houses, with burial chambers opening on to it.

(**a**) Plan of the hypogeum. The access stairway is on the west side of the court, and the principal rooms on the south. On the north side is a water-basin which was supplied from a well in the north-west burial-chamber. Most of the burials took the form of rectangular *loculi* which would have been closed with stone slabs, each carrying a painted representation of a door; but the central recess opening from the long cult-room on the south side of the court contained a funerary *kline* or sarcophagus.

(**b**) The court, looking south. The central altar, when excavated, still carried traces of the last sacrifices conducted on it. Behind, the three doorways giving access to the cult-room had their own elaborate frames, as well as being fitted within the openings of an engaged Doric order; and they were flanked by guardian sphinxes on pedestals. The façade, like the other sides of the court and the interiors of the chambers, was richly coloured.

A. Adriani, *La nécropole de Moustafa Pacha* (*Annuaire du Musée Gréco-Romain* 1933–35) (1936) 15–44 and *passim*; *id. Repertorio d'arte dell'Egitto greco-romano* C. I–II (1966) 130–4 no. 84, figs. 181–6, 193, 195, 197–8, 201–2.

7. Philosophy and science

The Hellenistic period was the hey-day of Greek science. In the Classical age scientific enquiry had, in most fields, been confined to the realm of abstract speculation; it was, in fact, closely interwoven with philosophy. But in the second half of the fourth century Aristotle established the principle of collecting data as a necessary preliminary to understanding the physical world; and this principle was propagated by Alexander, who took a staff of scientists on his eastern expedition to study the botany, zoology, geography, hydrography and other aspects of the areas conquered. This signalled the beginnings of a divorce between philosophical speculation and research in the natural and physical sciences (cf. *CAH* VII².1, ch. 9). While the former continued to flourish in Athens with the successors of Plato and Aristotle, and more especially with the new schools of the Stoa (**255**) and Epicurus (**256**), scientific research made remarkable progress on quite separate lines, notably in the fields of geography, astronomy, mathematics and practical mechanics. An important factor was the patronage of the early Ptolemies, whose two great research institutes in Alexandria, the Museum and the Library, attracted many of the leading scientists and philologists of the day (cf. **257**).

The achievements of Hellenistic geographers included the production of more accurate maps of the known world (aided by information brought back by Alexander and the explorers) and Eratosthenes' (cf. **257**) famous calculation of the earth's circumference, in which he used the principle of the sun-dial (cf. **258**) to take readings on the position of the noonday sun at Alexandria and Syene (Aswan). In astronomy Aristarchus' heliocentric theory of the universe was not widely accepted but important work was done on the recording of stellar and planetary movements, especially by Hipparchus of Nicaea, who measured the precession of the equinoxes, and calculated the length of the solar year to within six minutes and that of the lunar month to within one second. It was this sort of information which enabled mechanicians to construct instruments like the Anticythera computer (**261**). Physical and mathematical research included Archimedes' work on statics, hydrostatics, and the measurement of curvilinear areas and volumes: among other things he established close limits for the value of π, and calculated the ratio of volume between a cylinder and a sphere inscribed within it. Such research in solid geometry is presupposed by the papyrus illustrated in **259**, though the writer falls sadly short of the standards set by Archimedes.

In practical mechanics much energy was devoted to the creation of machines of war, notably catapults powered by torsion or (in theory at least) by compressed air (cf. chapter 7, **111**). Other, more peaceable, machines exploited the principles of water-pressure, air-pressure or flotation, and employed new transmission devices, such as the screw and the cogwheel (**260–1**). Perhaps the most fertile inventor of antiquity was Ctesibius of Alexandria, whose contrivances included a force-pump, a water-organ and a water-clock. A water-clock in the Tower of the Winds in Athens (**262**) may have worked on the same principles as that of Ctesibius.

One science which had already achieved a degree of maturity in Classical times was medicine, and here the Alexandrian school continued where the Hippocratics had left off, making particular progress in the understanding of anatomy and physiology, where they were greatly helped by the use of dissection. But actual medical practice, as illustrated by surviving prescriptions (**263**), representations of surgical instruments (**265–6**), and pictures of physiotherapists at work (**267**), probably differed little from what had gone before. In medicine, as in other sciences, practical application was not necessarily in step with theoretical knowledge, and in any case further progress was hampered by technological restrictions, in this case the lack of good optical instruments.

255

256

255. Portrait of Zenon of Citium (*c.* 333–*c.* 263 B.C.), founder of the Stoic school of philosophy. Roman copy of the head of a statue of the third century B.C. Named after the Stoa Poecile (Painted Stoa) in Athens, where Zenon started teaching, the Stoics preached a view of the universe as a great state ruled by one supreme power called Destiny or Nature. Virtue, and with it happiness, consisted in living according to the divine will, which was all-wise and all-good. This system, which in its monotheism and its code of morals to some extent foreshadowed Christianity, enjoyed great success in Hellenistic times and was the most popular philosophy of the Roman Imperial period.

(Naples, National Museum 1089, formerly Farnese collection. Marble; upper part of herm, inscribed ΖΗΝΩΝ. Nose, rims of ears restored. Height 44 cm (head 31 cm).)

Richter, *Portraits* 187f. no. 1, figs. 1084–5, 1089.

256. Portrait of Epicurus of Samos (341–270 B.C.), founder of the second of the two great schools of philosophy which flourished in Athens in Hellenistic times. Roman copy of the head and shoulders of a statue of the third century B.C. His physical system was based on the atomic theory of Democritus; there was no life after death (when the body dissolved into its constituent atoms) and the gods had no interest in our world. The goal of the Epicurean was to live a life of freedom from pain in the body and from disturbance in the mind (*ataraxia*). This almost amoral philosophy was much less successful than Stoicism but had influential followers in first-century B.C. Rome, notably Lucretius, who expounded the system in his poem *De Rerum Natura*.

(Rome, Capitoline Museum 53. Marble bust; end of nose restored. Height 48.5 cm (head 35.9 cm).)

Richter, *Portraits* 195 no. 2, figs. 1151–2.

257. Detail of a papyrus from Oxyrhynchus listing some of the early heads of the Library in Alexandria. Second century A.D. (copy of list of first century B.C.?). The first name surviving is Apollonius 'the Rhodian' (author of the epic *Argonautica*), the pupil of Callimachus and tutor of Ptolemy III Euergetes; after him come Eratosthenes (the great polymath, who wrote on literary criticism, chronology, mathematics, astronomy, geography and philosophy, as well as composing poetry), Aristophanes of Byzantium (famous for his linguistic and literary studies), Apollonius of Alexandria 'the Classifier'

257

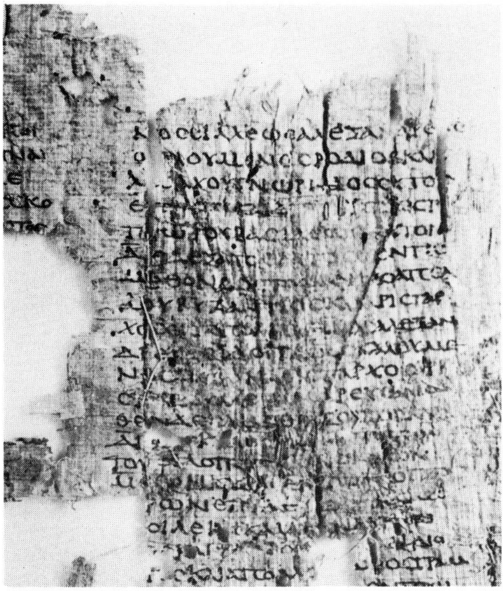

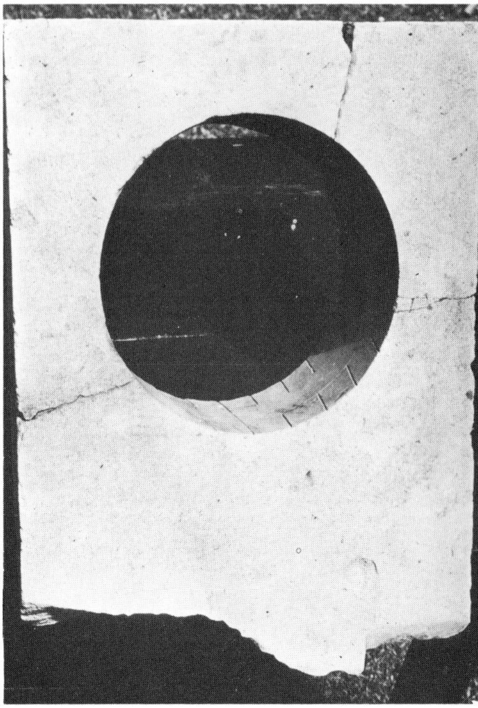

258

(otherwise unknown), and Aristarchus of Samothrace, an influential literary critic who acted as tutor to the children of Ptolemy VI Philometor. There follows an obscure military officer named Cydas, perhaps put in charge of the Library when Ptolemy VIII conducted a purge of scholars in 145/4 B.C.; and the final names are four grammarians who are said to have flourished in the time of Ptolemy IX (between 116 and 80 B.C.).

(Dublin, Trinity College Library D 10–11 (col. ii, lines 1–20).)

B. P. Grenfell and A. S. Hunt, eds., *The Oxyrhynchus Papyri* x (1914) 99ff. no. 1241.

258. Sundial found at Aï Khanum in Afghanistan. Third or second century B.C. The first scientifically designed sun-dials were probably produced in the third century B.C. as astronomical and mathematical science became able to define the path of the sun at different seasons and at different latitudes with increasing precision and to project that path on to a shadow-receiving surface. Most commonly Hellenistic sun-dials took the form of sections of a cone or hemisphere engraved with a network of radiating lines for the hours and curving lines for the seasons (winter and summer solstice and equinox); since the length of the hour in the ancient world depended upon the length of the day, the hour-lines spread further apart as they approached the curve which represented the summer solstice. By tracking the shadow of a bronze pointer across the dial, the reader could not only tell the time of day but also gain a crude estimate of the month. The Aï Khanum sun-dial, however, is of an unique type consisting of a circular hole cut in a stone slab. The slab was set as shown in the photograph but with its south face (at the rear) tilted towards the equator at an angle of 37° from the vertical. Since 37° is the approximate latitude of Aï Khanum, this means that the sun fell on its north face in the spring and summer and on its south face in the autumn and winter; the lower half of the cylindrical cavity was therefore graduated with two separate hour-scales, one for each half of the year. Shadows were cast by a horizontal rod suspended within the cavity.

(Kabul Museum? From the gymnasium at Aï Khanum (1975 excavations). White limestone; lower part damaged. Height 45 cm; width 35 cm; thickness 15 cm.)

P. Bernard, *CRAI* (1976) 299–302, fig. 10.

259. Fragment of a late-Hellenistic papyrus containing a collection of problems in stereo-

259

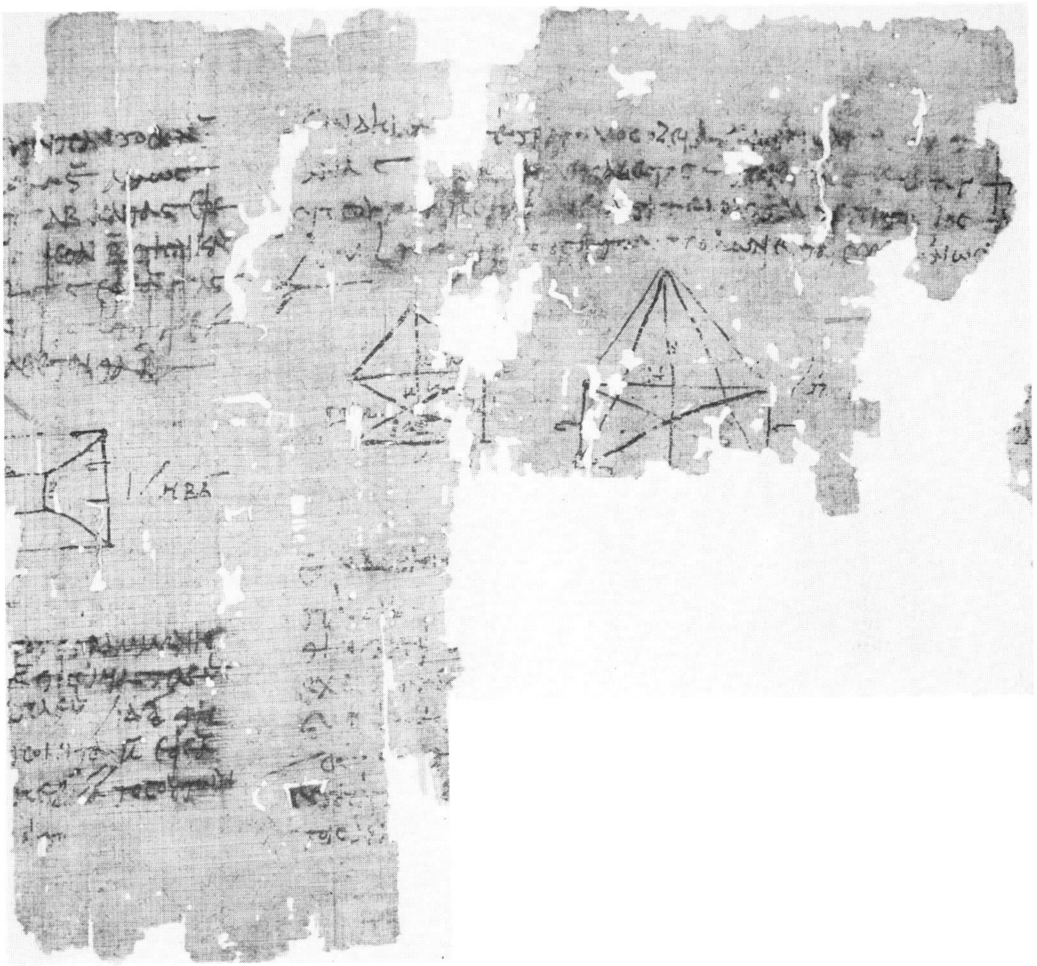

metry. First century B.C. Perhaps intended as a school manual, the collection illustrates the sort of exercises in solid geometry which became commonplace after Euclid and Archimedes. Of those illustrated (nos. 28–30 in the papyrus), the first involves calculations of the height and volume of a truncated pyramid with square base, the second the height and volume of a complete pyramid with square base, and the third the volume of a pyramid with rectangular base. The writer is concerned with purely practical demonstrations rather than the proof of theorems, and his accuracy is marred by the use of approximations (e.g. $\pi = 3$, and $\sqrt{200} = 14\frac{1}{7}$).

(Vienna, National Library G 19, 996 F (frag. 6). From Dimêh (Fayûm), discovered about 1890. Papyrus about 2.50 m long; at least 20 cm wide. This fragment approx. 22 cm by 20 cm.)

H. Gerstinger and K. Vogel, *Mitteilungen aus der Papyrus Sammlung der National Bibliothek in Wien*, n.s. 1 (1932) 11–76.

260. Terracotta relief depicting a negro treading an Archimedean 'snail' (*cochlea*), or water-screw, a machine by which water was wound up the thread of a screw set within a pipe (cf. Vitr. x.6). First century B.C.? He supports himself on a pole and treads a series of steps fitted to the middle of the cylinder which contained the screw. The vines in the background indicate that the device is being used to irrigate a vineyard. Similar devices are still employed in parts of the Nile Delta and Middle Egypt.

(London, British Museum EA 37563. From Alexandria. Red clay with traces of yellow, black and white paint. Height 18.0 cm; width 9.5 cm; thickness 4.0 cm.)

260

T. A. Rickard, *JRS* 18 (1928) 131, pl. XII, 1; *id. Man and Metals* (1932) 424f., fig. 50; H. Hodges, *Technology in the Ancient World* (1971) 184, fig. 211; J. F. Healy, *Mining and Metallurgy in the Greek and Roman World* (1978) 95, fig. 25.

261. Astronomical calculator from the Anticythera shipwreck (cf. **133**). Early first century B.C. This is the most complicated and sophisticated piece of machinery known from the ancient world, and it apparently used differential gearing, a technique which did not reappear until the late sixteenth century. Archimedes in the third century B.C. probably used simple gearing to make a kind of planetarium in global form, described by Cicero (*Rep.* I.14.21–2); but the conception of the differential gear may be the achievement of an anonymous genius of the late second or early first century. It was used here to drive a series of dials carrying different astronomical data. These dials, when read in conjunction, would produce a synchronization of calendar dates, zodiacal signs, phases of the moon, and possibly positions of the planets.

(**a**) The three main fragments in their present state. The mechanism was originally installed in a wooden casing approximately 15.8 cm wide,

261a

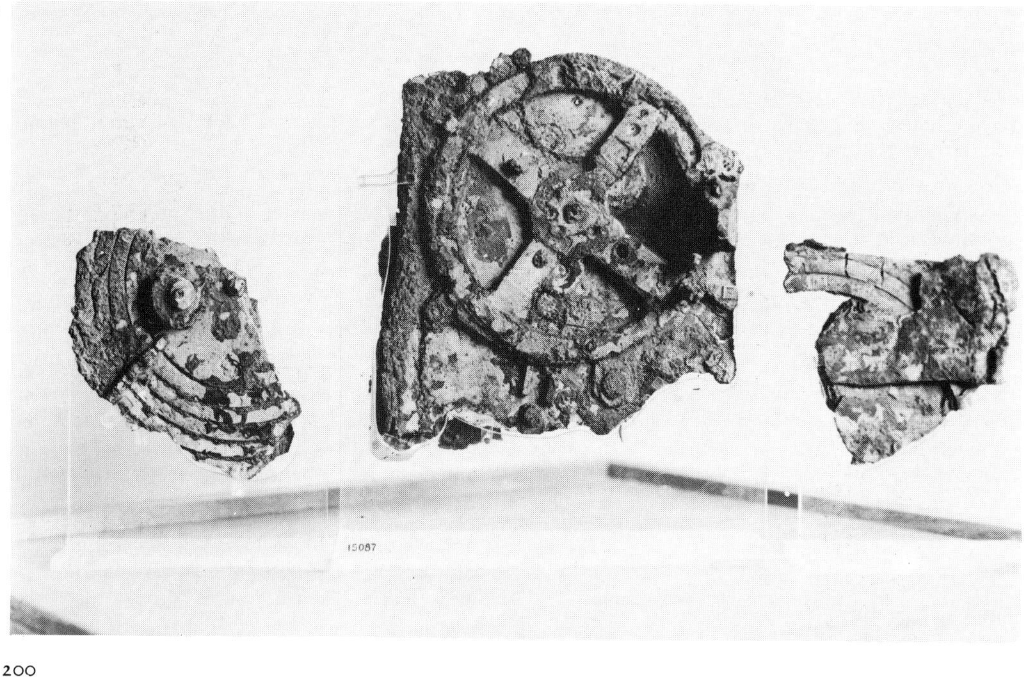

261b

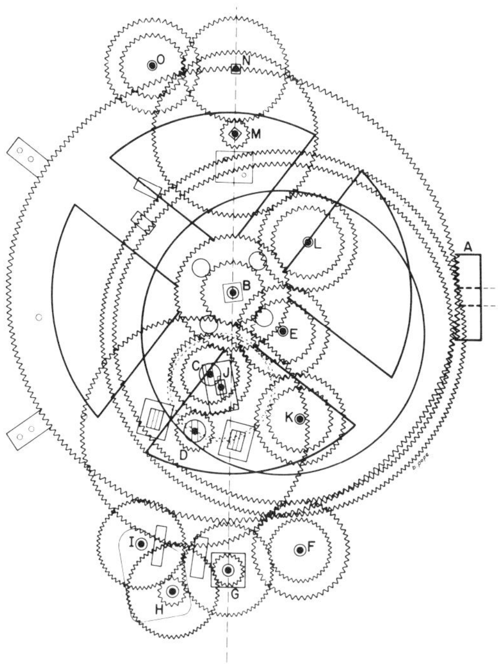

31.6 cm high, and 7.5 cm thick. The central piece shows the main drive-wheel in the front part, while the right-hand fragment, which belonged (the other way up) to the bottom left corner, carries part of the graduated rings turned directly by the drive-wheel. The left-hand fragment, which fitted at the top left corner, shows part of the upper back dial.

(**b**) Diagrammatic reconstruction of the gearing. The main drive-wheel (on axis B) was operated by a crown-wheel set at right-angles to it (A). Whether this was designed to be driven by water-power, like the clock in the Tower of the Winds (**262**), or, as seems more likely, was turned manually with a crank-handle, it is impossible to know for certain. One revolution of the drive-wheel represented the annual solar cycle, and the attached rings were graduated in terms of the zodiac and the Egyptian calendar. They also gave references to an inscription on plates above and below, which recorded the dates of the rising and setting of various constellations. The solar cycle was translated, via a differential turntable on axis E, to dials at the back of the mechanism for lunar months (axis G), lunar years (axis I), and perhaps cycles of 47 lunar months, five revolutions of which would complete the so-called 'Metonic cycle', which equated an exact number of lunations (235) with an exact number of solar years (19) (axis N). This reconstruction has been worked out with the aid of gamma-radiography.

(Athens, National Museum 15087. Bronze, much encrusted and corroded. Largest fragment approx. 13.5 cm wide by 16.0 cm high.)

D. J. de Solla Price, *Gears from the Greeks. The Antikythera Mechanism – a Calendar Computer from ca. 80 B.C.* (*Transactions of the American Philosophical Society* n.s. 64.7) (1974).

262a

262. The Tower of the Winds in Athens, an octagonal marble tower built by Andronicus of Cyrrhus (whether the Macedonian or the Syrian city is uncertain) in the mid-first century B.C. Vitruvius (1.6.4) refers merely to the crowning weather-vane and the reliefs of the Winds on the eight faces, but Varro (*Rust.* III.5.17) calls it a *horologium* (clock), and modern investigation has suggested that it was an elaborate combination of weather-station and astronomical timepiece.

(**a**) General view from the south east. The weather-vane, now missing, was in the form of a bronze Triton holding a rod in his right hand, with which he indicated the respective Winds (portrayed as flying male and female figures).

262b

Beneath the winds were sun-dials, of which the radiating grooves still survive (not visible in the photograph). At the left, partially hidden by a later wall, are the remains of a cylindrical annexe which probably contained the mechanism of a water-clock which was the main attraction of the interior.

(**b**) Hypothetical reconstruction of the water-clock. It probably belonged to the inflow type invented, according to Vitruvius, by Ctesibius. A head of water in an upper tank maintained a steady drip into a lower container, thus raising the level of a float which operated the timepiece. Emptying of the container, presumably every twenty-four hours, had the effect of 'rewinding' the clock. What visual device was used to display the passage of time is a matter for conjecture, but an attractive possibility (shown here) is the anaphoric clock described by Vitruvius (IX.8.8–14). The essence of this is a revolving

263

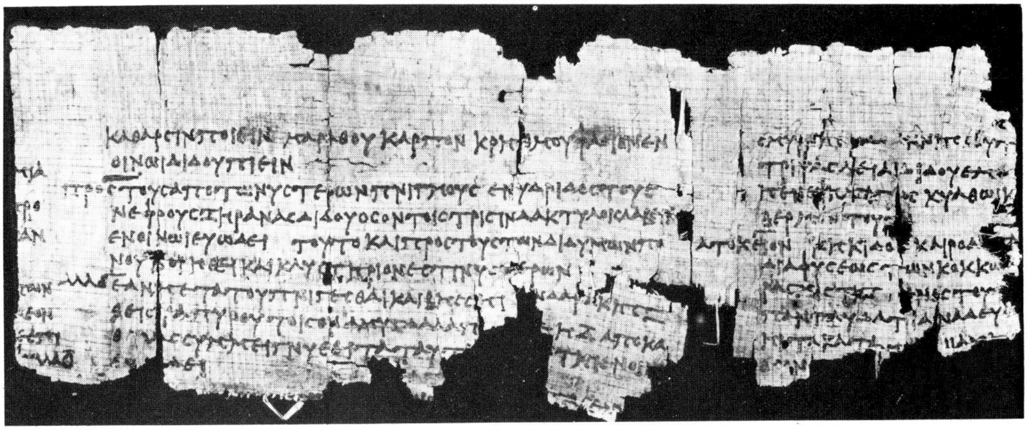

264

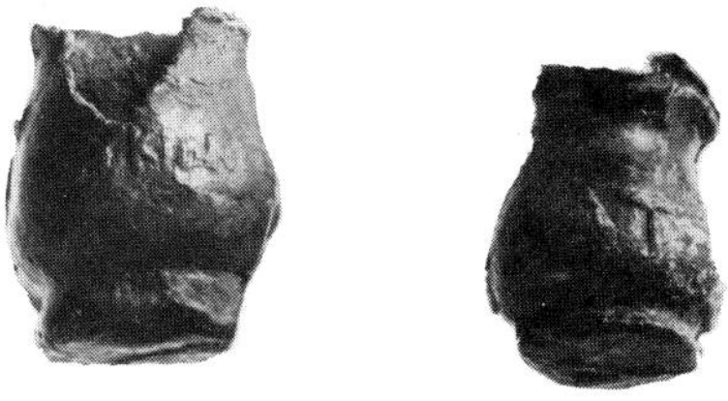

disc on which the position of sun and stars can be read off from hour to hour by means of a superposed frame of reference wires. The position of the sun on the disc could be adjusted each day to take account of the movement of the ecliptic. This marvellous showpiece, more like a modern planetarium than a simple reference-clock, would accord well with the ancient tendency to treat gadgets as a means of stimulating curiosity, or simply as a source of entertainment, rather than for purely utilitarian purposes.

J. V. Noble and D. J. de Solla Price, *AJA* 72 (1968) 345–55, pls. 111–18; J. Travlos, *Pictorial Dictionary of Ancient Athens* (1971) 281–8, figs. 362–78.

263. Prescribed medicines for various disorders. Third or second century B.C. The recipes include the fruit of fennel and the outer leaf of samphire, taken in wine, as a purgative; dried otters' kidneys in sweet-smelling wine as a remedy for hysterical choking and pains in the testicles; and a concoction of arsenic, brimstone and almonds, again in wine, in cases where choking is combined with coughing. Such prescriptions, the last of which goes back to Hippocrates (*De Morbis Mulierum* 200), give a good idea of the remedies available in Hellenistic medicine.

(Manchester, John Rylands Library 531 recto. Provenance uncertain (bought 1920). Upper part of papyrus scroll. Length 21.5 cm; width 8.4 cm.)

Catalogue of the Greek and Latin Papyri in the John Rylands Library Manchester III: C. H. Roberts, ed., *Theological and Literary Texts* (1938) 165–8, no. 531, pl. 8.

264. Tiny lead jugs used for medicine or eye-salve. Such containers, widespread in the Hellenistic period, may be of terracotta as well as lead, and are commonly stamped with the name of the maker and of the contents. Especially common are thimble-sized lead containers of *lykion* (left), a purgative.

(London, British Museum 1842.7–28.569 (formerly Burgon collection) and 1868.1–10.219. Provenance unknown. Both examples broken on one side. Left: height 2.6 cm; diameter 2.5 cm. Right: height 2.2 cm; diameter 2.1 cm.)

Unpublished.

265. Funerary relief in honour of a heroized doctor. First century B.C. The dead man, seated at the right, is represented on a larger scale than the petitioners at the left, who are probably (to judge from the veil of mourning worn by the woman) surviving members of his family. That a real doctor rather than a healing-god is meant, is indicated by the clean-shaven, portrait-like features. The snake twined round the tree was traditionally associated with healing, especially in the cult of Asclepius (and also with heroes: cf. **239**); but the instrument-case in the background, containing different forms of surgical knives and two pairs of forceps, suggests that

265

this doctor owed his success to more practical methods.

(Berlin, Pergamon Museum SK 804, formerly Grimani collection (Venice). Provenance unknown. Coarse white marble, restored at top corners. Height 67.5 cm; width 83.7 cm; depth 8.5 cm (relief 5 cm).)

Königliche Museen zu Berlin. Beschreibung der antiken Skulpturen mit Ausschluss der pergamenischen Fundstücke (1891) 306f. no. 804; E. Rohde, *Griechische und römische Kunst in den Staatlichen Museen zu Berlin* (1968) 107; G. Snyder, *Instrumentum medici* (1972) 33, pl. 16.

266. Rectangular base with relief of medical instruments. Third or second century B.C. At the extremities are represented cupping-vessels; in the middle is a case containing surgical knives and scalpels. The function of the hooked instrument in the right half of the case is uncertain; it is most probably some form of probe. Bleeding was a favourite method of treatment in the ancient world (as it remained until the nineteenth century), being recommended for maladies as diverse as loss of speech, eye disease, and indigestion.

266

(Athens, National Museum 1378. From the sanctuary of Asclepius in Athens (1877 excavations). Marble; chip missing at lower left corner. Height 33 cm; length 44 cm; depth 37.5 cm.)

F. von Duhn, *AZ* 35 (1877) 166 no. 86; A. Anagnostakis, *BCH* I (1877) 212–14, pl. IX; Svoronos, *Ath. Mus.* 324–7, no. 75, pl. XLVII; E. Berger, *Das Basler Arztrelief* (1970) 72–4, 77, 177 n. 151, figs. 87, 98.

267a

268

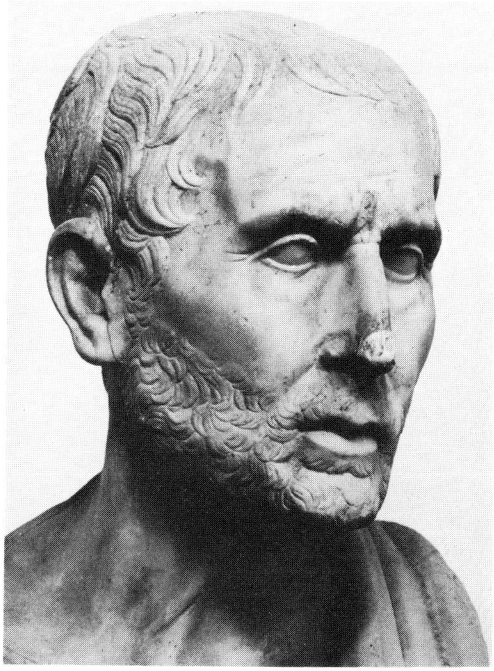

267b

267. Manuscript illuminations representing manipulative surgery of the Hellenistic period. The work which they illustrate, a commentary by the first-century B.C. physician Apollonius of Citium on Hippocrates' treatise *On Joints*, was intended from the start to be illustrated by diagrams, and these tenth-century miniatures certainly go back in their essentials to a Hellenistic source, even if the architectural backdrop was added later.

(**a**) Reduction of a broken or dislocated jaw.

(**b**) Reduction of vertebrae. The patient is subjected to traction, while at the same time the physiotherapist stands on his back.

(Florence, Biblioteca Medicea Laurenziana MS Laur. Plut. 74.7, fol. 198 v and 203 v.)

Corpus Medicorum Graecorum XI.1.1: *Apollonios von Kition* (1965) figs. XIV, XVIII; E. D. Phillips, *Greek Medicine* (1973) pls. 11, 13; *Istoria tou ellinikou ethnous* V, 2 (1974) 342 right.

268. Detail of portrait-bust of Posidonius of Apamea (*c.* 135–50 B.C.), the last great polymath of the Hellenistic world. Copy of the head of a statue of the mid-first century B.C. He founded a school on Rhodes, where he and his pupils worked on geography, natural history and astronomy, and he constructed an orrery which, to judge from the description by Cicero (*Nat. D.* II.34.88), was very similar to the Anticythera mechanism (**261**). But in many ways he epitomizes the ultimate failure of Hellenistic science, since the breadth of his interests, which included history and philosophy as well as the physical sciences, prevented him from making headway in any one field, and his flirtation with pseudo-sciences, such as astrology, demonology and divination, confused the picture of the physical world which had begun to emerge from the work of enquirers such as Eratosthenes and Aristarchus. His influence on writers of the Roman age was to some extent a factor in the decline of ancient scientific achievement.

(Naples, National Museum 1088, formerly Farnese collection. Marble; end of nose and part of ears restored. Height of bust 44 cm (head 24 cm).)

Richter, *Portraits* 282, fig. 2020 (with bibliography).

EPILOGUE

The eventual failure of Hellenistic science provides a slightly despondent note on which to conclude. But the very real achievements of the Hellenistic age should not be belittled. For all the neglect that it has suffered, this period in some ways embodies the highest achievements of Greek civilization, especially in the fields of science and engineering and in the arts of government and economics. It is also the period that saw Greek ideas and experiences carried almost to the limits of the known world – into the hinterland of Egypt and Anatolia, and throughout the Near and Middle East as far as Afghanistan and India. But it is above all the period in which Greek culture was transmitted to the Romans.

It is not within the scope of the present volume to consider the gradual absorption of the Hellenistic world by the Romans in the second and first centuries B.C. Suffice it to say that the Roman conquest, so far from extinguishing Hellenistic culture, helped to preserve it. In the eastern Mediterranean, under the new masters, the Greek way of life continued in much the same form, with the Greek language as its common tongue and the Greek urban model as the basis of its organization, till half a millennium later it was handed on to the Christian world of Byzantium. In the west, though subordinated to new ideals and modified by new requirements, it contributed much to the shaping of the Roman Imperial pattern, and thus, indirectly, to the culture of medieval and Renaissance Europe. The major contribution here was in fields not covered by the present volume: in literature, architecture and the arts. But in other fields too – water technology, housing and its associated amenities, medicine, education, sport and hygiene, theatrical entertainments, philosophy – the Greeks gave a good deal to their conquerors. It must not be forgotten that the form of Greek civilization to which the Romans were primarily exposed was not that of classical times but rather that of the much neglected 'twilight' years, the two or three centuries that we call the Hellenistic age.